Sing the
Word

Sing to the Word

Suggested Hymns from the
Church Hymnal FIFTH EDITION
for use with the
Revised Common Lectionary
and other special occasions

EDWARD DARLING

UNIVERSITY PRESS

OXFORD

UNIVERSITY PRESS

Great Clarendon Street, Oxford OX2 6DP

Oxford University Press is a department of the University of Oxford.
It furthers the University's objective of excellence in research, scholarship,
and education by publishing worldwide in

Oxford New York

Athens Auckland Bangkok Bogotá Buenos Aires Calcutta
Cape Town Chennai Dar es Salaam Delhi Florence Hong Kong Istanbul
Karachi Kuala Lumpur Madrid Melbourne Mexico City Mumbai
Nairobi Paris São Paulo Singapore Taipei Tokyo Toronto Warsaw

and associated companies in Berlin Ibadan

Oxford is a registered trade mark of Oxford University Press
in the UK and in certain other countries

© Oxford University Press 2000

First published 2000

British Library Cataloguing in Publication Data

Data available

ISBN 0–19–145609–8

1 3 5 7 9 10 8 6 4 2

Typeset in Swift and Gill Sans
by The Spartan Press Ltd,
Printed in Great Britain
on acid-free paper by
Bookcraft, Midsomer Norton

TO PATRICIA
who has given me loyal support
and encouragement
throughout my entire ministry

Contents

Foreword

by The Right Reverend Harold Miller (Bishop of Down and Dromore)

I AM so pleased that Bishop Edward Darling has provided us with *Sing to the Word* to accompany the new edition of the *Church Hymnal*. The revised hymn book is a wide range of material and styles, giving us 'windows' into a variety of 'psalms, hymns and spiritual songs'. But it does not, and cannot, help us adequately to relate these to the liturgical setting and context in which worship is offered. In relation to the Revised Common Lectionary, which is the new pattern of Sunday Bible-reading embraced by the Church of Ireland, this book helps to fill the gap. Bishop Edward has, in his own characteristic way, done the painstaking work of reading every Bible passage (Old Testament Readings, Psalms, New Testament Readings and Gospels), and, with a mind soaked in both scripture and hymnody, has found hymns which resonate with, and are often rooted in, the Bible texts.

This book is published as a companion volume to the 5th edition of the *Church Hymnal*. If Bishop Edward's earlier volume *Choosing the Hymns,* and regular contributions to the *Church of Ireland Gazette* are anything to go by, it will be found in the hands of every pastor, organist and music leader in the Church of Ireland and will be a well-thumbed resource.

May it help us to discover a thoroughly biblical base for our singing, a variety in our choice of music, and the great joy of the Lord in answering our oft-uttered prayer 'O Lord, open our lips, and our mouths will proclaim your praise.'

✠ HAROLD DOWN AND DROMORE

Compiler's Introduction

THE choice of hymns is something which is often taken far too lightly. Many clergy and organists tend to choose hymns which are popular and well known, but which bear little or no relevance to the passages of scripture prescribed in the Lectionary. This can lead to a lack of imagination, and even stagnation, in our worship, and presents no great challenge to the average congregation.

The good ordering of worship is something which demands an immense amount of thought and preparation. Most clergy are conscientious about the way they prepare their sermons for preaching. Sadly, many others give insufficient serious thought to the preparation of the hymns to be incorporated into that same act of worship.

Perhaps the reason for this is that they can take the easy way out and shelve their responsibility by delegating this particular task entirely to the organist. Ideally, the selection of hymns for any act of worship should be a task that is shared equally by the clergy and organists alike, the clergy ensuring that the words of the hymns are as relevant as possible to the lections of the day, and the organists ensuring that the music is both suitable and challenging for the occasion.

The Revised Common Lectionary

In recent years the Revised Common Lectionary has become widely used throughout numerous parts of the world by Christians of many traditions, and, as a result, has become a unifying factor in Christian worship. It is this Lectionary which is giving a new shape and meaning to the regular worship of the Church of Ireland and which is increasingly becoming the norm at all principal services in our parish churches. It is on this Lectionary, therefore, that the suggested choice of hymns for worship throughout the normal Christian calendar is based. No hymns have been suggested for use with the additional prescribed Lectionaries for a Second and a Third Service, as not only will these Lectionaries have a limited use in most churches, but space would not permit the same detailed choice of hymns to be printed. There are, however, hymns selected for other occasions, such as Saints' Days, Harvest Thanksgiving services,

Ember Days and the Dedication Festival of a church, to mention but a few. (See the note on page 245).

The lists outlined in the following pages, however, are comprehensive and could easily lead to confusion if not used intelligently and with care.

Choosing the most suitable hymns

In using this book, the first thing to bear in mind is that some lections have a huge amount of suitable hymns suggested, while others have no suggestions at all. It should not be considered essential, or even necessary, that one hymn should be chosen to relate to each part of the Lectionary for the day or occasion. Two hymns, or even only one, might well be sufficient to highlight the most relevant thoughts being expressed in all the readings. This will automatically leave room for a eucharistic hymn, or a suitable hymn of praise or thanksgiving, to be incorporated into the service.

Adequate time, therefore, should be given to the task of selecting the best hymns for the occasion. This could become ineffective, however, if one simply reads through the suggested list and picks out the best known of the relevant hymns. It would be more beneficial if clergy and organists, when preparing for worship, were to read the passages of scripture recommended in the Lectionary, and to meditate and reflect carefully on the words of all the suggested hymns. This could be a spiritual exercise, carried out on a regular basis, that would prepare them well for the act of worship which is being planned. Indeed, this is an exercise which might well be profitably undertaken by any member of the congregation, and not just by the clergy and organists.

The purpose of this book, therefore, is not just to assist those who have a specific responsibility for ordering our worship, but to be a spiritual companion for anyone who wishes to make private preparation beforehand. Indeed, the book itself could be used daily as an aid to one's private prayer and meditation.

Seasonal Hymns

Users of this book could be somewhat disconcerted to find a Christmas hymn being recommended as suitable in the middle of the month of July or a Harvest hymn in the season of Advent. It should be understood, at the outset, that the hymns itemised under each reading bear some relevance to that particular passage of scripture, but that is not to say that such hymns should necessarily be chosen. Hymns which are obviously 'out-of-season' are, accordingly, shown in brackets, and, while they probably will not be chosen to be sung in church on a particular Sunday, they still may be very useful aids to private meditation and can be helpful towards the choice of other more suitable hymns.

It should also be recognised that the hymns suggested under each reading are printed in alphabetical order of their first lines and not in order of importance, relevance, or suitability.

Indexes

Towards the back of this book are three different types of indexes. One is a list of hymns, referred to as 'Control Hymns', which simply relate to more than one of the readings appointed for a particular Sunday or occasion. They might well, therefore, be the most appropriate hymns to choose.

The second index gives a list of all the hymns recommended throughout this book; but one should not necessarily assume that those not mentioned in this list are inappropriate. One has only to examine the index of hymns in the *Church Hymnal* to realise that there are others which can profitably be used, even though they may have no obvious relevance to the readings of the day.

The third index provides a complete list of all the readings that are appointed to be read over the course of the three-year Revised Common Lectionary and the additional Lectionaries for use on Saints' Days, Holy Days and other special occasions. This will be of value to clergy in particular who wish at any time to find a hymn based on a passage of scripture from which they might be preaching.

Acknowledgements

I should like to express my appreciation to the Hymnal Revision Committee for encouraging me to compile this book; my wife, Patricia, who so readily helped to proofread the material compiled; Bishop Harold Miller (himself a lover of hymnody and liturgy) for writing the Foreword; Canon Brian Mayne whose advice and guidance on the use of the Revised Common Lectionary has always been so helpful.

I am also indebted to Michael Perry (sadly no longer with us) for the helpful suggestions in his book *Preparing for Worship*; the compilers of *Sing His Glory*—the Church of England guide to the choice of hymns with the Revised Common Lectionary; the Revised Common Lectionary Index for *Hymns Old and New*; *Hymnal Studies Five* —the American Episcopal Church's Liturgical Index to the Hymnal 1982; *Sunday by Sunday*—the Royal School of Church Music's quarterly guide for all who plan and lead weekly worship; and the Warden and staff of St. Deiniol's Library, Hawarden, North Wales where much of the preparatory work for this book was carried out. Such assistance has made my task so much easier, a task which I both enjoyed and counted a privilege to undertake.

It is my hope that those who use this book will find it a useful companion in helping to enrich the liturgy and worship of the Church of Ireland so that Almighty God may be given the glory, honour and praise that rightly belong to him.

✠ EDWARD DARLING

Codes and their interpretation

Throughout this book a system of coding for the Sundays and other occasions is used for ease and convenience.

Where a particular passage of scripture appears more than once in the course of a complete year, a code indicates on what other occasions that same biblical passage appears. The codes are also used beside each reading itemised in the 'Lectionary Index' at the back of the book.

The codes show the season of the year, the particular Sunday of that season being indicated by a number following, and the year is shown by the letters A, B, or C at the end: e.g. The First Sunday of Advent in Year A is shown as A1A.

Saints' Days and other Holy Days are shown by the month and day hyphenated: e.g. St Patrick's Day is shown as 3–17.

A more detailed explanation of the codes is shown below:

Codes for the Christian Calendar

A	Advent
C	Christmas
Ep	Epiphany
Pres	Presentation of Christ in the Temple
AW	Ash Wednesday
L	Lent
	Sundays before Lent show the number preceding the 'L'. As Mothering Sunday is always the Fourth Sunday of Lent, it is shown as L4MS
HW	Holy Week
	The Monday, Tuesday, and Wednesday are shown as M, T, and W
MT	Maundy Thursday
GF	Good Friday
EE	Easter Eve
EV	Easter Vigil
E	Easter
	Easter Day, being the First Sunday of Easter, is shown as E1
An	Ascension

P	Pentecost
TS	Trinity Sunday
Pr	Proper

An asterisk following a particular Proper refers to a Paired Reading. When there is no asterisk, the reading is from the Continuous lections

AS	All Saints

Codes for Special Occasions

BS	Bible Sunday
DF	Dedication Festival
Ember	Ember Days
GHS	The Guidance of the Holy Spirit
HT	Harvest Thanksgiving
Ms	Mission
Peace	Peace
Rog	Rogation Days
Unity	Unity

The Season of
Advent

The First Sunday of Advent   Year A
between November 27 and December 3

1st Reading   **Isaiah 2: 1–5**

118	Behold, the mountain of the Lord
501	Christ is the world's true light
263	Crown him with many crowns
496	For the healing of the nations
538	O Lord, the clouds are gathering
539	Rejoice, O land, in God thy might
509	Your kingdom come, O God!

Psalm   **Psalm 122**   *[DFBC/Ember]*

683	All people that on earth do dwell
670	Jerusalem the golden
506	Pray that Jerusalem may have

2nd Reading   **Romans 13: 11–14**

549	Dear Lord and Father of mankind
74	First of the week and finest day
126	Hark! a thrilling voice is sounding
487	Soldiers of Christ, arise
488	Stand up, stand up for Jesus

The Gospel   **Matthew 24: 36–44**

119	Come, thou long-expected Jesus
127	Hark what a sound, and too divine for hearing
132	Lo! he comes with clouds descending
140	The Lord will come and not be slow
145	You servants of the Lord

The First Sunday of Advent   Year B
between November 27 and December 3

1st Reading   **Isaiah 64: 1–9**

122	Drop down, ye heavens, from above
336	Jesus, where'er thy people meet
132	Lo! he comes with clouds descending
594	O Lord of creation, to you be all praise!

3

Psalm		**Psalm 80: 1–7, 17–19**	*[A4A]*
	10	All my hope on God is founded	
	695	God of mercy, God of grace	
	614	Great Shepherd of your people, hear	
	305	O Breath of life, come sweeping through us	

2nd Reading		**1 Corinthians 1: 3–9**
	327	Christ is our corner-stone
	508	Peace to you

The Gospel		**Mark 13: 24–37**
	119	Come, thou long-expected Jesus
	567	Forth, in thy name, O Lord, I go
	668	God is our fortress and our rock
	125	Hail to the Lord's anointed
	127	Hark what a sound, and too divine for hearing
	130	Jesus came, the heavens adoring
	132	Lo! he comes with clouds descending
	369	Songs of praise the angels sang
	197	Songs of thankfulness and praise
	678	Ten thousand times ten thousand
	73	The day thou gavest, Lord, is ende'd
	140	The Lord will come and not be slow
	142	Wake, O wake! With tidings thrilling
	145	You servants of the Lord

The First Sunday of Advent   Year C
between November 27 and December 3

1st Reading		**Jeremiah 33: 14–16**
	642	Amazing grace (how sweet the sound!)
	323	The God of Abraham praise

Psalm		**Psalm 25: 1–10**	*[LIB/Pr1OC*]*
	17	Lead me, Lord, lead me in thy righteousness	
		(Treoraigh mé, treoraigh mé, a Thiarna)	
	652	Lead us, heavenly Father, lead us	
	712	Tell out, my soul, the greatness of the Lord	

2nd Reading		**1 Thessalonians 3: 9–13**
	343	We love the place, O God
The Gospel		**Luke 21: 25–36**
	567	Forth, in thy name, O Lord, I go
	668	God is our fortress and our rock
	126	Hark! a thrilling voice is sounding
	127	Hark what a sound, and too divine for hearing
	131	Lift up your heads, you mighty gates
	132	Lo! he comes with clouds descending
	369	Songs of praise the angels sang
	488	Stand up, stand up for Jesus
	73	The day thou gavest, Lord, is ended
	509	Your kingdom come, O God!

The Second Sunday of Advent   Year A
between December 4 and 10

1st Reading		**Isaiah 11: 1–10**
	250	All hail the power of Jesu's name
	296	Come, Holy Ghost, our souls inspire
	297	Come, thou Holy Spirit, come
	263	Crown him with many crowns
	481	God is working his purpose out as year succeeds to year
	161	I know a rose-tree springing
	431	Lord, enthroned in heavenly splendour
	636	May the mind of Christ my Saviour
	135	O come, O come, Emmanuel
	197	Songs of thankfulness and praise (*omit v.4*)
Psalm		**Psalm 72: 1–7, 18–19**
	688	Come, bless the Lord, God of our forebears
	353	Give to our God immortal praise
	481	God is working his purpose out as year succeeds to year
	125	Hail to the Lord's anointed
	97	Jesus shall reign where'er the sun
	706	O bless the God of Israel
	140	The Lord will come and not be slow

5

2nd Reading		Romans 15: 4–13
	250	All hail the power of Jesu's name
	263	Crown him with many crowns
	381	God has spoken—by his prophets
	382	Help us, O Lord, to learn
	161	I know a rose-tree springing
	383	Lord, be thy word my rule
	384	Lord, thy word abideth
	385	Rise and hear! The Lord is speaking
	386	Spirit of God, unseen as the wind
	387	Thanks to God, whose Word was spoken
	372	Through all the changing scenes of life

The Gospel		Matthew 3: 1–12
	126	Hark! a thrilling voice is sounding
	303	Lord of the Church, we pray for our renewing
	136	On Jordan's bank the Baptist's cry
	204	When Jesus came to Jordan

The Second Sunday of Advent   Year B
between December 4 and 10

1st Reading		Isaiah 40: 1–11	[6–24]
	120	Comfort, comfort ye my people	
	122	Drop down, ye heavens, from above	
	644	Faithful Shepherd, feed me	
	6	Immortal, invisible, God only wise	
	535	Judge eternal, throned in splendour	
	134	Make way, make way, for Christ the King	
	141	These are the days of Elijah	

Psalm		Psalm 85: 1–2, 8–13
	695	God of mercy, God of grace
	539	Rejoice, O land, in God thy might
	140	The Lord will come and not be slow

2nd Reading		2 Peter 3: 8–15a
	567	Forth, in thy name, O Lord, I go
	162	In the bleak mid-winter
	164	It came upon the midnight clear

| 634 | Love divine, all loves excelling |
| 537 | O God, our help in ages past |

The Gospel   **Mark 1: 1–8**

126	Hark! a thrilling voice is sounding ✓
419	I am not worthy, holy Lord
134	Make way, make way, for Christ the King
136	On Jordan's bank the Baptist's cry
491	We have a gospel to proclaim
204	When Jesus came to Jordan

The Second Sunday of Advent   Year C
between December 4 and 10

1st Reading   **Baruch 5: 1–9**

| 418 | Here, O my Lord, I see thee face to face |
| 671 | Jesus, thy blood and righteousness |

Alternative 1st Reading   **Malachi 3: 1–4** ✓   *[PresABC]*

52	Christ, whose glory fills the skies
634	Love divine, all loves excelling
134	Make way, make way, for Christ the King
640	Purify my heart

Canticle for Psalm   **Benedictus (Luke 1: 68–79)**   *[Pr29C]*

685	Blessed be the God of Israel
52	Christ, whose glory fills the skies
119	Come, thou long-expected Jesus
381	God has spoken—by his prophets
706	O bless the God of Israel

2nd Reading   **Philippians 1: 3–11**

518	Bind us together, Lord
413	Father, we thank thee who hast planted
567	Forth, in thy name, O Lord, I go

The Gospel   **Luke 3: 1–6**

| 126 | Hark! a thrilling voice is sounding |
| 134 | Make way, make way, for Christ the King |

306   O Spirit of the living God
136   On Jordan's bank the Baptist's cry
204   When Jesus came to Jordan

The Third Sunday of Advent   Year A
between December 11 and 17

1st Reading   **Isaiah 35: 1–10**

146   A great and mighty wonder
166   Joy to the world, the Lord is come!
231   My song is love unknown (*vv. 1, 2, 4, 7*)
104   O for a thousand tongues to sing
113   There is singing in the desert, there is laughter in
        the skies

Psalm   **Psalm 146: 5–10**   *[A3C]*

4   God, who made the earth
125   Hail to the Lord's anointed
92   How sweet the name of Jesus sounds
357   I'll praise my maker while I've breath
97   Jesus shall reign where'er the sun
99   Jesus, the name high over all
535   Judge eternal, throned in splendour
363   O Lord of heaven and earth and sea
712   Tell out, my soul, the greatness of the Lord
8   The Lord is king! Lift up your voice
376   Ye holy angels bright

Alternative Canticle   **Magnificat (Luke 1: 47–55)**   *[A3B/A4BC]*

704   Mary sang a song, a song of love
712   Tell out, my soul, the greatness of the Lord
139   The angel Gabriel from heaven came
373   To God be the glory! Great things he has done!

2nd Reading   **James 5: 7–10**

41   [God, whose farm is all creation]
535   Judge eternal, throned in splendour
281   Rejoice, the Lord is King!

The Gospel **Matthew 11: 2–11**

417	He gave his life in selfless love
104	O for a thousand tongues to sing
136	On Jordan's bank the Baptist's cry
324	God, whose almighty word

The Third Sunday of Advent Year B
between December 11 and 17

1st Reading **Isaiah 61: 1–4, 8–11**

218	And can it be that I should gain
494	Beauty for brokenness
481	God is working his purpose out as year succeeds to year
324	God, whose almighty word
125	Hail to the Lord's anointed
569	Hark, my soul, it is the Lord
124	Hark the glad sound! the Saviour comes
418	Here, O my Lord, I see thee face to face
574	I give you all the honour
357	I'll praise my maker while I've breath
97	Jesus shall reign where'er the sun
99	Jesus, the name high over all
671	Jesus, thy blood and righteousness
134	Make way, make way, for Christ the king
706	O bless the God of Israel
104	O for a thousand tongues to sing

Psalm **Psalm 126** [L5C/Pr25B*/7–25/HTB]

567	Forth, in thy name, O Lord, I go
356	I will sing, I will sing a song unto the Lord
712	Tell out, my soul, the greatness of the Lord
373	To God be the glory! Great things he has done!

Alternative Canticle to Psalm **Magnificat (Luke 1: 47–55)** [A3A/A4BC]

704	Mary sang a song, a song of love
712	Tell out, my soul, the greatness of the Lord
373	To God be the glory! Great things he has done!

2nd Reading   **1 Thessalonians 5: 16–24**

455	Go forth for God; go forth to the world in peace
631	God be in my head
303	Lord of the Church, we pray for our renewing
634	Love Divine, all loves excelling
639	O thou who camest from above
341	Spirit divine, attend our prayers
73	The day thou gavest, Lord, is ended

The Gospel   **John 1: 6–8, 19–28**

124	Hark the glad sound! the Saviour comes
134	Make way, make way, for Christ the king
135	O come, O come, Emmanuel
136	On Jordan's bank the Baptist's cry

The Third Sunday of Advent   Year C
between December 11 and 17

1st Reading   **Zephaniah 3: 14–20**   *[EVABC]*

86	Christ is the King! O friends, rejoice
646	Glorious things of thee are spoken
281	Rejoice, the Lord is King!

Canticle for Psalm   **'The Song of Isaiah' (Isaiah 12: 2–6)**   *[EVABC]*

370	Stand up, and bless the Lord
373	To God be the glory! Great things he has done!
492	Ye servants of God, your master proclaim

Alternative Psalm   **Psalm 146: 5–10**   *[A3A]*

4	God, who made the earth
125	Hail to the Lord's anointed
92	How sweet the name of Jesus sounds
357	I'll praise my maker while I've breath
97	Jesus shall reign where'er the sun
99	Jesus, the name high over all
535	Judge eternal, throned in splendour
363	O Lord of heaven and earth and sea
712	Tell out, my soul, the greatness of the Lord
8	The Lord is king! Lift up your voice
376	Ye holy angels bright

2nd Reading   **Philippians 4: 4–7**   *[Rog]*

349	Fill thou my life, O Lord my God
225	In the cross of Christ I glory
16	Like a mighty river flowing
636	May the mind of Christ my Saviour
507	Put peace into each other's hands
281	Rejoice, the Lord is King!
627	What a friend we have in Jesus

The Gospel   **Luke 3: 7–18**

419	I am not worthy, holy Lord
303	Lord of the Church, we pray for our renewing
306	O Spirit of the living God
136	On Jordan's bank the Baptist's cry
341	Spirit divine, attend our prayers
204	When Jesus came to Jordan

The Fourth Sunday of Advent   Year A
between December 18 and 24

1st Reading   **Isaiah 7: 10–16**

151	Child in the manger
160	Hark! the herald-angels sing
168	Lord, you were rich beyond all splendour
135	O come, O come, Emmanuel
174	O little town of Bethlehem

Psalm   **Psalm 80: 1–7, 17–19**   *[AIB]*

10	All my hope on God is founded
695	God of mercy, God of grace
614	Great Shepherd of your people, hear
305	O Breath of life, come sweeping through us

2nd Reading   **Romans 1: 1–7**

524	May the grace of Christ our Saviour
508	Peace to you

The Gospel   **Matthew 1: 18–25**

250	All hail the power of Jesu's name
148	As Joseph was a-walking

152	Come and join the celebration
119	Come, thou long-expected Jesus
159	Good Christians all, rejoice
160	Hark! the herald-angels sing
92	How sweet the name of Jesus sounds
94	In the name of Jesus
99	Jesus, the name high over all
168	Lord, you were rich beyond all splendour
102	Name of all majesty
135	O come, O come, Emmanuel
174	O little town of Bethlehem
175	Of the Father's heart begotten
139	The angel Gabriel from heaven came
117	To the name of our salvation

The Fourth Sunday of Advent
between December 18 and 24

Year B

1st Reading		**2 Samuel 7: 1–11, 16**	
	342	Sweet is the solemn voice that calls	
	73	The day thou gavest, Lord, is ended	
	343	We love the place, O God	
Canticle for Psalm		**Magnificat (Luke 1: 47–55)**	*[A3AB/A4C]*
	704	Mary sang a song, a song of love	
	712	Tell out, my soul, the greatness of the Lord	
	373	To God be the glory! Great things he has done!	
Alternative Psalm		**Psalm 89: 1–4, 19–26**	
	690	Come, worship God, who is worthy of honour	
	374	When all thy mercies, O my God	
2nd Reading		**Romans 16: 25–37**	
	636	May the mind of Christ my Saviour	
	175	Of the Father's heart begotten	
The Gospel		**Luke 1: 26–38**	*[3–25]*
	119	Come, thou long-expected Jesus	
	263	Crown him with many crowns (*vv. 1, 2, 5, 6*)	
	462	For Mary, mother of our Lord	

123   God the Father sends his angel
125   Hail to the Lord's anointed
 92   How sweet the name of Jesus sounds
 94   In the name of Jesus
 97   Jesus shall reign where'er the sun
 99   Jesus, the name high over all
133   Long ago, prophets knew
704   Mary sang a song, a song of love
175   Of the Father's heart begotten
472   Sing we of the blessed mother
139   The angel Gabriel from heaven came
 73   The day thou gavest, Lord, is ended
185   Virgin-born, we bow before thee
477   We praise you, Lord, today

The Fourth Sunday of Advent   Year C
between December 18 and 24

1st Reading   **Micah 5: 2–5a**

194   Earth has many a noble city (*vv. 1, 2, 5*)
158   God rest you merry, gentlemen
160   Hark! the herald-angels sing
431   Lord, enthroned in heavenly splendour
171   O Bethl'hem is a small place
174   O little town of Bethlehem
179   See amid the winter's snow
197   Songs of thankfulness and praise (*omit v. 4*)
198   The first Nowell the angel did say (*vv. 1, 2, 4, 6*)

Canticle for Psalm   **Magnificat (Luke 1: 47–55)**   *[A3AB/A4B]*

704   Mary sang a song, a song of love
712   Tell out, my soul, the greatness of the Lord
373   To God be the glory! Great things he has done!

Alternative Psalm   **Psalm 80: 1–7**

695   God of mercy, God of grace
614   Great Shepherd of your people, hear

2nd Reading   **Hebrews 10: 5–10**

400   And now, O Father, mindful of the love
431   Lord, enthroned in heavenly splendour

The Gospel **Luke 1: 39–45 (46–55)**

470 Let God's people join in worship
472 Sing we of the blessed mother
185 Virgin-born, we bow before thee
476 Ye watchers and ye holy ones

If Psalm 80: 1–7 is used and the optional extra Gospel verses are accordingly read, see hymns for Psalm Canticle above

2 The Seasons of Christmas and Epiphany

*concluding with the
Presentation of Christ in the Temple*

Christmas Day
December 25

Years A, B, C

CHRISTMAS PROPER I

1st Reading		**Isaiah 9: 2–7**
	151	Child in the manger
	52	Christ, whose glory fills the skies
	124	Hark the glad sound! the Saviour comes
	174	O little town of Bethlehem
	369	Songs of praise the angels sang
	323	The God of Abraham praise
	199	The people that in darkness walked
	184	Unto us is born a Son

Psalm		**Psalm 96**	*[Pr4C/Pr24A*]*
	166	Joy to the world, the Lord is come!	
	705	New songs of celebration render	
	196	O worship the Lord in the beauty of holiness!	
	710	Sing to God new songs of worship	
	8	The Lord is king! Lift up your voice	
	373	To God be the glory! Great things he has done!	
	377	You shall go out with joy	

2nd Reading		**Titus 2: 11–14**
	160	Hark! the herald-angels sing

The Gospel		**Luke 2: 1–14 (15–20)**
	146	A great and mighty wonder
	147	Angels, from the realms of glory
	149	Away in a manger, no crib for a bed
	151	Child in the manger
	156	Don oíche úd i mBeithil *(About that night in Bethl'hem)*
	693	Glory in the highest to the God of heaven!
	157	'Glory to God!' all heav'n with joy is ringing *(omit v.3)*
	692	Glory to God in highest heav'n
	158	God rest you merry, gentlemen
	162	In the bleak mid-winter
	163	Infant holy, infant lowly
	585	Jesus, good above all other *(vv. 1, 2, 5)*

Christmas Day

December 25

Years A, B, C

CHRISTMAS PROPER 2

| **1st Reading** | **Isaiah 62: 6–12** |
| | 134   Make way, make way, for Christ the King |

Psalm	**Psalm 97** *[E7C/8–6]*
	34 O worship the King all-glorious above
	281 Rejoice, the Lord is King!
	8 The Lord is King! Lift up your voice

| **2nd Reading** | **Titus 3: 4–7** |
| | 305   O Breath of life, come sweeping through us |

| **The Gospel** | **Luke 2: (1–7) 8–20** |

146   A great and mighty wonder
147   Angels, from the realms of glory
149   Away in a manger, no crib for a bed
151   Child in the manger
156   Don oíche úd i mBeithil
     (*About that night in Bethl'hem*)
693   Glory in the highest to the God of heaven!
157   'Glory to God!' all heav'n with joy is ringing
     (*omit v.3*)
692   Glory to God in highest heaven
158   God rest you merry, gentlemen
162   In the bleak mid-winter
163   Infant holy, infant lowly
585   Jesus, good above all other (*vv. 1, 2, 5*)
170   Love came down at Christmas

172	O come, all ye faithful (*Adeste, fideles*) (*omit v. 4*)
176	On Christmas night all Christians sing
177	Once in royal David's city
182	Silent night, holy night
198	The first Nowell the angel did say (*vv. 1, 2, 6*)
187	When the crimson sun had set
188	While shepherds watched their flocks by night

Christmas Day
December 25

Years A, B, C

CHRISTMAS PROPER 3

1st Reading   **Isaiah 52: 7–10**   *[4–25/11–30]*

479	Go, tell it on the mountain
125	Hail to the Lord's anointed
129	How lovely on the mountains are the feet of him
597	Take my life, and let it be
387	Thanks to God, whose Word was spoken

Psalm   **Psalm 98**   *[EVABC/E6B/ Pr27C/Pr28C*]*

146	A great and mighty wonder
125	Hail to the Lord's anointed
166	Joy to the world, the Lord is come!
705	New songs of celebration render
710	Sing to God new songs of worship
369	Songs of praise the angels sang

2nd Reading   **Hebrews 1: 1–4 (5–12)**

84	Alleluia! raise the anthem
381	God has spoken—by his prophets
3	God is love: let heaven adore him
696	God, we praise you! God, we bless you!
94	In the name of Jesus
164	It came upon the midnight clear
276	Majesty, worship his majesty
228	Meekness and majesty (*omit v. 2*)
7	My God, how wonderful thou art
175	Of the Father's heart begotten
387	Thanks to God, whose Word was spoken

The Gospel		**John 1: 1–14 (15–18)**
	146	A great and mighty wonder
	84	Alleluia! raise the anthem
	87	Christ is the world's Light, he and none other
	259	Christ triumphant, ever reigning
	410	Dearest Jesus, at your word
	160	Hark! the herald-angels sing
	427	Let all mortal flesh keep silence
	195	Lord, the light of your love is shining
	172	O come, all ye faithful (*Adeste, fideles*)
	175	Of the Father's heart begotten
	491	We have a gospel to proclaim

The First Sunday of Christmas   Year A
between December 26 and January 1

1st Reading		**Isaiah 63: 7–9**
		No suggested hymns

Psalm		**Psalm 148**	*[CIBC/ESC]*
	682	All created things, bless the Lord	
	24	All creatures of our God and King	
	683	All people that on earth do dwell	
	711	All you heavens, bless the Lord (*Surrexit Christus*)	
	708	O praise ye the Lord! Praise him in the height	
	366	Praise, my soul, the King of heaven	
	709	Praise the Lord! You heavens, adore him	

2nd Reading		**Hebrews 2: 10–18**
	501	Christ is the world's true light
	94	In the name of Jesus
	584	Jesus calls us! O'er the tumult
	652	Lead us, heavenly Father, lead us
	108	Praise to the Holiest in the height

The Gospel		**Matthew 2: 13–23**
	460	For all your saints in glory (*vv. 1, 2v, 3*)
	184	Unto us is born a Son

The First Sunday of Christmas   Year B
between December 26 and January 1

1st Reading	**Isaiah 61: 10 – 62: 3**	
	218	And can it be that I should gain
	418	Here, O my Lord, I see thee face to face
	671	Jesus, thy blood and righteousness
	638	O for a heart to praise my God

Psalm	**Psalm 148**	*[CIAC/E5C]*
	682	All created things, bless the Lord
	24	All creatures of our God and King
	683	All people that on earth do dwell
	711	All you heavens, bless the Lord (*Surrexit Christus*)
	708	O praise ye the Lord! Praise him in the height
	366	Praise, my soul, the King of heaven
	709	Praise the Lord! You heavens, adore him

2nd Reading	**Galatians 4: 4–7**	*[1–1/9–8]*
	558	Abba Father, let me be
	241	[Sing, my tongue, the glorious battle (*vv. 1, 2, 5*)]
	185	Virgin-born, we bow before thee

The Gospel	**Luke 2: 15–21**	*[1–1]*
	250	All hail the power of Jesu's name
	152	Come and join the celebration
	92	How sweet the name of Jesus sounds
	94	In the name of Jesus
	98	Jesus! Name of wondrous love!
	99	Jesus, the name high over all
	102	Name of all majesty
	179	See amid the winter's snow
	180	Shepherds came, their praises bringing (*omit v. 2*)
	182	Silent night, holy night

The First Sunday of Christmas   Year C
between December 26 and January 1

1st Reading	**1 Samuel 2: 18–20, 26**	
	717	May the Lord bless you and keep you

Psalm	**Psalm 148**	*[CIAB/E5C]*
	682	All created things, bless the Lord
	24	All creatures of our God and King
	683	All people that on earth do dwell
	711	All you heavens, bless the Lord (*Surrexit Christus*)
	708	O praise ye the Lord! Praise him in the height
	366	Praise, my soul, the King of heaven
	709	Praise the Lord! You heavens, adore him

2nd Reading	**Colossians 3: 12–17**	*[L4MS/BSA]*
	346	Angel voices, ever singing
	294	Come down, O Love divine
	550	'Forgive our sins as we forgive'
	454	Forth in the peace of Christ we go
	300	Holy Spirit, truth divine
	360	Let all the world in every corner sing
	525	Let there be love shared among us
	503	Make me a channel of your peace
	361	Now thank we all our God
	369	Songs of praise the angels sang
	601	Teach me, my God and King
	374	When all thy mercies, O my God
	458	When, in our music, God is glorified

The Gospel	**Luke 2: 41–52**	
	347	Children of Jerusalem
	453	Come to us, creative Spirit
	632	I love to hear the story
	651	Jesus, friend of little children
	177	Once in royal David's city

The Second Sunday of Christmas   Years A, B, C
between January 2 and 5

1st Reading	**Jeremiah 31: 7–14**
644	Faithful Shepherd, feed me
481	God is working his purpose out as year succeeds to year
Alternative 1st Reading	**Sirach 24: 1–12**
646	Glorious things of thee are spoken
Psalm	**Psalm 147: 12–20**
350	For the beauty of the earth
6	Immortal, invisible, God only wise
Alternative Canticle to Psalm	**Wisdom 10: 15–21**
254	[At the Lamb's high feast we sing]
643	Be thou my vision, O Lord of my heart
262	[Come, ye faithful, raise the strain]
13	God moves in a mysterious way
104	O for a thousand tongues to sing
2nd Reading	**Ephesians 1: 3–14** [Pr10B]
84	Alleluia! raise the anthem
189	As with gladness men of old
318	Father, Lord of all creation
352	Give thanks with a grateful heart
99	Jesus, the name high over all
652	Lead us, heavenly Father, lead us
524	May the grace of Christ our Saviour
363	O Lord of heaven and earth and sea
313	The Spirit came, as promised
9	There's a wideness in God's mercy
373	To God be the glory! Great things he has done!
451	We come as guests invited
The Gospel	**John 1: 1–9 (10–18)**
146	A great and mighty wonder
215	[Ah, holy Jesu, how hast thou offended]
250	All hail the power of Jesu's name
84	Alleluia! raise the anthem
147	Angels, from the realms of glory

151	Child in the manger
87	Christ is the world's Light, he and none other
501	Christ is the world's true light
259	Christ triumphant, ever reigning
52	Christ, whose glory fills the skies
381	God has spoken—by his prophets
89	God is love—his the care
553	Jesu, lover of my soul
425	Jesus, thou joy of loving hearts
166	Joy to the world, the Lord is come!
427	Let all mortal flesh keep silence
195	Lord, the light of your love is shining
634	Love divine, all loves excelling
172	O come, all ye faithful (*Adeste, fideles*)
175	Of the Father's heart begotten
387	Thanks to God, whose Word was spoken
491	We have a gospel to proclaim

The Epiphany

Years A, B, C

January 6

1st Reading

Isaiah 60: 1–6

190	Brightest and best of the suns of the morning
125	Hail to the Lord's anointed
192	How brightly beams the morning star!
195	Lord, the light of your love is shining
196	O worship the Lord in the beauty of holiness!

Psalm

Psalm 72: 1–7, 10–14

250	All hail the power of Jesu's name
688	Come, bless the Lord, God of our forebears
353	Give to our God immortal praise
125	Hail to the Lord's anointed
97	Jesus shall reign where'er the sun
140	The Lord will come and not be slow

2nd Reading

Ephesians 3: 1–12

642	Amazing grace (how sweet the sound!)
562	Blessed assurance, Jesus is mine
11	Can we by searching find out God
352	Give thanks with a grateful heart

522	In Christ there is no east or west
103	O Christ the same, through all our story's pages
112	There is a Redeemer

The Gospel **Matthew 2: 1–12**

147	Angels, from the realms of glory
189	As with gladness men of old
190	Brightest and best of the suns of the morning
152	Come and join the celebration
194	Earth has many a noble city
162	In the bleak mid-winter
170	Love came down at Christmas
196	O worship the Lord in the beauty of holiness!
198	The first Nowell the angel did say
600	The wise may bring their learning
201	We three kings of Orient are
202	What child is this, who, laid to rest

The First Sunday of Epiphany   Year A
The Baptism of Christ   between January 7 and 13

1st Reading **Isaiah 42: 1–9** *[HW-MABC]*

643	Be thou my vision, O Lord of my heart
691	Faithful vigil ended
353	Give to our God immortal praise
330	God is here! As we his people
124	Hark the glad sound! the Saviour comes
357	I'll praise my maker while I've breath
97	Jesus shall reign where'er the sun
99	Jesus, the name high over all
134	Make way, make way, for Christ the King
305	O Breath of life, come sweeping through us
104	O for a thousand tongues to sing
605	Will you come and follow me

Psalm **Psalm 29** *[EpIBC/TSB]*

349	Fill thou my life, O Lord my God
30	Let us, with a gladsome mind
431	Lord, enthroned in heavenly splendour
196	O worship the Lord in the beauty of holiness!
45	Praise, O praise our God and king

2nd Reading   **Acts 10: 34–43**   [E/ABC]

250   All hail the power of Jesu's name
263   Crown him with many crowns (vv. 1–4)
163   Infant holy, infant lowly (v. 1 only)
 96   Jesus is Lord! Creation's voice proclaims it
102   Name of all majesty
306   O Spirit of the living God
177   Once in royal David's city (vv. 1, 2, 5, 6)
197   Songs of thankfulness and praise
491   We have a gospel to proclaim

The Gospel   **Matthew 3: 13–17**

295   Come, gracious Spirit, heavenly Dove
324   God, whose almighty word
322   I bind unto myself today (vv. 1, 2, 8, 9)
652   Lead us, heavenly Father, lead us
214   O Love, how deep, how broad, how high!
136   On Jordan's bank the Baptist's cry
197   Songs of thankfulness and praise
341   Spirit divine, attend our prayers
386   Spirit of God, unseen as the wind
200   The sinless one to Jordan came
204   When Jesus came to Jordan

The First Sunday of Epiphany   Year B
The Baptism of Christ   between January 7 and 13

1st Reading   **Genesis 1: 1–5**

 66   Before the ending of the day
121   Creator of the starry height
 74   First of the week and finest day
  3   God is love: let heaven adore him
  4   God, who made the earth
 67   God, who made the earth and heaven
324   God, whose almighty word
 58   Morning has broken
537   O God, our help in ages past
369   Songs of praise the angels sang
341   Spirit divine, attend our prayers
 35   The spacious firmament on high
 77   This day, at God's creating word

Psalm	**Psalm 29**	*[EpIAC/TSB]*

349	Fill thou my life, O Lord my God
30	Let us, with a gladsome mind
431	Lord, enthroned in heavenly splendour
196	O worship the Lord in the beauty of holiness!
45	Praise, O praise our God and king

2nd Reading **Acts 19: 1–7**

295	Come, gracious Spirit, heavenly Dove
318	Father, Lord of all creation
299	Holy Spirit, come, confirm us
98	Jesus! Name of wondrous love!
305	O Breath of life, come sweeping through us
306	O Spirit of the living God
310	Spirit of the living God
111	There is a name I love to hear

The Gospel **Mark 1: 4–11**

295	Come, gracious Spirit, heavenly Dove
324	God, whose almighty word
419	I am not worthy, holy Lord
322	I bind unto myself today (*vv. 1, 2, 8, 9*)
652	Lead us, heavenly Father, lead us
214	O Love, how deep, how broad, how high!
136	On Jordan's bank the Baptist's cry
197	Songs of thankfulness and praise
341	Spirit divine, attend our prayers
386	Spirit of God, unseen as the wind
200	The sinless one to Jordan came
204	When Jesus came to Jordan

The First Sunday of Epiphany   Year C
The Baptism of Christ   between January 7 and 13

1st Reading **Isaiah 43: 1–7**

642	Amazing grace (how sweet the sound!)
12	God is our strength and refuge
557	Rock of ages, cleft for me
595	Safe in the shadow of the Lord
22	You shall cross the barren desert

Psalm		**Psalm 29**	*[Ep|AB/TSB]*
	349	Fill thou my life, O Lord my God	
	30	Let us, with a gladsome mind	
	431	Lord, enthroned in heavenly splendour	
	196	O worship the Lord in the beauty of holiness!	
	45	Praise, O praise our God and king	

2nd Reading		**Acts 8: 14–17**	
	294	Come down, O Love divine	
	297	Come, thou Holy Spirit, come	
	318	Father, Lord of all creation	
	312	Gracious Spirit, Holy Ghost	
	91	He is Lord, he is Lord	
	299	Holy Spirit, come, confirm us	
	421	I come with joy, a child of God	
	301	Let every Christian pray	
	306	O Spirit of the living God	
	313	The Spirit came, as promised	

The Gospel		**Luke 3: 15–17, 21–22**	
	295	Come, gracious Spirit, heavenly Dove	
	324	God, whose almighty word	
	419	I am not worthy, holy Lord	
	322	I bind unto myself today (*vv. 1, 2, 8, 9*)	
	652	Lead us, heavenly Father, lead us	
	214	O Love, how deep, how broad, how high?	
	136	On Jordan's bank the Baptist's cry	
	197	Songs of thankfulness and praise	
	341	Spirit divine, attend our prayers	
	386	Spirit of God, unseen as the wind	
	200	The sinless one to Jordan came	
	204	When Jesus came to Jordan	

The Second Sunday of Epiphany   Year A
between January 14 and 20

1st Reading		**Isaiah 49: 1–7**	*[HW-TABC]*
	685	Blessed be the God of Israel	
	691	Faithful vigil ended	
	481	God is working his purpose out as year succeeds to year	

	125	Hail to the Lord's anointed
	192	How brightly beams the morning star!
	706	O bless the God of Israel
	595	Safe in the shadow of the Lord
Psalm		**Psalm 40: 1–11**
	642	Amazing grace (how sweet the sound!)
	597	Take my life, and let it be
	712	Tell out, my soul, the greatness of the Lord
	492	Ye servants of God, your master proclaim
2nd Reading		**1 Corinthians 1: 1–9**
	80	Great is thy faithfulness, O God my Father
	268	Hail, thou once-despised Jesus
	431	Lord, enthroned in heavenly splendour
	508	Peace to you
	112	There is a Redeemer
The Gospel		**John 1: 29–42**
	258	[Christ the Lord is risen again!]
	295	Come, gracious Spirit, heavenly Dove
	332	Come, let us join our cheerful songs
	263	Crown him with many crowns
	693	Glory in the highest to the God of heaven!
	692	Glory to God in highest heav'n
	268	Hail, thou once-despised Jesus
	126	Hark! a thrilling voice is sounding
	584	Jesus calls us! O'er the tumult
	587	Just as I am, without one plea
	652	Lead us, heavenly Father, lead us
	431	Lord, enthroned in heavenly splendour
	200	The sinless one to Jordan came
	112	There is a Redeemer
	204	When Jesus came to Jordan
	395	When Jesus taught by Galilee
	492	Ye servants of God, your master proclaim

The Second Sunday of Epiphany   Year B
between January 14 and 20

1st Reading		**1 Samuel 3: 1–10 (11–20)**	*[Pr4B]*
	608	Be still and know that I am God	
✓	581	I, the Lord of sea and sky	
	589	Lord, speak to me that I may speak	
	624	Speak, Lord, in the stillness	

Psalm		**Psalm 139: 1–6, 13–18**	*[Pr4B/Pr18C*]*
	51	Awake, my soul, and with the sun	
	567	Forth, in thy name, O Lord, I go	
	226	It is a thing most wonderful	
	19	There is no moment of my life	

2nd Reading   **Revelation 5: 1–10**

398	Alleluia! sing to Jesus
332	Come, let us join our cheerful songs
454	Forth in the peace of Christ we go
694	Glory, honour, endless praises
697	Great and wonderful your deeds
699	Hail, gladdening Light of his pure glory poured
702	Light of the world, in grace and beauty
132	Lo! he comes with clouds descending
678	Ten thousand times ten thousand
112	There is a Redeemer
373	To God be the glory! Great things he has done!
292	Ye choirs of new Jerusalem

Alternative 2nd Reading   **1 Corinthians 6: 12–20**

630	Blessed are the pure in heart
382	Help us, O Lord, to learn
313	The Spirit came, as promised
244	There is a green hill far away

The Gospel   **John 1: 43–51**

549	Dear Lord and Father of mankind
460	For all your saints in glory, for all your saints at rest (*vv. 1, 2n, 3*)
219	From heav'n you came, helpless babe
584	Jesus calls us! O'er the tumult

97	Jesus shall reign where'er the sun
395	When Jesus taught by Galilee
605	Will you come and follow me

The Second Sunday of Epiphany   Year C
between January 14 and 20

1st Reading   **Isaiah 62: 1–5**

| 638 | O for a heart to praise my God |
| 528 | The Church's one foundation |

Psalm   **Psalm 36: 5–10**

| 6 | Immortal, invisible, God only wise |
| 553 | Jesu, lover of my soul |

2nd Reading   **1 Corinthians 12: 1–11**

294	Come down, O Love divine
408	Come, risen Lord, and deign to be our guest
297	Come, thou Holy Spirit, come
318	Father, Lord of all creation
312	Gracious Spirit, Holy Ghost
91	He is Lord, he is Lord
299	Holy Spirit, come, confirm us
421	I come with joy, a child of God
96	Jesus is Lord! Creation's voice proclaims it
301	Let every Christian pray
102	Name of all majesty
306	O Spirit of the living God
438	O thou, who at thy eucharist didst pray
440	One bread, one body, one Lord of all
313	The Spirit came, as promised
491	We have a gospel to proclaim

The Gospel   **John 2: 1–11**

197	Songs of thankfulness and praise
445	Soul, array thyself with gladness
528	The Church's one foundation
448	The trumpets sound, the angels sing

The Third Sunday of Epiphany

Year A

between January 21 and 27

1st Reading   **Isaiah 9: 1–4**

52	Christ, whose glory fills the skies
362	O God beyond all praising
306	O Spirit of the living God
199	The people that in darkness walked

Psalm   **Psalm 27: 1, 4–9**

87	Christ is the world's Light, he and none other
501	Christ is the world's true light
431	Lord, enthroned in heavenly splendour
362	O God beyond all praising
620	O Lord, hear my prayer
557	Rock of ages, cleft for me
20	The King of love my shepherd is

2nd Reading   **1 Corinthians 1: 10–18**

86	Christ is the King! O friends, rejoice
318	Father, Lord of all creation
478	Go forth and tell! O Church of God, awake!
479	Go, tell it on the mountain
520	God is love, and where true love is, God himself is there
523	Help us to help each other, Lord
421	I come with joy, a child of God
522	In Christ there is no east or west
525	Let there be love shared among us
484	Lift high the cross, the love of Christ proclaim
438	O thou, who at thy eucharist didst pray
486	People of God, arise
507	Put peace into each others' hands
485	Rise up and serve the Lord!
488	Stand up, stand up for Jesus
490	The Spirit lives to set us free
530	Ubi caritas et amor
491	We have a gospel to proclaim
531	Where love and loving-kindness dwell
492	Ye servants of God, your master proclaim

The Gospel	**Matthew 4: 12–23**
52	Christ, whose glory fills the skies
549	Dear Lord and Father of mankind
460	For all your saints in glory, for all your saints at rest (*vv. 1, 2s, 3*)
219	From heav'n you came, helpless babe
584	Jesus calls us! O'er the tumult
593	O Jesus, I have promised
199	The people that in darkness walked
395	When Jesus taught by Galilee
605	Will you come and follow me

The Third Sunday of Epiphany

Year B

between January 21 and 27

1st Reading	**Jonah 3: 1–5, 10**
381	God has spoken—by his prophets
Psalm	**Psalm 62: 5–12**
381	God has spoken—by his prophets
668	God is our fortress and our rock
557	Rock of ages, cleft for me
2nd Reading	**1 Corinthians 7: 29–31**
353	Give to our God immortal praise
646	Glorious things of thee are spoken
The Gospel	**Mark 1: 14–20**
549	Dear Lord and Father of mankind
460	For all your saints in glory, for all your saints at rest (*vv. 1, 2s, 3*)
219	From heav'n you came, helpless babe
584	Jesus calls us! O'er the tumult
395	When Jesus taught by Galilee
605	Will you come and follow me

The Third Sunday of Epiphany

Year C

between January 21 and 27

1st Reading		**Nehemiah 8: 1–3, 5–6, 8–10**
	381	God has spoken—by his prophets
	380	God has spoken to his people, alleluia!
	382	Help us, O Lord, to learn
	383	Lord, be thy word my rule
	384	Lord, thy word abideth
	386	Spirit of God, unseen as the wind
	387	Thanks to God, whose Word was spoken
	388	Word of the living God

Psalm		**Psalm 19**	*[L3B/EVABC/Pr19B/Pr22A]*
	606	As the deer pants for the water	
	153	Come, thou Redeemer of the earth	
	351	From all that dwell below the skies	
	631	God be in my head	
	696	God, we praise you! God, we bless you!	
	616	In my life, Lord, be glorified	
	97	Jesus shall reign where'er the sun	
	384	Lord, thy word abideth	
	432	Love is his word, love is his way	
	638	O for a heart to praise my God	
	34	O worship the King all-glorious above	
	35	The spacious firmament on high	

2nd Reading		**1 Corinthians 12: 12–31a**
	318	Father, Lord of all creation
	523	Help us to help each other, Lord
	303	Lord of the Church, we pray for our renewing
	438	O thou, who at thy eucharist didst pray
	440	One bread, one body, one Lord of all

The Gospel		**Luke 4: 14–21**
	218	And can it be that I should gain
	494	Beauty for brokenness
	501	Christ is the world's true light
	119	[Come, thou long-expected Jesus]
	380	God has spoken to his people, alleluia!
	125	Hail to the Lord's anointed
	569	Hark, my soul, it is the Lord

124	Hark the glad sound! the Saviour comes
357	I'll praise my maker while I've breath
97	Jesus shall reign where'er the sun
99	Jesus, the name, high over all
483	Jesus went to worship
134	Make way, make way, for Christ the King
706	O bless the God of Israel
104	O for a thousand tongues to sing
605	Will you come and follow me

The Fourth Sunday of Epiphany   Year A
between January 28 and February 1

1st Reading		**Micah 6: 1–8**
	190	Brightest and best of the suns of the morning
	567	Forth, in thy name, O Lord, I go
	211	Immortal love, for ever full
	358	King of glory, King of peace
	637	O for a closer walk with God
	498	What does the Lord require for praise and offering?

| **Psalm** | | **Psalm 15** | *[PrIIC*/PrI7B*/5–14]* |
| | 631 | God be in my head | |

2nd Reading		**1 Corinthians 1: 18–31**	*[HW-TABC]*
	643	Be thou my vision, O Lord of my heart	
	646	Glorious things of thee are spoken	
	225	In the cross of Christ I glory	
	698	Jesus, Saviour of the world	
	671	Jesus, thy blood and righteousness	
	484	Lift high the cross, the love of Christ proclaim	
	232	Nature with open volume stands	
	600	The wise may bring their learning	
	248	We sing the praise of him who died	
	247	When I survey the wondrous cross	

The Gospel		**Matthew 5: 1–12**	*[ASA]*
	630	Blessed are the pure in heart	
	293	Breathe on me, Breath of God	
	503	Make me a channel of your peace	

507	Put peace into each other's hands
308	Revive your Church, O Lord
712	Tell out, my soul, the greatness of the Lord
22	You shall cross the barren desert

The Fourth Sunday of Epiphany   Year B
between January 28 and February 1

1st Reading   **Deuteronomy 18: 15–20**

319	Father, of heaven, whose love profound
92	How sweet the name of Jesus sounds
535	Judge eternal, throned in splendour

Psalm   **Psalm 111**   *[Pr15B/Pr23C*]*

84	Alleluia! raise the anthem
352	Give thanks with a grateful heart
574	I give you all the honour
130	Jesus came, the heavens adoring
529	Thy hand, O God, has guided
373	To God be the glory! Great things he has done!

2nd Reading   **1 Corinthians 8: 1–13**

518	Bind us together, Lord
103	O Christ the same, through all our story's pages
529	Thy hand, O God, has guided

The Gospel   **Mark 1: 21–28**

211	Immortal love for ever full
99	Jesus, the name high over all
513	O Christ, the Healer, we have come
104	O for a thousand tongues to sing
112	There is a Redeemer
514	We cannot measure how you heal

The Fourth Sunday of Epiphany   Year C
between January 28 and February 1

1st Reading		**Ezekiel 43: 27–44**
	316	Bright the vision that delighted
	670	Jerusalem the golden
Psalm		**Psalm 48** [Pr9B]
	646	Glorious things of thee are spoken
	380	God has spoken to his people, alleluia!
	354	Great is the Lord and most worthy of praise
	593	O Jesus, I have promised
2nd Reading		**1 Corinthians 13: 1–13**
	515	'A new commandment I give unto you'
	86	Christ is the King! O friends, rejoice
	520	God is love, and where true love is, God himself is there
	89	God is love—his the care
	3	God is love: let heaven adore him
	312	Gracious Spirit, Holy Ghost
	523	Help us to help each other, Lord
	418	Here, O my Lord, I see thee face to face
	525	Let there be love shared among us
	195	Lord, the light of your love is shining
	634	Love divine, all loves excelling
	655	Loving Shepherd of your sheep
	7	My God, how wonderful thou art
	229	My God I love thee; not because
	105	O the deep, deep love of Jesus
	323	The God of Abraham praise (vv. 1, 2, 5)
	530	Ubi caritas et amor
The Gospel		**Luke 2: 22–40** [PresABC]
	119	Come, thou long-expected Jesus
	88	Fairest Lord Jesus
	691	Faithful vigil ended
	191	Hail to the Lord who comes
	193	In his temple now behold him
	634	Love divine, all loves excelling
	472	Sing we of the blessed mother
	203	When candles are lighted on Candlemas Day

The Presentation of Christ in the Temple Years A, B, C
February 2 also known as Candlemas Day

1st Reading		**Malachi 3: 1–4**	*[A2C]*
	52	Christ, whose glory fills the skies	
	634	Love divine, all loves excelling	
	134	Make way, make way, for Christ the King	
	640	Purify my heart	

Psalm		**Psalm 24: 1–10 (or 7–10)**	
	696	God, we praise you! God, we bless you!	
	266	[Hail the day that sees him rise *(vv. 1, 2)*]	
	358	King of glory, King of peace	
	337	Lift up your heads, O ye gates	
	131	Lift up your heads, you mighty gates	
	134	Make way, make way, for Christ the King	
	488	Stand up, stand up for Jesus	
	284	[The golden gates are lifted up]	

Alternative Psalm		**Psalm 84**	*[Pr16B]*
	400	And now, O Father, mindful of the love	
	333	How lovely are thy dwellings fair!	
	95	Jesu, priceless treasure	
	425	Jesus, thou joy of loving hearts	
	360	Let all the world in every corner sing	
	634	Love divine, all loves excelling	
	620	O Lord, hear my prayer	
	487	Soldiers of Christ, arise	
	342	Sweet is the solemn voice that calls	
	343	We love the place, O God	

2nd Reading		**Hebrews 2: 14–18**	
	212	Jesus, grant me this, I pray	
	652	Lead us, heavenly Father, lead us	
	635	Lord, be my guardian and my guide	
	108	Praise to the Holiest in the height	
	114	Thou didst leave thy throne and thy kingly crown	
	627	What a friend we have in Jesus	

The Gospel **Luke 2: 22–40** *[Ep4C]*

119 Come, thou long-expected Jesus
88 Fairest Lord Jesus
691 Faithful vigil ended
191 Hail to the Lord who comes
193 In his temple now behold him
634 Love divine, all loves excelling
472 Sing we of the blessed mother
203 When candles are lighted on Candlemas Day

3 ORDINARY TIME
The Sundays before Lent

(PROPERS 0–3)

The Fifth Sunday before Lent   Year A

(occurrence of this Sunday depends on the dates of Easter Day and Ash Wednesday)

PROPER 0

1st Reading		**Isaiah 58: 1–9a (9b–12)**	*[AWABC]*
	647	Guide me, O thou great Jehovah	
	125	Hail to the Lord's anointed	
	535	Judge eternal, throned in splendour	
	712	Tell out, my soul, the greatness of the Lord	
	497	The Church of Christ, in every age	
	510	We pray for peace	

Psalm **Psalm 112: 1–9 (10)**

591   O happy day that fixed my choice

2nd Reading **1 Corinthians 2: 1–12 (13–16)**

11   Can we by searching find out God
567   Forth, in thy name, O Lord, I go
220   [Glory be to Jesus]
232   Nature with open volume stands
594   O Lord of creation, to you be all praise!
248   We sing the praise of him who died
247   [When I survey the wondrous cross]

The Gospel **Matthew 5: 13–20**

86   Christ is the King! O friends, rejoice
589   Lord, speak to me that I may speak
503   Make me a channel of your peace
526   Risen Lord, whose name we cherish

The Fifth Sunday before Lent   Year B

(occurrence of this Sunday depends on the dates of Easter Day and Ash
Wednesday)

PROPER 0

1st Reading		**Isaiah 40: 21–31**
	566	Fight the good fight with all thy might!
	3	God is love: let heaven adore him
	306	O Spirit of the living God
	323	The God of Abraham praise

Psalm		**Psalm 147: 1–11, 20c**
	16	Like a mighty river flowing

2nd Reading		**1 Corinthians 9: 16–23**
	478	Go forth and tell! O Church of God, awake!
	589	Lord, speak to me that I may speak
	306	O Spirit of the living God
	491	We have a gospel to proclaim

The Gospel		**Mark 1: 29–39**
	65	At evening, when the sun had set
	512	From you all skill and science flow
	211	Immortal love for ever full
	213	Jesus' hands were kind hands, doing good to all
	513	O Christ, the Healer, we have come

The Fifth Sunday before Lent   Year C

(occurrence of this Sunday depends on the dates of Easter Day and Ash
Wednesday)

PROPER 0

1st Reading		**Isaiah 6: 1–8 (9–13)**	*[TSB]*
	316	Bright the vision that delighted	
	415	For the bread which you have broken	
	454	Forth in the peace of Christ we go	
	331	God reveals his presence	

696	God, we praise you! God, we bless you!
355	Holy, holy, holy is the Lord
321	Holy, holy, holy! Lord God almighty
714	Holy, holy, holy Lord, God of power and might
715	Holy, holy, holy, Lord God, the Lord almighty
581	I, the Lord of sea and sky
6	Immortal, invisible, God only wise
427	Let all mortal flesh keep silence
7	My God, how wonderful thou art
639	O thou who camest from above
370	Stand up, and bless the Lord
323	The God of Abraham praise

Psalm **Psalm 138** *[Pr5B/Pr12C*/Pr16A*]*

250	All hail the power of Jesu's name
358	King of glory, King of peace
21	The Lord's my shepherd, I'll not want

2nd Reading **1 Corinthians 15: 1–11** *[EIB]*

218	And can it be that I should gain
257	Christ is the world's Redeemer
264	Finished the strife of battle now
286	The strife is o'er, the battle done
248	We sing the praise of him who died

The Gospel **Luke 5: 1–11**

454	Forth in the peace of Christ we go
567	Forth, in thy name, O Lord, I go
419	I am not worthy, holy Lord
553	Jesu, lover of my soul

The Fourth Sunday before Lent   Year A

(occurrence of this Sunday depends on the dates of Easter Day and Ash Wednesday)

PROPER I

Ist Reading		**Deuteronomy 30: 15–20**	[Pr18C]
	206	Come, let us to the Lord our God	
	56	Lord, as I wake I turn to you	
	591	O happy day that fixed my choice	
	597	Take my life, and let it be	

Alternative Ist Reading		**Sirach 15: 15–20**
	206	Come, let us to the Lord our God
	56	Lord, as I wake I turn to you
	591	O happy day that fixed my choice
	597	Take my life, and let it be

Psalm		**Psalm 119: 1–8**	[Pr26B*/5–I]
	630	Blessed are the pure in heart	
	649	Happy are they, they that love God	
	601	Teach me, my God and King	

2nd Reading		**1 Corinthians 3: 1–9**
	481	God is working his purpose out as year succeeds to year
	42	[Good is the Lord, our heavenly King]
	43	[Holy is the seed-time, when the buried grain]
	303	Lord of the Church, we pray for our renewing
	526	Risen Lord, whose name we cherish
	47	[We plough the fields, and scatter]

The Gospel		**Matthew 5: 21–37**
	550	'Forgive our sins as we forgive'
	421	I come with joy, a child of God
	589	Lord, speak to me that I may speak

The Fourth Sunday before Lent   Year B

(occurrence of this Sunday depends on the dates of Easter Day and Ash Wednesday)

PROPER I

1st Reading		**2 Kings 5: 1–14**	*[Pr9C]*
	553	Jesu, lover of my soul	
	587	Just as I am, without one plea	
	557	Rock of ages, cleft for me	

Psalm		**Psalm 30**	*[E3C/Pr5C*/Pr8B*/Pr9C]*
	554	Lord Jesus, think on me	
	592	O Love that wilt not let me go	
	196	O worship the Lord in the beauty of holiness!	
	528	The Church's one foundation	

2nd Reading		**1 Corinthians 9: 24–27**
	566	Fight the good fight with all thy might!
	101	Jesus, the very thought of thee
	636	May the mind of Christ my Saviour
	376	Ye holy angels bright

The Gospel		**Mark 1: 40–45**
	511	Father of mercy, God of consolation
	512	From you all skill and science flow
	553	Jesu, lover of my soul
	513	O Christ, the Healer, we have come
	514	We cannot measure how you heal

The Fourth Sunday before Lent   Year C

(occurrence of this Sunday depends on the dates of Easter Day and Ash Wednesday)

PROPER 1

1st Reading		**Jeremiah 17: 5–10**
	10	All my hope on God is founded
	257	Christ is the world's Redeemer
	553	Jesu, lover of my soul

Psalm		**Psalm 1**	*[E7B/Pr18C*/Pr20B/Pr25A*]*
	649	Happy are they, they that love God	
	56	Lord, as I wake I turn to you	
	383	Lord, be thy word my rule	

2nd Reading		**1 Corinthians 15: 12–20**
	251	[Alleluia! Alleluia! Hearts to heaven and voices raise]
	703	[Now lives the Lamb of God]
	289	[This joyful Eastertide]

The Gospel		**Luke 6: 17–26**
	494	Beauty for brokenness
	324	God, whose almighty word
	513	O Christ, the Healer, we have come
	448	The trumpets sound, the angels sing

The Third Sunday before Lent   Year A

(occurrence of this Sunday depends on the dates of Easter Day and Ash Wednesday)

PROPER 2

1st Reading		**Leviticus 19: 1–2, 9–18**	*[E5C/Pr25A*]*
	515	'A new commandment I give unto you'	
	494	Beauty for brokenness	
	39	For the fruits of his creation	
	321	Holy, holy, holy! Lord God Almighty	

535	Judge eternal, throned in splendour
525	Let there be love shared among us
497	The Church of Christ, in every age
509	Your kingdom come, O God!

Psalm **Psalm 119: 33–40** *[Pr18A*]*

594	O Lord of creation, to you be all praise!

2nd Reading **1 Corinthians 3: 10–11, 16–23**

218	And can it be that I should gain
643	Be thou my vision, O Lord of my heart
630	Blessed are the pure in heart
326	Blessed city, heavenly Salem (*Christ is made the sure foundation*)
327	Christ is our corner-stone
294	Come down, O Love divine
330	God is here! As we his people
528	The Church's one foundation
8	The Lord is king! Lift up your voice
313	The Spirit came, as promised

The Gospel **Matthew 5: 38–48**

516	Beloved, let us love: love is of God
517	Brother, sister, let me serve you
523	Help us to help each other, Lord
513	O Christ, the Healer, we have come
499	When I needed a neighbour, were you there
531	Where love and loving-kindness dwell
500	Would you walk by on the other side

The Third Sunday before Lent   Year B

(occurrence of this Sunday depends on the dates of Easter Day and Ash Wednesday)

PROPER 2

1st Reading **Isaiah 43: 18–25**

125	Hail to the Lord's anointed

Psalm **Psalm 41**

366	Praise, my soul, the King of heaven

2nd Reading		**2 Corinthians 1: 18–22**
	313	The Spirit came, as promised
	451	We come as guests invited

The Gospel		**Mark 2: 1–12**
	197	Songs of thankfulness and praise
	370	Stand up, and bless the Lord

The Third Sunday before Lent   Year C

(occurrence of this Sunday depends on the dates of Easter Day and Ash Wednesday)

PROPER 2

1st Reading		**Genesis 45: 3–11, 15**
	563	Commit your ways to God
	649	Happy are they, they that love God
	522	In Christ there is no east or west
	525	Let there be love shared among us
	527	Son of God, eternal Saviour
	531	Where love and loving-kindness dwell

Psalm		**Psalm 37: 1–11, 39–40**
	608	Be still and know that I am God
	325	Be still, for the presence of the Lord, the Holy One, is here
	563	Commit your ways to God
	12	God is our strength and refuge
	639	O thou who camest from above

2nd Reading		**1 Corinthians 15: 35–38, 42–50**
	250	All hail the power of Jesu's name
	703	Now lives the Lamb of God
	108	Praise to the Holiest in the height
	186	What Adam's disobedience cost

The Gospel		**Luke 6: 27–38**
	517	Brother, sister, let me serve you
	550	'Forgive our sins as we forgive'

416	Great God, your love has called us here
523	Help us to help each other, Lord
503	Make me a channel of your peace
598	Take this moment, sign and space

The Second Sunday before Lent   Year A

(occurrence of this Sunday depends on the dates of Easter Day and Ash Wednesday)

Option A THE CREATION

As there are very many hymns suitable to this theme, no hymn appears under more than one of the following readings:

1st Reading   **Genesis 1: 1–2: 3**

23	Álainn farraige spéirghlas (*Beautiful the green-blue sea*)
25	All things bright and beautiful
66	Before the ending of the day
121	Creator of the starry height
74	First of the week and finest day
48	God in his love for us lent is this planet
3	God is love: let heaven adore him
26	God sends us refreshing rain
4	God, who made the earth
67	God, who made the earth and heaven
27	God, who stretched the spangled heavens
324	God, whose almighty word
94	In the name of Jesus
29	Lord of beauty, thine the splendour
31	Lord of the boundless curves of space
58	Morning has broken
537	O God, our help in ages past
32	O Lord my God! When I in awesome wonder
33	O Lord of every shining constellation
34	O worship the King all-glorious above
369	Songs of praise the angels sang
341	Spirit divine, attend our prayers
35	The spacious firmament on high
77	This day, at God's creating word
36	We thank you, God our Father

Psalm		**Psalm 136 (or 136: 1–9, 22–36)**
	682	All created things, bless the Lord
	711	All you heavens, bless the Lord (*Surrexit Christus*)
	353	Give to our God immortal praise
	30	Let us, with a gladsome mind
	45	Praise, O praise our God and King

2nd Reading		**Romans 8: 18–25**
	501	Christ is the world's true Light
	654	Light of the lonely pilgrim's heart
	49	Lord, bring the day to pass

The Gospel		**Matthew 6: 25–34**
	28	I sing the almighty power of God
	6	Immortal, invisible, God only wise
	657	O God of Bethel, by whose hand
	365	Praise to the Lord, the Almighty, the King of creation
	596	Seek ye first the kingdom of God

Option B PROPER 3

1st Reading		**Isaiah 49: 8–16a**
	643	Be thou my vision, O Lord of my heart
	644	Faithful Shepherd, feed me
	569	Hark, my soul, it is the Lord
	466	Here from all nations, all tongues, and all peoples
	128	Hills of the north, rejoice
	467	How bright those glorious spirits shine!
	6	Immortal, invisible, God only wise
	363	O Lord of heaven and earth and sea
	20	The King of love my shepherd is

Psalm		**Psalm 131**
	10	All my hope on God is founded
	569	Hark, my soul, it is the Lord
	661	Through the night of doubt and sorrow

2nd Reading   **1 Corinthians 4: 1-5**

119	Come, thou long-expected Jesus
127	Hark what a sound, and too divine for hearing
132	Lo! he comes with clouds descending
457	Pour out thy Spirit from on high
527	Son of God, eternal Saviour
140	The Lord will come and not be slow

The Gospel   **Matthew 6: 24-34**

28	I sing the almighty power of God
6	Immortal, invisible, God only wise
57	Lord, for tomorrow and its needs
657	O God of Bethel, by whose hand
365	Praise to the Lord, the Almighty, the King of creation
596	Seek ye first the kingdom of God

The Second Sunday before Lent   Year B

(occurrence of this Sunday depends on the dates of Easter Day and Ash Wednesday)

Option A THE CREATION

1st Reading   **Proverbs 8: 1, 22-31**

| 84 | Alleluia! raise the anthem |

Other hymns on the Creation theme are suitable

Psalm   **Psalm 104: 24-35**   *[PABC]*

346	Angel voices, ever singing
42	Good is the Lord, our heavenly King
356	I will sing, I will sing a song unto the Lord
357	I'll praise my maker while I've breath
6	Immortal, invisible, God only wise
305	O Breath of life, come sweeping through us

2nd Reading   **Colossians 1: 15-20**

643	Be thou my vision, O Lord of my heart
220	Glory be to Jesus
160	[Hark! the herald-angels sing]

53

522 In Christ there is no east or west
94   In the name of Jesus
431 Lord, enthroned in heavenly splendour
303 Lord of the Church, we pray for our renewing
7   My God, how wonderful thou art
103 O Christ the same, through all our story's pages
306 O Spirit of the living God
675 Peace, perfect peace, in this dark world of sin?

The Gospel   **John 1: 1–14**

146 [A great and mighty wonder]
84   Alleluia! raise the anthem
87   Christ is the world's Light, he and none other
259 Christ triumphant, ever reigning
160 [Hark! the herald-angels sing]
427 Let all mortal flesh keep silence
195 Lord, the light of your love is shining
172 [O come, all ye faithful (*Adeste, fideles*)]
175 [Of the Father's heart begotten]
491 We have a gospel to proclaim

PROPER 3

1st Reading   **Hosea 2: 14–20**

528 The Church's one foundation

Psalm   **Psalm 103: 1–13, 22**

1   Bless the Lord, my soul
686 Bless the Lord, the God of our forebears
688 Come, bless the Lord, God of our forebears
349 Fill thou my life, O Lord my God
33   O Lord of every shining constellation
366 Praise, my soul, the King of heaven
365 Praise to the Lord, the Almighty, the King of
         creation
660 Thine for ever! God of love
47   [We plough the fields, and scatter]
374 When all thy mercies, O my God

2nd Reading   **2 Corinthians 3: 1–6**

382 Help us, O Lord, to learn
306 O Spirit of the living God

The Gospel		**Mark 2: 13–22**
	218	And can it be that I should gain
	608	Be still and know that I am God
	549	Dear Lord and Father of mankind
	417	He gave his life in selfless love
	418	Here, O my Lord, I see thee face to face
	94	In the name of Jesus
	584	Jesus calls us! O'er the tumult
	130	Jesus came, the heavens adoring
	605	Will you come and follow me

The Second Sunday before Lent   Year C

(occurrence of this Sunday depends on the dates of Easter Day and Ash Wednesday)

Option A THE CREATION

1st Reading		**Genesis 2: 4b–9, 15–25**
	293	Breathe on me, Breath of God
	58	Morning has broken
	102	Name of all majesty
	305	O Breath of life, come sweeping through us
	34	O worship the King all-glorious above

Other hymns on the Creation theme are suitable

Psalm		**Psalm 65**	*[Pr10A*/Pr25C/HTA]*
	612	Eternal Father, strong to save	
	645	Father, hear the prayer we offer	
	42	Good is the Lord, our heavenly King	
	581	I, the Lord of sea and sky	
	709	Praise the Lord! You heavens, adore him	

2nd Reading		**Revelation 4**
	398	Alleluia! sing to Jesus
	346	Angel voices, ever singing
	686	Bless the Lord, the God of our forebears
	688	Come, bless the Lord, God of our forebears
	694	Glory, honour, endless praises
	331	God reveals his presence

696	God, we praise you! God, we bless you!
221	Hark! the voice of love and mercy
355	Holy, holy, holy is the Lord
321	Holy, holy, holy! Lord God Almighty
714	Holy, holy, holy Lord, God of power and might
715	Holy, holy, holy, Lord God, the Lord Almighty
427	Let all mortal flesh keep silence
592	O Love that wilt not let me go
238	[Ride on, ride on in majesty]
557	Rock of ages, cleft for me

The Gospel　　　　　　　　**Luke 8: 22–35**

563	Commit your ways to God
612	Eternal Father, strong to save
553	Jesu, lover of my soul
584	Jesus call us! O'er the tumult
652	Lead us, heavenly Father, lead us
588	Light of the minds that know him
527	Son of God, eternal Saviour
47	[We plough the fields, and scatter]

Option B PROPER 3

1st Reading　　　　　　　　**Sirach 27: 4–7**

| 311 | Fruitful trees, the Spirit's sowing |

Alternative 1st Reading　　**Isaiah 55: 10–13**　　　　　　*[Pr10A*]*

65	At evening, when the sun had set
454	Forth in the peace of Christ we go
384	Lord, thy word abideth
710	Sing to God new songs of worship
47	[We plough the fields, and scatter]
377	You shall go out with joy

Psalm　　　　　　　　　　**Psalm 92: 1–4, 12–15**　　　　*[Pr6B*]*

668	God is our fortress and our rock
361	Now thank we all our God
76	Sweet is the work, my God and King
36	We thank you, God our Father

2nd Reading   **1 Corinthians 15: 51–58**

62	Abide with me, fast falls the eventide
261	[Christ, above all glory seated!]
255	[Christ is risen, alleluia!]
264	[Finished the strife of battle now]
67	God, who made the earth and heaven
420	'I am the bread of life'
270	I know that my Redeemer lives
272	[Jesus lives: thy terrors now]
277	[Love's redeeming work is done]
102	Name of all majesty
392	Now is eternal life
135	[O come, O come, Emmanuel]
107	One day when heaven was filled with his praises
281	Rejoice, the Lord is King!
526	Risen Lord, whose name we cherish
286	[The strife is o'er, the battle done]
288	[Thine be the glory, risen, conquering Son]
289	[This joyful Eastertide]

The Gospel   **Luke 6: 39–49**

2	Faithful one, so unchanging
646	Glorious things of thee are spoken
668	God is our fortress and our rock
12	God is our strength and refuge
526	Risen Lord, whose name we cherish
557	Rock of ages, cleft for me
676	Safe in the arms of Jesus

The Sunday before Lent   Year A
observed as 'Transfiguration Sunday'

The provisions of PROPER 4 listed for the Sunday between May 29 and June 4 may be used, if desired, instead of the Readings shown below

1st Reading   **Exodus 24: 12–18**

325	Be still, for the presence of the Lord, the Holy One, is here
647	Guide me, O thou great Jehovah

Psalm		**Psalm 2**	
	646	Glorious things of thee are spoken	
	238	[Ride on, ride on in majesty]	
	509	Your kingdom come, O God!	

Alternative Psalm		**Psalm 99**	*[ILC/Pr24A]*
	686	Bless the Lord, the God of our forebears	
	688	Come, bless the Lord, God of our forebears	
	431	Lord, enthroned in heavenly splendour	
	281	Rejoice, the Lord is King!	
	8	The Lord is king! Lift up your voice	

2nd Reading		**2 Peter 1: 16–21**	
	501	Christ is the world's true light	
	52	Christ, whose glory fills the skies	
	613	Eternal light, shine in my heart	
	381	God has spoken—by his prophets	
	654	Light of the lonely pilgrim's heart	

The Gospel		**Matthew 17: 1–9**	*[L2A]*
	325	Be still, for the presence of the Lord, the Holy One, is here	
	643	Be thou my vision, O Lord of my heart	
	501	Christ is the world's true light	
	205	Christ, upon the mountain peak	
	52	Christ, whose glory fills the skies	
	331	God reveals his presence ₋	
	209	Here in this holy time and place	
	101	Jesus, the very thought of thee	
	195	Lord, the light of your love is shining	
	102	Name of all majesty	
	60	O Jesus, Lord of heavenly grace	
	449	Thee we adore, O hidden Saviour, thee	
	112	There is a Redeemer	
	374	When all thy mercies, O my God	

The Sunday before Lent

Year B

observed as 'Transfiguration Sunday'

The provisions of PROPER 4 listed for the Sunday between May 29 and June 4 may be used, if desired, instead of the Readings shown below

1st Reading **2 Kings 2: 1–12**

643	Be thou my vision, O Lord of my heart
297	Come, thou Holy Spirit, come
298	Filled with the Spirit's power, with one accord
647	Guide me, O thou great Jehovah
386	Spirit of God, unseen as the wind
310	Spirit of the living God

Psalm **Psalm 50: 1–6**

501	Christ is the world's true light
381	God has spoken—by his prophets
97	Jesus shall reign where'er the sun
362	O God beyond all praising

2nd Reading **2 Corinthians 4: 3–6**

684	All praise to thee, for thou, O King divine
613	Eternal light, shine in my heart
481	God is working his purpose out as year succeeds to year
324	God, whose almighty word
482	Jesus bids us shine with a pure clear light
484	Lift high the cross, the love of Christ proclaim
195	Lord, the light of your love is shining
228	Meekness and majesty
486	People of God, arise
341	Spirit divine, attend our prayers
490	The Spirit lives to set us free
491	We have a gospel to proclaim
493	Ye that know the Lord is gracious

The Gospel **Mark 9: 2–9** *[L2B]*

325	Be still, for the presence of the Lord, the Holy One, is here
643	Be thou my vision, O Lord of my heart
501	Christ is the world's true light
205	Christ, upon the mountain peak

52	Christ, whose glory fills the skies
331	God reveals his presence
209	Here in this holy time and place
101	Jesus, the very thought of thee
195	Lord, the light of your love is shining
102	Name of all majesty
60	O Jesus, Lord of heavenly grace
449	Thee we adore, O hidden Saviour, thee
112	There is a Redeemer
374	When all thy mercies, O my God

The Sunday before Lent   Year C
observed as 'Transfiguration Sunday'

The provisions of PROPER 4 listed for the Sunday between May 29 and June 4 may be used, if desired, instead of the Readings shown below

1st Reading		**Exodus 34: 29–35**	*[8–6]*
	325	Be still, for the presence of the Lord, the Holy One, is here	

Psalm		**Psalm 99**	*[ILA/Pr24A]*
	686	Bless the Lord, the God of our forebears	
	688	Come, bless the Lord, God of our forebears	
	431	Lord, enthroned in heavenly splendour	
	281	Rejoice, the Lord is King!	
	8	The Lord is king! Lift up your voice	

2nd Reading		**2 Corinthians 3: 12 – 4: 2**	
	300	Holy Spirit, truth divine	
	616	In my life, Lord, be glorified	
	195	Lord, the light of your love is shining	
	634	Love divine, all loves excelling	
	106	O Jesus, King most wonderful	
	490	The Spirit lives to set us free	

The Gospel		**Luke 9: 28–36 (37–43)**	*[L2C/8–6]*
	325	Be still, for the presence of the Lord, the Holy One, is here	
	643	Be thou my vision, O Lord of my heart	
	501	Christ is the world's true light	

4 The Season of Lent

*Ash Wednesday to
Easter Eve (morning)*

Ash Wednesday
The First Day of Lent

Years A, B, C

1st Reading		Joel 2: 1-2, 12-17	
	210	Holy God of righteous glory	
	538	O Lord, the clouds are gathering	

Alternative 1st Reading		Isaiah 58: 1-12	[5LA]
	647	Guide me, O thou great Jehovah	
	125	Hail to the Lord's anointed	
	535	Judge eternal, throned in splendour	
	712	Tell out, my soul, the greatness of the Lord	
	497	The Church of Christ, in every age	
	510	We pray for peace	

Psalm		Psalm 51: 1-17
	630	Blessed are the pure in heart
	297	Come, thou Holy Spirit, come
	614	Great Shepherd of your people, hear
	208	Hearken, O Lord, have mercy upon us
	553	Jesu, lover of my soul
	305	O Breath of life, come sweeping through us
	638	O for a heart to praise my God
	557	Rock of ages, cleft for me

2nd Reading		2 Corinthians 5: 20b - 6: 10
	643	Be thou my vision, O Lord of my heart
	566	Fight the good fight with all thy might!
	352	Give thanks with a grateful heart
	417	He gave his life in selfless love
	587	Just as I am, without one plea
	652	Lead us, heavenly Father, lead us
	487	Soldiers of Christ, arise
	488	Stand up, stand up for Jesus

The Gospel		Matthew 6: 1-6, 16-21
	646	Glorious things of thee are spoken
	619	Lord, teach us how to pray aright
	363	O Lord of heaven and earth and sea
	625	Prayer is the soul's sincere desire

The First Sunday of Lent   Year A

1st Reading		**Genesis 2: 15–17; 3: 1–17**
	250	All hail the power of Jesu's name
	212	Jesus, grant me this, I pray
	484	Lift high the cross, the love of Christ proclaim
	555	Lord of creation, forgive us, we pray
	102	Name of all majesty
	108	Praise to the Holiest in the height
	545	Sing of Eve and sing of Adam
	290	Walking in a garden at the close of day
	186	What Adam's disobedience cost

Psalm **Psalm 32** *[L4C/Pr6C*]*

562 Blessed assurance, Jesus is mine
92 How sweet the name of Jesus sounds

2nd Reading **Romans 5: 12–19**

218 And can it be that I should gain
108 Praise to the Holiest in the height

The Gospel **Matthew 4: 1–11**

66 Before the ending of the day (*vv. 1, 2, 3d*)
207 Forty days and forty nights
668 God is our fortress and our rock
652 Lead us, heavenly Father, lead us
635 Lord, be my guardian and my guide
214 O Love, how deep, how broad, how high! (*vv. 1–4, 7*)
595 Safe in the shadow of the Lord
596 Seek ye first the kingdom of God
641 Yield not to temptation, for yielding is sin

The First Sunday of Lent   Year B

1st Reading **Genesis 9: 8–17**

592 O Love that wilt not let me go

Psalm **Psalm 25: 1–10** *[AlC/Pr10C*]*

17 Lead me, Lord, lead me in thy righteousness
    (*Treoraigh mé, treoraigh mé, a Thiarna*)
652 Lead us, heavenly Father, lead us
712 Tell out, my soul, the greatness of the Lord

2nd Reading   **1 Peter 3: 18–22**

218	And can it be that I should gain
260	Christ is alive! Let Christians sing
257	Christ is the world's Redeemer
417	He gave his life in selfless love
553	Jesu, lover of my soul
431	Lord, enthroned in heavenly splendour
102	Name of all majesty
214	O Love, how deep, how broad, how high! (vv. 1–3, 7)
177	[Once in royal David's city (vv. 1, 2, 5, 6)]
439	Once, only once, and once for all
200	The sinless one to Jordan came
244	There is a green hill far away

The Gospel   **Mark 1: 9–15**

66	Before the ending of the day (vv. 1, 2, 3d)
207	Forty days and forty nights
668	God is our fortress and our rock
324	God, whose almighty word
322	I bind unto myself today
652	Lead us, heavenly Father, lead us
635	Lord, be my guardian and my guide
637	O for a closer walk with God
363	O Lord of heaven and earth and sea
136	On Jordan's bank the Baptist's cry
595	Safe in the shadow of the Lord
197	Songs of thankfulness and praise
341	Spirit divine, attend our prayers
200	The sinless one to Jordan came
204	When Jesus came to Jordan

The First Sunday of Lent   Year C

1st Reading   **Deuteronomy 26: 1–11**   [HTC]

39	For the fruits of his creation

Psalm   **Psalm 91: 1–2, 9–16**

66	Before the ending of the day (vv. 1, 2, 3d)
12	God is our strength and refuge
322	I bind unto myself today (vv. 1, 6, 8, 9)
357	I'll praise my maker while I've breath

537	O God, our help in ages past
366	Praise, my soul, the King of heaven
595	Safe in the shadow of the Lord
372	Through all the changing scenes of life

2nd Reading **Romans 10: 8b–13**

91	He is Lord, he is Lord
522	In Christ there is no east or west
96	Jesus is Lord! Creation's voice proclaims it
425	Jesus, thou joy of loving hearts
303	Lord of the Church, we pray for our renewing
306	O Spirit of the living God
71	Saviour, again to thy dear name we raise
117	To the name of our salvation
491	We have a gospel to proclaim

The Gospel **Luke 4: 1–13**

66	Before the ending of the day (vv. 1, 2, 3d)
207	Forty days and forty nights
668	God is our fortress and our rock
652	Lead us, heavenly Father, lead us
635	Lord, be my guardian and my guide
214	O Love, how deep, how broad, how high (vv. 1–4, 7)
595	Safe in the shadow of the Lord
596	Seek ye first the kingdom of God
641	Yield not to temptation, for yielding is sin

The Second Sunday of Lent Year A

1st Reading **Genesis 12: 1–4a**

349	Fill thou my life, O Lord my God
657	O God of Bethel, by whose hand
545	Sing of Eve and sing of Adam
323	The God of Abraham praise⁔

Psalm **Psalm 121** *[Pr24C*/Rog]*

349	Fill thou my life, O Lord my God
14	I lift my eyes to the quiet hills
16	Like a mighty river flowing
664	To Zion's hill I lift my eyes

2nd Reading		**Romans 4: 1–5, 13–17**
	400	And now, O Father, mindful of the love

The Gospel		**John 3: 1–17**	*[TSB]*
	562	Blessed assurance, Jesus is mine	
	87	Christ is the world's Light, he and none other	
	319	Father, of heaven, whose love profound	
	352	Give thanks 'with a grateful heart	
	353	Give to our God immortal praise	
	226	It is a thing most wonderful	
	698	Jesus, Saviour of the world	
	484	Lift high the cross, the love of Christ proclaim	
	303	Lord of the Church, we pray for our renewing	
	227	Man of sorrows! What a name	
	102	Name of all majesty	
	305	O Breath of life, come sweeping through us	
	307	Our great Redeemer, as he breathed	
	108	Praise to the Holiest in the height	
	241	Sing, my tongue, the glorious battle	
	341	Spirit divine, attend our prayers	
	386	Spirit of God, unseen as the wind	
	373	To God be the glory! Great things he has done!	

*An alternative Gospel Reading **Matthew 17: 1–9** may be used if it has not already been used on the Sunday before Lent with the Readings for Transfiguration Sunday. Hymns suitable for this passage can be found amongst the selection for that day.*

The Second Sunday of Lent

Year B

1st Reading		**Genesis 17: 1–7, 15–16**
	545	Sing of Eve and sing of Adam
	323	The God of Abraham praise

Psalm		**Psalm 22: 23–31**
	581	I, the Lord of sea and sky
	8	The Lord is king! Lift up your voice
	492	Ye servants of God, your master proclaim

2nd Reading	**Romans 4: 13–25**	*[Pr5A]*
	418	Here, O my Lord, I see thee face to face
	545	Sing of Eve and sing of Adam
	244	There is a green hill far away

The Gospel **Mark 8: 31–38**

608	Be still and know that I am God
94	In the name of Jesus
588	Light of the minds that know him
59	New every morning is the love
108	Praise to the Holiest in the height
599	'Take up thy cross', the Saviour said
605	Will you come and follow me

*An alternative Gospel Reading **Mark 9: 2–9** may be used if it has not already been used on the Sunday before Lent with the Readings for Transfiguration Sunday. Hymns suitable for this passage can be found amongst the selection for that day.*

The Second Sunday of Lent Year C

1st Reading **Genesis 15: 1–12, 17–18**

10	All my hope on God is founded
501	Christ is the world's true light
383	Lord, be thy word my rule
595	Safe in the shadow of the Lord
545	Sing of Eve and sing of Adam
323	The God of Abraham praise

Psalm **Psalm 27**

87	Christ is the world's Light, he and none other
501	Christ is the world's true light
566	Fight the good fight with all thy might!
431	Lord, enthroned in heavenly splendour
362	O God beyond all praising
620	O Lord, hear my prayer
557	Rock of ages, cleft for me
20	The King of love my shepherd is
627	What a friend we have in Jesus

2nd Reading   **Philippians 3: 17 – 4: 1**

    566   Fight the good fight with all thy might!
    468   How shall I sing that majesty
    672   Light's abode, celestial Salem
    370   Stand up, and bless the Lord

The Gospel   **Luke 13: 31–35**

    369   Songs of praise the angels sang
    143   Waken, O sleeper, wake and rise
    145   You servants of the Lord

*An alternative Gospel Reading **Luke 9: 28–36** [ILC/8–6] may be used if it has not already been used on the Sunday before Lent with the Readings for Transfiguration Sunday. Hymns suitable for this passage can be found amongst the selection for that day.*

The Third Sunday of Lent   Year A

1st Reading   **Exodus 17: 1–7**   *[PR2IA]*

    607   As pants the hart for cooling streams
    606   As the deer pants for the water
    645   Father, hear the prayer we offer
    646   Glorious things of thee are spoken
    647   Guide me, O thou great Jehovah
    431   Lord, enthroned in heavenly splendour
    557   Rock of ages, cleft for me

Psalm   **Psalm 95**

    346   Angel voices, ever singing
    327   Christ is our corner-stone
    687   Come, let us praise the Lord
    689   Come, sing praises to the Lord above
    690   Come, worship God, who is worthy of honour
    360   Let all the world in every corner sing
    196   O worship the Lord in the beauty of holiness!
    369   Songs of praise the angels sang
    529   Thy hand, O God, has guided

2nd Reading   **Romans 5: 1–11**

    215   Ah, holy Jesu, how hast thou offended
    218   And can it be that I should gain
    294   Come down, O Love divine

268   Hail, thou once-despised Jesus!
671   Jesus, thy blood and righteousness
358   King of glory, King of peace
652   Lead us, heavenly Father, lead us
429   Lord Jesus Christ, you have come to us
618   Lord of all hopefulness, Lord of all joy
634   Love divine, all loves excelling
636   May the mind of Christ my Saviour
621   O Love divine, how sweet thou art!
373   To God be the glory! Great things he has done!

The Gospel   **John 4: 5–42**

411   Draw near and take the body of the Lord
646   Glorious things of thee are spoken
330   God is here! As we his people
300   Holy Spirit, truth divine
92   How sweet the name of Jesus sounds
576   I heard the voice of Jesus say
553   Jesu, lover of my soul
425   Jesus, thou joy of loving hearts
303   Lord of the Church, we pray for our renewing
305   O Breath of life, come sweeping through us
557   Rock of ages, cleft for me
339   Saviour, send a blessing to us

The Third Sunday of Lent   Year B

1st Reading   **Exodus 20: 1–17**

383   Lord, be thy word my rule
135   [O come, O come, Emmanuel]
76   Sweet is the work, my God and King

Psalm   **Psalm 19**   *[Ep3C/EVABC/Pr19B/Pr22A]*

606   As the deer pants for the water
153   [Come, thou Redeemer of the earth]
351   From all that dwell below the skies
631   God be in my head
696   God, we praise you! God, we bless you!
616   In my life, Lord, be glorified
97   Jesus shall reign where'er the sun
384   Lord, thy word abideth

432	Love is his word, love is his way
638	O for a heart to praise my God
34	O worship the King all-glorious above
35	The spacious firmament on high

2nd Reading **1 Corinthians 1: 18–25**

10	All my hope on God is founded
643	Be thou my vision, O Lord of my heart
232	Nature with open volume stands
248	We sing the praise of him who died

The Gospel **John 2: 13–22** *[DFA]*

453	Come to us, creative Spirit
336	Jesus, where'er thy people meet
343	We love the place, O God

The Third Sunday of Lent Year C

1st Reading **Isaiah 55: 1–9**

646	Glorious things of thee are spoken ✓
576	I heard the voice of Jesus say ✓
557	Rock of ages, cleft for me
448	The trumpets sound, the angels sing

Psalm **Psalm 63: 1–8**

63	All praise to thee, my God, this night
607	As pants the hart for cooling streams
606	As the deer pants for the water
357	I'll praise my maker while I've breath
553	Jesu, lover of my soul
95	Jesu, priceless treasure
425	Jesus, thou joy of loving hearts

2nd Reading **1 Corinthians 10: 1–13**

2	Faithful one, so unchanging
459	For all the saints, who from their labours rest
646	Glorious things of thee are spoken
668	God is our fortress and our rock
647	Guide me, O thou great Jehovah
92	How sweet the name of Jesus sounds
431	Lord, enthroned in heavenly splendour

557   Rock of ages, cleft for me
676   Safe in the arms of Jesus

The Gospel   **Luke 13: 1–9**

311   Fruitful trees, the Spirit's sowing

The Fourth Sunday of Lent   Year A

1st Reading   **1 Samuel 16: 1–13**

630   Blessed are the pure in heart
125   Hail to the Lord's anointed
306   O Spirit of the living God
498   What does the Lord require for praise and
       offering?

Psalm   **Psalm 23**   *[E4ABC/PrIIB*/Pr23A*]*

644   Faithful Shepherd, feed me
645   Father, hear the prayer we offer
466   Here from all nations, all tongues, and all
       peoples
467   How bright those glorious spirits shine!
655   Loving Shepherd of your sheep
433   My God, your table here is spread
235   O sacred head, sore wounded
365   Praise to the Lord, the Almighty, the King of
       creation
20   The King of love my shepherd is
21   The Lord's my shepherd, I'll not want
448   The trumpets sound, the angels sing

2nd Reading   **Ephesians 5: 8–14**

51   Awake, my soul, and with the sun
74   First of the week and finest day
126   [Hark! a thrilling voice is sounding]
142   Wake, O wake! With tidings thrilling
143   Waken, O sleeper, wake and rise

The Gospel   **John 9: 1–41**

642   Amazing grace (how sweet the sound!)
87   Christ is the world's Light, he and none other
501   Christ is the world's true light

52	Christ, whose glory fills the skies
296	Come, Holy Ghost, our souls inspire
324	God, whose almighty word
417	He gave his life in selfless love
576	I heard the voice of Jesus say
357	I'll praise my maker while I've breath
553	Jesu, lover of my soul
587	Just as I am, without one plea
231	My song is love unknown
104	O for a thousand tongues to sing
106	O Jesus, King most wonderful
373	To God be the glory! Great things he has done!

The Fourth Sunday of Lent   Year B

1st Reading   **Numbers 21: 4–9**

647 Guide me, O thou great Jehovah

Psalm   **Psalm 107: 1–3, 17–22**

683 All people that on earth do dwell
353 Give to our God immortal praise
128 Hills of the north, rejoice
30 Let us, with a gladsome mind
484 Lift high the cross, the love of Christ proclaim

2nd Reading   **Ephesians 2: 1–10**

250 All hail the power of Jesu's name
642 Amazing grace (how sweet the sound!)
258 [Christ the Lord is risen again!]
352 Give thanks with a grateful heart
583 Jesu, my Lord, my God, my all
99 Jesus, the name high over all
56 Lord, as I wake I turn to you
277 [Love's redeeming work is done]
557 Rock of ages, cleft for me

The Gospel   **John 3: 14–21**

352 Give thanks with a grateful heart
353 Give to our God immortal praise
226 It is a thing most wonderful
484 Lift high the cross, the love of Christ proclaim

227	Man of sorrows! What a name
102	Name of all majesty
106	O Jesus, King most wonderful
237	O my Saviour, lifted
241	Sing, my tongue, the glorious battle
373	To God be the glory! Great things he has done!

The Fourth Sunday of Lent   Year C

1st Reading   **Joshua 5: 9–12**

No suggested hymns

Psalm   **Psalm 32**   *[LIA/Pr6C*]*

| 562 | Blessed assurance, Jesus is mine |
| 92 | How sweet the name of Jesus sounds |

2nd Reading   **2 Corinthians 5: 16–21**

268	Hail, thou once-despised Jesus
417	He gave his life in selfless love
299	Holy Spirit, come, confirm us
522	In Christ there is no east or west
634	Love divine, all loves excelling
231	My song is love unknown
59	New every morning is the love
306	O Spirit of the living God
528	The Church's one foundation

The Gospel   **Luke 15: 1–3, 11b–32**

642	Amazing grace (how sweet the sound!)
328	Come on and celebrate!
329	Father, again in Jesus' name we meet
319	Father, of heaven, whose love profound
570	Give me oil in my lamp, keep me burning *(omit v. 1)*
	(Give me joy in my heart, keep me praising)
268	Hail, thou once-despised Jesus!
419	I am not worthy, holy Lord
130	Jesus came, the heavens adoring
587	Just as I am, without one plea
594	O Lord of creation, to you be all praise!
366	Praise, my soul, the King of heaven
448	The trumpets sound, the angels sing

Provisions for **Mothering Sunday**

The following provisions may replace those provided for the Fourth Sunday of Lent in any year

Ist Reading		**Exodus 2: 1–10**
	541	God of Eve and God of Mary
	569	Hark, my soul, it is the Lord

Alternative Ist Reading		**1 Samuel 1: 20–28**
	391	Father, now behold us (*at a Baptism only*)
	651	Jesus, friend of little children

Psalm		**Psalm 34: 11–20**
	657	O God of Bethel, by whose hand
	507	Put peace into each other's hands
	372	Through all the changing scenes of life

Alternative Psalm		**Psalm 127: 1–4**
	63	All praise to thee, my God, this night
	481	God is working his purpose out as year succeeds to year
	543	Lord of the home, your only Son
	288	Thine be the glory, risen, conquering Son

2nd Reading		**2 Corinthians 1: 3–7**
	361	Now thank we all our God
	508	Peace to you

Alternative 2nd Reading		**Colossians 3: 12–17**	[CIC/BSA]
	346	Angel voices, ever singing	
	294	Come, down, O Love divine	
	550	'Forgive our sins as we forgive'	
	454	Forth in the peace of Christ we go	
	300	Holy Spirit, truth divine	
	360	Let all the world in every corner sing	
	525	Let there be love shared among us	
	503	Make me a channel of your peace	
	361	Now thank we all our God	
	369	Songs of praise the angels sang	
	601	Teach me, my God and King	
	374	When all thy mercies, O my God	
	458	When, in our music, God is glorified	

The Gospel   **Luke 2: 33–35**

691   Faithful vigil ended
125   Hail to the Lord's anointed

Alternative Gospel   **John 19: 25–27**

523   Help us to help each other, Lord
226   It is a thing most wonderful
495   Jesu, Jesu, fill us with your love
472   Sing we of the blessed mother (*vv. 1–2*)

The Fifth Sunday of Lent   Year A
formerly called Passion Sunday

1st Reading   **Ezekiel 37: 1–14**   *[EVABC/PB]*

293   Breathe on me, Breath of God
319   Father, of heaven, whose love profound
305   O Breath of life, come sweeping through us
306   O Spirit of the living God
308   Revive your Church, O Lord
310   Spirit of the living God

Psalm   **Psalm 130**   *[Pr5B*/Pr8B/Prl4B]*

564   Deus meus, adiuva me (*O my God, in help draw near*)
620   O Lord, hear my prayer
  9   There's a wideness in God's mercy
627   What a friend we have in Jesus

2nd Reading   **Romans 8: 6–11**

294   Come down, O Love divine
319   Father, of heaven, whose love profound
 74   First of the week and finest day
299   Holy Spirit, come, confirm us
104   O for a thousand tongues to sing

The Gospel   **John 11: 1–45**

293   Breathe on me, Breath of God
613   Eternal light, shine in my heart
511   Father of mercy, God of consolation
569   Hark, my soul, it is the Lord
420   'I am the bread of life'
226   It is a thing most wonderful

99	Jesus, the name high over all
671	Jesus, thy blood and righteousness
513	O Christ, the Healer, we have come
308	Revive your Church, O Lord
490	The Spirit lives to set us free
115	Thou art the Way: to thee alone

The Fifth Sunday of Lent   Year B
formerly called Passion Sunday

1st Reading   **Jeremiah 31: 31–34**   *[ASA]*

125	Hail to the Lord's anointed
382	Help us, O Lord, to learn
638	O for a heart to praise my God

Psalm   **Psalm 51: 1–12**   *[Pr13B]*

397	Alleluia! Alleluia! Opening our hearts to him
297	Come, thou Holy Spirit, come
614	Great Shepherd of your people, hear
208	Hearken, O Lord, have mercy upon us
553	Jesu, lover of my soul
305	O Breath of life, come sweeping through us
638	O for a heart to praise my God
557	Rock of ages, cleft for me

Alternative Psalm   **Psalm 119: 9–16**   *[4–25]*

383	Lord, be thy word my rule
384	Lord, thy word abideth
638	O for a heart to praise my God

2nd Reading   **Hebrews 5: 5–10**

226	It is a thing most wonderful
652	Lead us, heavenly Father, lead us
431	Lord, enthroned in heavenly splendour
228	Meekness and majesty
291	Where high the heavenly temple stands

The Gospel   **John 12: 20–33**

668	God is our fortress and our rock
43	[Holy is the seed-time, when the buried grain]
484	Lift high the cross, the love of Christ proclaim

227 Man of sorrows! What a name
278 Now the green blade rises from the buried grain
   (*omit v. 3*)
237 O my Saviour, lifted ⌐
241 Sing, my tongue, the glorious battle
473 Síormholadh is glóir duit, a Athair shíorai
   (*All glory and praise to you, Father, above*)

The Fifth Sunday of Lent   Year C
formerly called Passion Sunday

| **1st Reading** | | **Isaiah 43: 16–21** | |

262 [Come, ye faithful, raise the strain]
81 Lord, for the years your love has kept and guided

Psalm   **Psalm 126**   *[A3B/7–25/Pr25B*/HTB]*

567 Forth, in thy name, O Lord, I go
356 I will sing, I will sing a song unto the Lord
712 Tell out, my soul, the greatness of the Lord
373 To God be the glory! Great things he has done!

2nd Reading   **Philippians 3: 4b–14**   *[Pr22A]*

218 And can it be that I should gain
561 Beneath the Cross of Jesus
11 Can we by searching find out God
566 Fight the good fight with all thy might!
418 Here, O my Lord, I see thee face to face
99 Jesus, the name high over all
425 Jesus, thou joy of loving hearts ⌐
671 Jesus, thy blood and righteousness
588 Light of the minds that know him
81 Lord, for the years your love has kept and guided
248 We sing the praise of him who died
247 When I survey the wondrous cross
376 Ye holy angels bright

The Gospel   **John 12: 1–8**

517 Brother, sister, let me serve you
523 Help us to help each other, Lord
495 Jesu, Jesu, fill us with your love
101 Jesus, the very thought of thee

587 Just as I am, without one plea
7 My God, how wonderful thou art
499 When I needed a neighbour, were you there

The Sixth Sunday of Lent   Year A
Palm Sunday

LITURGY OF THE PALMS

The Gospel   **Matthew 21: 1–11**

217 All glory, laud, and honour
347 Children of Jerusalem
    Give me oil in my lamp, keep me burning *(omit*
570   *v.1)*
    (Give me joy in my heart, keep me praising)
125 Hail to the Lord's anointed
124 [Hark the glad sound! the Saviour comes]
714 Holy, holy, holy Lord, God of power and might
715 Holy, holy, holy, Lord God, the Lord Almighty
223 Hosanna, hosanna, hosanna in the highest
131 Lift up your heads, you mighty gates
431 Lord, enthroned in heavenly splendour
134 Make way, make way, for Christ the King
231 My song is love unknown
238 Ride on, ride on in majesty

Psalm   **Psalm 118: 1–2, 19–29**   *[L6BC]*

683 All people that on earth do dwell
326 Blessed city, heavenly Salem
    (Christ is made the sure foundation)
327 Christ is our corner-stone
714 Holy, holy, holy Lord, God of power and might
715 Holy, holy, holy, Lord God, the Lord Almighty
334 I will enter his gates with thanksgiving in my
    heart
678 Ten thousand times ten thousand
78 This is the day that the Lord has made
493 Ye that know the Lord is gracious

LITURGY OF THE PASSION

1st Reading		**Isaiah 50: 4–9a**	*[L6BC/HW-WABC/Pr19B*]*
	23	My Lord, what love is this	
	235	O sacred head, sore wounded	
	239	See, Christ was wounded for our sake	

Psalm		**Psalm 31: 9–16**	*[L6BC]*
	227	Man of sorrows! What a name	

2nd Reading		**Philippians 2: 5–11**	*[L6BC]*
	250	All hail the power of Jesu's name	
	684	All praise to thee, for thou, O King divine	
	218	And can it be that I should gain	
	630	Blessed are the pure in heart	
	219	From heav'n you came, helpless babe	
	417	He gave his life in selfless love	
	91	He is Lord, he is Lord	
	523	Help us to help each other, Lord	
	211	Immortal love for ever full	
	94	In the name of Jesus	
	275	Look, ye saints, the sight is glorious	
	168	Lord, you were rich beyond all splendour	
	636	May the mind of Christ my Saviour	
	228	Meekness and majesty	
	102	Name of all majesty	
	285	The head that once was crowned with thorns	
	112	There is a Redeemer	
	114	Thou didst leave thy throne and thy kingly crown	
	117	To the name of our salvation	

The Gospel		**Matthew 26: 14 – 27: 66 (or 27: 11–54)**	
		Hymns are listed for the shorter option only	
	215	Ah, holy Jesu, how hast thou offended	
	219	From heav'n you came, helpless babe	
	90	Hail, Redeemer, King divine!	
	268	Hail, thou once-despisèd Jesus!	
	221	Hark! the voice of love and mercy	
	226	It is a thing most wonderful	
	429	Lord Jesus Christ, you have come to us	

229   My God, I love thee; not because
230   My Lord, what love is this
233   O dearest Lord, thy sacred head
241   Sing, my tongue, the glorious battle
244   There is a green hill far away
247   When I survey the wondrous cross

Other Passiontide hymns are suitable

The Sixth Sunday of Lent
Palm Sunday

Year B

LITURGY OF THE PALMS

The Gospel   **Mark 11: 1–11**

217   All glory, laud, and honour
347   Children of Jerusalem
        Give me oil in my lamp, keep me burning (*omit*
570   *v.1*)
        (Give me joy in my heart, keep me praising)
125   Hail to the Lord's anointed
124   [Hark the glad sound! the Saviour comes]
714   Holy, holy, holy Lord, God of power and might
715   Holy, holy, holy, Lord God, the Lord Almighty
223   Hosanna, hosanna, hosanna in the highest
131   Lift up your heads, you mighty gates
431   Lord, enthroned in heavenly splendour
134   Make way, make way, for Christ the King
231   My song is love unknown
238   Ride on, ride on in majesty

Alternative Gospel   **John 12: 12–16**

Hymns as from the Gospel passage from Mark 11

Psalm   **Psalm 118: 1–2, 19–29**   *[L6AC]*

683   All people that on earth do dwell
326   Blessed city, heavenly Salem
        (Christ is made the sure foundation)
327   Christ is our corner-stone
714   Holy, holy, holy Lord, God of power and might
715   Holy, holy, holy, Lord God, the Lord Almighty

334 I will enter his gates with thanksgiving in my
       heart
678 Ten thousand times ten thousand
 78 This is the day that the Lord has made
493 Ye that know the Lord is gracious

LITURGY OF THE PASSION

1st Reading		**Isaiah 50: 4–9a**	*[L6AC/HW-WABC/Pr19B*]*

230 My Lord, what love is this
235 O sacred head, sore wounded
239 See, Christ was wounded for our sake

Psalm		**Psalm 31: 9–16**	*[L6AC]*

227 Man of sorrows! What a name

2nd Reading		**Philippians 2: 5–11**	*[L6AC]*

250 All hail the power of Jesu's name
684 All praise to thee, for thou, O King divine
218 And can it be that I should gain
630 Blessed are the pure in heart
219 From heav'n you came, helpless babe
417 He gave his life in selfless love
 91 He is Lord, he is Lord
523 Help us to help each other, Lord
211 Immortal love for ever full
 94 In the name of Jesus
275 Look, ye saints, the sight is glorious
168 Lord, you were rich beyond all splendour
636 May the mind of Christ my Saviour
228 Meekness and majesty
102 Name of all majesty
285 The head that once was crowned with thorns
112 There is a Redeemer
114 Thou didst leave thy throne and thy kingly crown
117 To the name of our salvation

The Gospel **Mark 14: 1 – 15: 47 (or 15: 1–39 (40–47))**

Hymns are listed for the shorter option only

215 Ah, holy Jesu, how hast thou offended
 90 Hail, Redeemer, King divine!

268	Hail, thou once-despised Jesus!
221	Hark! the voice of love and mercy
226	It is a thing most wonderful
429	Lord Jesus Christ, you have come to us
229	My God, I love thee; not because
231	My song is love unknown
233	O dearest Lord, thy sacred head
241	Sing, my tongue, the glorious battle
285	The head that once was crowned with thorns
244	There is a green hill far away
247	When I survey the wondrous cross

Other Passiontide hymns are suitable

The Sixth Sunday of Lent   Year C
Palm Sunday

LITURGY OF THE PALMS

The Gospel   **Luke 19: 28–40**

217	All glory, laud, and honour
347	Children of Jerusalem
570	Give me oil in my lamp, keep me burning (*omit v.1*)
	(*Give me joy in my heart, keep me praising*)
125	Hail to the Lord's anointed
124	[Hark the glad sound! the Saviour comes]
714	Holy, holy, holy Lord, God of power and might
715	Holy, holy, holy, Lord God, the Lord Almighty
223	Hosanna, hosanna, hosanna in the highest
131	Lift up your heads, you mighty gates
431	Lord, enthroned in heavenly splendour
134	Make way, make way, for Christ the King
231	My song is love unknown
238	Ride on, ride on in majesty

Psalm   **Psalm 118: 1–2, 19–29**   [L6AB]

683	All people that on earth do dwell
326	Blessed city, heavenly Salem
	(*Christ is made the sure foundation*)
327	Christ is our corner-stone

714 Holy, holy, holy Lord, God of power and might
715 Holy, holy, holy, Lord God, the Lord Almighty
334 I will enter his gates with thanksgiving in my heart
678 Ten thousand times ten thousand
78 This is the day that the Lord has made
493 Ye that know the Lord is gracious

LITURGY OF THE PASSION

| **1st Reading** | **Isaiah 50: 4–9a** | *[L6AB/HW-WABC/Pr19B*]* |

230 My Lord, what love is this
235 O sacred head, sore wounded
239 See, Christ was wounded for our sake

| **Psalm** | **Psalm 31: 9–16** | *[L6AB]* |

227 Man of sorrows! What a name

| **2nd Reading** | **Philippians 2: 5–11** | *[L6AB]* |

250 All hail the power of Jesu's name
684 All praise to thee, for thou, O King divine
218 And can it be that I should gain
630 Blessed are the pure in heart
219 From heav'n you came, helpless babe
417 He gave his life in selfless love
91 He is Lord, he is Lord
523 Help us to help each other, Lord
211 Immortal love for ever full
94 In the name of Jesus
275 Look, ye saints, the sight is glorious
168 Lord, you were rich beyond all splendour
636 May the mind of Christ my Saviour
228 Meekness and majesty
102 Name of all majesty
285 The head that once was crowned with thorns
112 There is a Redeemer
114 Thou didst leave thy throne and thy kingly crown
117 To the name of our salvation

| **The Gospel** | **Luke 22: 14 – 23: 56 (or 23: 1–49)** |
| | *Hymns are chosen for the shorter option only* |

396	According to thy gracious word
215	Ah, holy Jesu, how hast thou offended
550	'Forgive our sins as we forgive'
221	Hark! the voice of love and mercy
226	It is a thing most wonderful
617	Jesus, remember me when you come into your kingdom
554	Lord Jesus, think on me
229	My God I love thee; not because
231	My song is love unknown
241	Sing, my tongue, the glorious battle
244	There is a green hill far away
373	To God be the glory! Great things he has done!

Other Passiontide hymns are suitable

The Monday of Holy Week   Years A, B, C

| **1st Reading** | **Isaiah 42: 1–9** | [Ep/A] |

643	Be thou my vision, O Lord of my heart
691	Faithful vigil ended
353	Give to our God immortal praise
330	God is here! As we his people
124	[Hark the glad sound! the Saviour comes]
357	I'll praise my maker while I've breath
97	Jesus shall reign where'er the sun
99	Jesus, the name high over all
134	Make way, make way, for Christ the King
305	O Breath of life, come sweeping through us
104	O for a thousand tongues to sing
605	Will you come and follow me

| **Psalm** | **Psalm 36: 5–11** |

| 6 | Immortal, invisible, God only wise |
| 553 | Jesu, lover of my soul |

| **2nd Reading** | **Hebrews 9: 11–15** |

| 411 | Draw near and take the body of the Lord |
| 220 | Glory be to Jesus |

417 He gave his life in selfless love
418 Here, O my Lord, I see thee face to face
671 Jesus, thy blood and righteousness
439 Once, only once, and once for all
528 The Church's one foundation
  9 There's a wideness in God's mercy

The Gospel   **John 12: 1–11**

517 Brother, sister, let me serve you
548 Drop, drop, slow tears
523 Help us to help each other, Lord
495 Jesu, Jesu, fill us with your love
101 Jesus, the very thought of thee
587 Just as I am, without one plea
  7 My God, how wonderful thou art
499 When I needed a neighbour, were you there

The Tuesday of Holy Week   Years A, B, C

1st Reading   **Isaiah 49: 1–7**   *[Ep2A]*

685 Blessed be the God of Israel
691 Faithful vigil ended
481 God is working his purpose out as year succeeds
       to year
125 Hail to the Lord's anointed
192 [How brightly beams the morning star!]
706 O bless the God of Israel
595 Safe in the shadow of the Lord

Psalm   **Psalm 71: 1–14**

643 Be thou my vision, O Lord of my heart
459 For all the saints, who from their labours rest
       (*vv. 1–3*)
668 God is our fortress and our rock
620 O Lord, hear my prayer
557 Rock of ages, cleft for me
595 Safe in the shadow of the Lord

2nd Reading   **1 Corinthians 1: 18–31**   *[Ep4A]*

643 Be thou my vision, O Lord of my heart
646 Glorious things of thee are spoken
225 In the cross of Christ I glory
698 Jesus, Saviour of the world

671	Jesus, thy blood and righteousness
484	Lift high the cross, the love of Christ proclaim
232	Nature with open volume stands
241	Sing, my tongue, the glorious battle
600	The wise may bring their learning
248	We sing the praise of him who died
247	When I survey the wondrous cross

The Gospel **John 12: 20–36**

348	Father, we love you, we worship and adore you
668	God is our fortress and our rock
43	[Holy is the seed-time, when the buried grain]
484	Lift high the cross, the love of Christ proclaim
227	Man of sorrows! What a name
278	Now the green blade rises from the buried grain (*omit v.3*)
237	O my Saviour, lifted
241	Sing, my tongue, the glorious battle
473	[Síormholadh is glóir duit, a Athair shíorai] [(*All glory and praise to you, Father, above*)]
490	The Spirit lives to set us free

The Wednesday of Holy Week   Years A, B, C

1st Reading **Isaiah 50: 4–9a**   *[L6ABC/Pr19B*]*

230	My Lord, what love is this
235	O sacred head, sore wounded
239	See, Christ was wounded for our sake

Psalm **Psalm 70**   *[3APr27A*]*

| 620 | O Lord, hear my prayer |
| 596 | Seek ye first the kingdom of God |

2nd Reading **Hebrews 12: 1–3**

258	[Christ the Lord is risen again!]
566	Fight the good fight with all thy might!
463	Give us the wings of faith to rise
417	He gave his life in selfless love
636	May the mind of Christ my Saviour
240	Sweet the moments, rich in blessing
285	The head that once was crowned with thorns

247 When I survey the wondrous cross
376 Ye holy angels bright

The Gospel **John 13: 21–32**

215 Ah, holy Jesu, how hast thou offended
224 How deep the Father's love for us
226 It is a thing most wonderful
227 Man of sorrows! What a name
230 My Lord, what love is this
234 O Love divine, what hast thou done?
242 The heavenly Word proceeding forth

Maundy Thursday   Years A, B, C

1st Reading **Exodus 12: 1–4 (5–10) 11–14**

258 [Christ the Lord is risen again!]
328 Come on and celebrate!
268 Hail, thou once-despised Jesus!
431 Lord, enthroned in heavenly splendour
703 Now lives the Lamb of God

Psalm **Psalm 116: 1–2, 12–19**   *[Pr6A]*

10   All my hope on God is founded
51   Awake, my soul, and with the sun
411 Draw near and take the body of the Lord
362 O God beyond all praising
363 O Lord of heaven and earth and sea

2nd Reading **1 Corinthians 11: 23–26**

396 According to thy gracious word
403 Bread of the world, in mercy broken
404 Broken for me, broken for you
405 By Christ redeemed, in Christ restored
406 Christians, lift your hearts and voices
411 Draw near and take the body of the Lord
415 For the bread which you have broken
417 He gave his life in selfless love
421 I come with joy, a child of God
423 Jesus, our Master, on the night that they came
425 Jesus, thou joy of loving hearts
429 Lord Jesus Christ, you have come to us
432 Love is his word, love is his way

437   Now, my tongue, the mystery telling (*Part 1*)
438   O thou, who at thy eucharist didst pray
439   Once, only once, and once for all
451   We come as guests invited

The Gospel   **John 13: 1–17, 31b–35**

515   'A new commandment I give unto you'
399   An upper room did our Lord prepare
325   Be still, for the presence of the Lord,
           the Holy One, is here
630   Blessed are the pure in heart
312   Gracious Spirit, Holy Ghost
523   Help us to help each other, Lord
495   Jesu, Jesu, fill us with your love
525   Let there be love shared among us
432   Love is his word, love is his way
228   Meekness and majesty
438   O thou, who at thy eucharist didst pray
314   There's a spirit in the air

Good Friday

Years A, B, C

1st Reading   **Isaiah 52: 13 – 53: 12**

215   Ah, holy Jesu, how hast thou offended
404   Broken for me, broken for you
219   From heav'n you came, helpless babe
268   Hail, thou once-despised Jesus
417   He gave his life in selfless love
273   Led like a lamb to the slaughter (*omit v.2*)
275   Look, ye saints, the sight is glorious
227   Man of sorrows! What a name
230   My Lord, what love is this
231   My song is love unknown (*omit vv.4–6*)
235   O sacred head, sore wounded
107   One day when heaven was filled with his praises
239   See, Christ was wounded for our sake

Psalm   **Psalm 22**

671   Jesus, thy blood and righteousness
361   Now thank we all our God
233   O dearest Lord, thy sacred head
537   O God, our help in ages past

240	Sweet the moments, rich in blessing
247	When I survey the wondrous cross

2nd Reading **Hebrews 10: 16–25**

218	And can it be that I should gain
220	Glory be to Jesus
382	Help us, O Lord, to learn
222	Here is love, vast as the ocean
431	Lord, enthroned in heavenly splendour
619	Lord, teach us how to pray aright
638	O for a heart to praise my God
237	O my Saviour, lifted
341	Spirit divine, attend our prayers

Alternative 2nd Reading **Hebrews 4: 14–16; 5: 7–9**

218	And can it be that I should gain
65	At evening, when the sun had set
319	Father, of heaven, whose love profound
226	It is a thing most wonderful
652	Lead us, heavenly Father, lead us
431	Lord, enthroned in heavenly splendour
228	Meekness and majesty
291	Where high the heavenly temple stands

The Gospel **John 18: 1 – 19: 42**

215	Ah, holy Jesu, how hast thou offended
216	Alleluia, my Father, for giving us your Son
561	Beneath the Cross of Jesus
220	Glory be to Jesus
221	Hark! the voice of love and mercy
417	He gave his life in selfless love
222	Here is love, vast as the ocean
226	It is a thing most wonderful
132	[Lo! he comes with clouds descending]
275	Look, ye saints, the sight is glorious
227	Man of sorrows! What a name
229	My God, I love thee; not because
231	My song is love unknown
102	Name of all majesty
233	O dearest Lord, thy sacred head
234	O Love divine, what hast thou done?
237	O my Saviour, lifted
235	O sacred head, sore wounded

236	On a hill far away stood an old rugged cross
557	Rock of ages, cleft for me
239	See, Christ was wounded for our sake
241	Sing, my tongue, the glorious battle
240	Sweet the moments, rich in blessing
285	The head that once was crowned with thorns
243	The royal banners forward go
244	There is a green hill far away
245	To mock your reign, O dearest Lord
248	We sing the praise of him who died
246	Were you there when they crucified my Lord? (omit v.6)
247	When I survey the wondrous cross

Easter Eve
Years A, B, C

sometimes referred to as 'Holy Saturday'

The following Readings are for use at services other than the Easter Vigil. Provisions for the Easter Vigil will be found on pages 97–102.

1st Reading		**Job 14: 1–14**
	6	Immortal, invisible, God only wise
	537	O God, our help in ages past
	308	Revive your Church, O Lord

| **Alternative 1st Reading** | | **Lamentations 3: 1–9, 19–24** |
| | 59 | New every morning is the love |

Psalm		**Psalm 31: 1–4, 15–16**
	459	For all the saints, who from their labours rest (vv. 1–3)
	668	God is our fortress and our rock
	620	O Lord, hear my prayer
	557	Rock of ages, cleft for me
	595	Safe in the shadow of the Lord

2nd Reading		**1 Peter 4: 1–8**
	515	'A new commandment I give unto you'
	525	Let there be love shared among us

The Gospel **Matthew 27: 57–66**

    102   Name of all majesty

    239   See, Christ was wounded for our sake

Alternative Gospel **John 19: 38–42**

    231   My song is love unknown

    239   See, Christ was wounded for our sake

5 The Season of Easter

concluding with
The Day of Pentecost

The Easter Vigil Ceremonies

Traditionally the Vigil takes place after darkness has fallen on Easter Eve, but other times may be arranged as may be most pastorally convenient in a local situation. A minimum of three Old Testament readings should be chosen. The reading from Exodus 14 should always be used. The reading from Romans 6 should also always be used, and there are respective Gospel readings for years A, B, and C.

| Old Testament Reading | **Genesis 1: 1 – 2: 4a** | [TSA] |

23	Álainn farraige spéirghlas
	(Beautiful the green blue sea)
24	All creatures of our God and King
25	All things bright and beautiful
318	Father, Lord of all creation
74	First of the week and finest day
48	God in his love for us lent us this planet
3	God is love: let heaven adore him
26	God sends us refreshing rain
4	God, who made the earth
67	God, who made the earth and heaven
27	God, who stretched the spangled heavens
324	God, whose almighty word
28	I sing the almighty power of God
94	In the name of Jesus
30	Let us, with a gladsome mind
29	Lord of beauty, thine the splendour
31	Lord of the boundless curves of space
537	O God, our help in ages past
32	O Lord my God! When I in awesome wonder
33	O Lord of every shining constellation
34	O worship the King all-glorious above
35	The spacious firmament on high
77	This day, at God's creating word
36	We thank you, God our Father

Response — **Psalm 136: 1–9, 23–26**

683	All people that on earth do dwell
353	Give to our God immortal praise
581	I, the Lord of sea and sky
30	Let us, with a gladsome mind
45	Praise, O praise our God and king

2 **Old Testament Reading** **Genesis 7: 1–5, 11–18; 8: 6–18; 9: 8–13**

637	O for a closer walk with God
592	O Love that wilt not let me go
341	Spirit divine, attend our prayers

Response   **Psalm 46**   *[Pr4A/Pr29C*]*

608	Be still and know that I am God
325	Be still, for the presence of the Lord, the Holy One, is here
646	Glorious things of thee are spoken
668	God is our fortress and our rock
12	God is our strength and refuge
92	How sweet the name of Jesus sounds
211	Immortal love for ever full
95	Jesu, priceless treasure
659	Onward, Christian soldiers

3 **Old Testament Reading** **Genesis 22: 1–18**

13	God moves in a mysterious way
59	New every morning is the love
601	Teach me, my God and King
323	The God of Abraham praise

Response   **Psalm 16**   *[E2A/Pr8C*/Pr28B*]*

567	Forth, in thy name, O Lord, I go
300	Holy Spirit, truth divine
553	Jesu, lover of my soul
652	Lead us, heavenly Father, lead us
392	Now is eternal life
289	This joyful Eastertide

4 **Old Testament Reading** **Exodus 14: 10–31; 15: 20–21**
(obligatory)

254	At the Lamb's high feast we sing
262	Come, ye faithful, raise the strain
647	Guide me, O thou great Jehovah
652	Lead us, heavenly Father, lead us
657	O God of Bethel, by whose hand
537	O God, our help in ages past
661	Through the night of doubt and sorrow
679	When Israel was in Egypt's land

Response		**The Song of Miriam (Exodus 15: 1b–13, 17–18)**
	254	At the Lamb's high feast we sing
	259	Christ triumphant, ever reigning
	263	Crown him with many crowns
	647	Guide me, O thou great Jehovah
	90	Hail, Redeemer, King divine!
	125	Hail to the Lord's anointed
	97	Jesus shall reign where'er the sun
	281	Rejoice, the Lord is King!
	370	Stand up, and bless the Lord
	73	The day thou gavest, Lord, is ended
	8	The Lord is king! Lift up your voice
	199	[The people that in darkness walked]

---

5 **Old Testament Reading**		**Isaiah 55: 1–11**	*[BSB]*
	646	Glorious things of thee are spoken	
	576	I heard the voice of Jesus say	
	557	Rock of ages, cleft for me	
	448	The trumpets sound, the angels sing	

Response		**The Song of Isaiah (Isaiah 12: 2–6)**	*[A3C]*
	370	Stand up, and bless the Lord	
	373	To God be the glory! Great things he has done!	
	492	Ye servants of God, your master proclaim	

---

6 **Old Testament Reading**		**Baruch 3: 9–15, 32 – 4: 4**
	643	Be thou my vision, O Lord of my heart
or		**Proverbs 8: 1–8, 19–21; 9: 4b–6**
	643	Be thou my vision, O Lord of my heart

Response		**Psalm 19**	*[Ep3C/L3B/Pr19B/Pr22A]*
	606	As the deer pants for the water	
	153	Come, thou Redeemer of the earth	
	351	From all that dwell below the skies	
	631	God be in my head	
	696	God, we praise you! God, we bless you!	
	616	In my life, Lord, be glorified	
	97	Jesus shall reign, where'er the sun	
	384	Lord, thy word abideth	

432	Love is his word, love is his way
638	O for a heart to praise my God
34	O worship the King all-glorious above
35	The spacious firmament on high

———

7 **Old Testament Reading** **Ezekiel 36: 24–28**

553	Jesu, lover of my soul
638	O for a heart to praise my God
306	O Spirit of the living God
557	Rock of ages, cleft for me

Response   **Psalms 42 and 43**   *[Pr7C]*

607	As pants the hart for cooling streams
606	As the deer pants for the water
15	If thou but suffer God to guide thee
95	Jesu, priceless treasure
425	Jesus, thou joy of loving hearts
434	My Jesus, pierced for love of me

———

8 **Old Testament Reading** **Ezekiel 37: 1–14**   *[L5A/PB]*

293	Breathe on me, Breath of God
319	Father, of heaven, whose love profound
305	O Breath of life, come sweeping through us
306	O Spirit of the living God
308	Revive your Church, O Lord
310	Spirit of the living God

Response   **Psalm 143**

607	As pants the hart for cooling streams
606	As the deer pants for the water
553	Jesu, lover of my soul
95	Jesu, priceless treasure
425	Jesus, thou joy of loving hearts
17	Lead me, Lord, lead me in thy righteousness
	(Treoraigh mé, treoraigh mé, a Thiarna)
593	O Jesus, I have promised
620	O Lord, hear my prayer
557	Rock of ages, cleft for me

———

9 Old Testament Reading **Zephaniah 3: 14–20**   *[A3C]*

86	Christ is the King! O friends, rejoice
646	Glorious things of thee are spoken
125	Hail to the Lord's anointed
281	Rejoice, the Lord is King!

Response   **Psalm 98**   *[CPr3ABC/E6B/Pr27C/Pr28C*]*

146	[A great and mighty wonder]
125	Hail to the Lord's anointed
166	[Joy to the world, the Lord is come!]
705	New songs of celebration render
710	Sing to God new songs of worship
369	Songs of praise the angels sang

New Testament Reading **Romans 6: 3–11**

(obligatory)

389	All who believe and are baptized
84	Alleluia! raise the anthem
264	Finished the strife of battle now
403	Bread of the world, in mercy broken
81	Lord, for the years your love has kept and guided
392	Now is eternal life
436	Now let us from this table rise
703	Now lives the Lamb of God
638	O for a heart to praise my God
286	The strife is o'er, the battle done
661	Through the night of doubt and sorrow

Response   **Psalm 114**   *[Pr19A]*

325	Be still, for the presence of the Lord, the Holy One, is here
646	Glorious things of thee are spoken
557	Rock of ages, cleft for me

The Gospel (Year A) **Matthew 28: 1–10**   *[E1A]*

255	Christ is risen, alleluia!
256	Christ is risen as he said
258	Christ the Lord is risen again!
74	First of the week and finest day
693	Glory in the highest to the God of heaven!
269	Hark ten thousand voices sounding
271	Jesus Christ is risen today
274	Light's glittering morn bedecks the sky

277 Love's redeeming work is done
107 One day when heaven was filled with his praises
288 Thine be the glory, risen, conquering Son
115 Thou art the Way: to thee alone
491 We have a gospel to proclaim

The Gospel (Year B)   **Mark 16: 1–8**   *[EIB]*

255 Christ is risen, alleluia!
258 Christ the Lord is risen again!
74 First of the week and finest day
271 Jesus Christ is risen today
274 Light's glittering morn bedecks the sky
279 O sons and daughters, let us sing! (*vv. 1–3, 9*)
107 One day when heaven was filled with his praises
109 Sing alleluia to the Lord
115 Thou art the Way: to thee alone
491 We have a gospel to proclaim

The Gospel (Year C)   **Luke 24: 1–12**   *[EIC]*

255 Christ is risen, alleluia!
258 Christ the Lord is risen again!
264 Finished the strife of battle now
74 First of the week and finest day
271 Jesus Christ is risen today
274 Light's glittering morn bedecks the sky
277 Love's redeeming work is done
107 One day when heaven was filled with his praises
109 Sing alleluia to the Lord
286 The strife is o'er, the battle done
288 Thine be the glory, risen, conquering Son
115 Thou art the Way: to thee alone

Easter Day   Year A
The First Sunday of Easter

1st Reading   **Acts 10: 34–43**   *[EpIA/EIBC]*

250 All hail the power of Jesu's name
263 Crown him with many crowns (*vv.1–4*)
264 Finished the strife of battle now
91 He is Lord, he is Lord
271 Jesus Christ is risen today

96	Jesus is Lord! Creation's voice proclaims it
102	Name of all majesty
306	O Spirit of the living God
197	Songs of thankfulness and praise
286	The strife is o'er, the battle done
491	We have a gospel to proclaim

Alternative 1st Reading   **Jeremiah 31: 1–6**

| 569 | Hark, my soul, it is the Lord |

Psalm   **Psalm 118: 1–2, 14–24**   *[EIBC]*

683	All people that on earth do dwell
326	Blessed city, heavenly Salem
	(*Christ is made the sure foundation*)
327	Christ is our corner-stone
282	Give thanks to the Lord (*Surrexit Christus*)
714	Holy, holy, holy Lord, God of power and might
715	Holy, holy, holy, Lord God, the Lord Almighty
334	I will enter his gates with thanksgiving in my heart
340	Sing and be glad, for this is God's house!
678	Ten thousand times ten thousand
78	This is the day that the Lord has made
493	Ye that know the Lord is gracious

Alternative Canticle   Easter Anthems

1 Cor.5: 7–8; Rom.6: 9–11; 1 Cor.15: 20–22 *[EIBC]*

258	Christ the Lord is risen again!
328	Come on and celebrate!
264	Finished the strife of battle now
431	Lord, enthroned in heavenly splendour
703	Now lives the Lamb of God
108	Praise to the Holiest in the height (*vv. 1–4, 7*)
283	The Day of Resurrection
286	The strife is o'er, the battle done
186	What Adam's disobedience cost

2nd Reading   **Colossians 3: 1–4**

251	Alleluia! Alleluia! Hearts to heaven and voices raise
272	Jesus lives: thy terrors now
427	Let all mortal flesh keep silence
287	The whole bright world rejoices now

The Gospel		**John 20: 1–18**	*[EIBC]*
	256	Christ is risen as he said	
	87	Christ is the world's Light, he and none other	
	258	Christ the Lord is risen again!	
	74	First of the week and finest day	
	265	Good Joseph had a garden	
	338	Jesus, stand among us	
	424	Jesus, stand among us at the meeting of our lives	
	273	Led like a lamb to the slaughter	
	274	Light's glittering morn bedecks the sky	
	277	Love's redeeming work is done	
	107	One day when heaven was filled with his praises	
	288	Thine be the glory, risen, conquering Son	
	115	Thou art the Way: to thee alone	

Alternative Gospel		**Matthew 28: 1–10**	*[EVA]*
	255	Christ is risen, alleluia!	
	256	Christ is risen as he said	
	258	Christ the Lord is risen again!	
	74	First of the week and finest day	
	693	Glory in the highest to the God of heaven!	
	269	Hark ten thousand voices singing	
	271	Jesus Christ is risen today	
	274	Light's glittering morn bedecks the sky	
	277	Love's redeeming work is done	
	107	One day when heaven was filled with his praises	
	288	Thine be the glory, risen, conquering Son	
	115	Thou art the Way: to thee alone	
	491	We have a gospel to proclaim	

Easter Day

Year B

The First Sunday of Easter

1st Reading		**Acts 10: 34–43**	*[EpIA/EIAC]*
	250	All hail the power of Jesu's name	
	263	Crown him with many crowns (*vv.1–4*)	
	264	Finished the strife of battle now	
	91	He is Lord, he is Lord	
	271	Jesus Christ is risen today	
	96	Jesus is Lord! Creation's voice proclaims it	
	102	Name of all majesty	
	306	O Spirit of the living God	

197	Songs of thankfulness and praise
286	The strife is o'er, the battle done
491	We have a gospel to proclaim

Alternative Ist Reading   **Isaiah 25: 6–9**   *[ASB]*

251	Alleluia! Alleluia! Hearts to heaven and voices raise
254	At the Lamb's high feast we sing
264	Finished the strife of battle now
512	From you all skill and science flow
466	Here from all nations, all tongues, and all peoples
467	How bright those glorious spirits shine!
270	I know that my Redeemer lives
553	Jesu, lover of my soul
135	[O come, O come, Emmanuel]
280	Our Lord Christ hath risen

Psalm   **Psalm 118: 1–2, 14–24**   *[EIAC]*

683	All people that on earth do dwell
326	Blessed city, heavenly Salem (*Christ is made the sure foundation*)
327	Christ is our corner-stone
282	Give thanks to the Lord (*Surrexit Christus*)
714	Holy, holy, holy Lord, God of power and might
715	Holy, holy, holy, Lord God, the Lord Almighty
334	I will enter his gates with thanksgiving in my heart
340	Sing and be glad, for this is God's house!
678	Ten thousand times ten thousand
78	This is the day that the Lord has made
493	Ye that know the Lord is gracious

Alternative Canticle   Easter Anthems

1 Cor.5: 7–8; Rom.6: 9–11; 1 Cor.15: 20–22 *[EIAC]*

258	Christ the Lord is risen again!
328	Come on and celebrate!
264	Finished the strife of battle now
431	Lord, enthroned in heavenly splendour
703	Now lives the Lamb of God
108	Praise to the Holiest in the height (*vv. 1–4, 7*)
283	The Day of Resurrection
286	The strife is o'er, the battle done
186	What Adam's disobedience cost

2nd Reading		**1 Corinthians 15: 1–11**	*[5LC]*
	218	And can it be that I should gain	
	257	Christ is the world's Redeemer	
	286	The strife is o'er, the battle done	
	248	We sing the praise of him who died	

The Gospel		**John 20: 1–18**	*[EIAC]*
	256	Christ is risen as he said	
	87	Christ is the world's Light, he and none other	
	258	Christ the Lord is risen again!	
	74	First of the week and finest day	
	265	Good Joseph had a garden	
	338	Jesus, stand among us	
	424	Jesus, stand among us at the meeting of our lives	
	273	Led like a lamb to the slaughter	
	274	Light's glittering morn bedecks the sky	
	277	Love's redeeming work is done	
	107	One day when heaven was filled with his praises	
	288	Thine be the glory, risen, conquering Son	
	115	Thou art the Way: to thee alone	

Alternative Gospel		**Mark 16: 1–8**	*[EVB]*
	255	Christ is risen, alleluia!	
	258	Christ the Lord is risen again!	
	74	First of the week and finest day	
	271	Jesus Christ is risen today	
	274	Light's glittering morn bedecks the sky	
	279	O sons and daughters, let us sing! (*vv. 1–3, 9*)	
	107	One day when heaven was filled with his praises	
	109	Sing alleluia to the Lord	
	115	Thou art the Way: to thee alone	
	491	We have a gospel to proclaim	

Easter Day   Year C
The First Sunday of Easter

N

1st Reading		**Acts 10: 34–43**	*[EpIA/EIAB]*
	250	All hail the power of Jesu's name	
	263	Crown him with many crowns (*vv.1–4*)	
	264	Finished the strife of battle now	
	91	He is Lord, he is Lord	

271	Jesus Christ is risen today
96	Jesus is Lord! Creation's voice proclaims it
102	Name of all majesty
306	O Spirit of the living God
197	Songs of thankfulness and praise
286	The strife is o'er, the battle done
491	We have a gospel to proclaim

Alternative 1st Reading   **Isaiah 65: 17–25**   [2ACPr28C]

369	Songs of praise the angels sang
292	Ye choirs of new Jerusalem

Psalm   **Psalm 118: 1–2, 14–24**   [EIAB]

683	All people that on earth do dwell
326	Blessed city, heavenly Salem (*Christ is made the sure foundation*)
327	Christ is our corner-stone
282	Give thanks to the Lord (*Surrexit Christus*)
714	Holy, holy, holy Lord, God of power and might
715	Holy, holy, holy, Lord God, the Lord Almighty
334	I will enter his gates with thanksgiving in my heart
340	Sing and be glad, for this is God's house!
678	Ten thousand times ten thousand
78	This is the day that the Lord has made
493	Ye that know the Lord is gracious

Alternative Canticle   Easter Anthems

1 Cor.5: 7–8; Rom.6: 9–11; 1 Cor.15: 20–22 [EIAB]

258	Christ the Lord is risen again!
328	Come on and celebrate!
264	Finished the strife of battle now
431	Lord, enthroned in heavenly splendour
703	Now lives the Lamb of God
108	Praise to the Holiest in the height (*vv. 1–4, 7*)
283	The Day of Resurrection
286	The strife is o'er, the battle done
186	What Adam's disobedience cost

2nd Reading   **1 Corinthians 15: 19–26**

24	All creatures of our God and King
251	Alleluia! Alleluia! Hearts to heaven and voices raise

218	And can it be that I should gain
102	Name of all majesty
703	Now lives the Lamb of God
108	Praise to the Holiest in the height
8	The Lord is king! Lift up your voice

The Gospel **John 20: 1–18** *[EIAB]*

256	Christ is risen as he said
87	Christ is the world's Light, he and none other
258	Christ the Lord is risen again!
74	First of the week and finest day
265	Good Joseph had a garden
338	Jesus, stand among us
424	Jesus, stand among us at the meeting of our lives
273	Led like a lamb to the slaughter
274	Light's glittering morn bedecks the sky
277	Love's redeeming work is done
107	One day when heaven was filled with his praises
288	Thine be the glory, risen, conquering Son
115	Thou art the Way: to thee alone

Alternative Gospel **Luke 24: 1–12** *[EVC]*

255	Christ is risen, alleluia!
258	Christ the Lord is risen again!
264	Finished the strife of battle now
74	First of the week and finest day
271	Jesus Christ is risen today
274	Light's glittering morn bedecks the sky
277	Love's redeeming work is done
107	One day when heaven was filled with his praises
109	Sing alleluia to the Lord
286	The strife is o'er, the battle done
288	Thine be the glory, risen, conquering Son
115	Thou art the Way: to thee alone

The Second Sunday of Easter   Year A
also called 'Low Sunday'

1st Reading **Acts 2: 14a, 22–32**

567	Forth, in thy name, O Lord, I go
341	Spirit divine, attend our prayers
289	This joyful Eastertide

Alternative 1st Reading		**Genesis 8: 6–16; 9: 8–16**	
	295	Come, gracious Spirit, heavenly Dove	
	80	Great is thy faithfulness, O God my Father	
	637	O for a closer walk with God	
	592	O Love that wilt not let me go	

Psalm		**Psalm 16**	*[Pr8C*/Pr28B*]*
	567	Forth, in thy name, O Lord, I go	
	300	Holy Spirit, truth divine	
	553	Jesu, lover of my soul	
	652	Lead us, heavenly Father, lead us	
	392	Now is eternal life	
	289	This joyful Eastertide	

2nd Reading		**1 Peter 1: 3–9**	
	667	Blessed be the everlasting God	
	646	Glorious things of thee are spoken	
	425	Jesus, thou joy of loving hearts	
	106	O Jesus, King most wonderful	
	640	Purify my heart	
	283	The Day of Resurrection	
	681	There is a land of pure delight	
	373	To God be the glory! Great things he has done!	

The Gospel		**John 20: 19–31**	*[E2BC]*
	293	Breathe on me, Breath of God	
	255	Christ is risen, alleluia!	
	263	Crown him with many crowns	
	460	For all your saints in glory, for all your saints at rest (*vv.1, 2k, 3*)	
	415	For the bread which you have broken	
	454	Forth in the peace of Christ we go	
	219	From heav'n you came, helpless babe	
	268	Hail, thou once-despised Jesus	
	583	Jesu, my Lord, my God, my all	
	338	Jesus, stand among us	
	424	Jesus, stand among us at the meeting of our lives	
	652	Lead us, heavenly Father, lead us	
	305	O Breath of life, come sweeping through us	
	104	O for a thousand tongues to sing	
	279	O sons and daughters, let us sing! (*vv.1, 4–9*)	
	307	Our great Redeemer, as he breathed	

505	Peace be to this congregation
675	Peace, perfect peace, in this dark world of sin?
288	Thine be the glory, risen, conquering Son

The Second Sunday of Easter   Year B
also called 'Low Sunday'

1st Reading   **Acts 4: 32–35**

258	Christ the Lord is risen again!
523	Help us to help each other, Lord
277	Love's redeeming word is done
283	The Day of Resurrection

Alternative 1st Reading   **Isaiah 26: 2–9, 19**

563	Commit your ways to God
646	Glorious things of thee are spoken
668	God is our fortress and our rock
16	Like a mighty river flowing
505	Peace be to this congregation
557	Rock of ages, cleft for me

Psalm   **Psalm 133**   *[Pr7B/Pr15A/Unity]*

518	Bind us together, Lord
522	In Christ there is no east or west
525	Let there be love shared among us
438	O thou, who at thy eucharist didst pray
507	Put peace into each other's hands
661	Through the night of doubt and sorrow

2nd Reading   **1 John 1: 1 – 2: 2**

87	Christ is the world's Light, he and none other
501	Christ is the world's true light
613	Eternal light, shine in my heart
418	Here, O my Lord, I see thee face to face
553	Jesu, lover of my soul
587	Just as I am, without one plea
81	Lord, for the years your love has kept and guided
557	Rock of ages, cleft for me
624	Speak, Lord, in the stillness
490	The Spirit lives to set us free
373	To God be the glory! Great things he has done!

The Gospel   **John 20: 19–31**   *[E2AC]*

293	Breathe on me, Breath of God
255	Christ is risen, alleluia!
263	Crown him with many crowns
460	For all your saints in glory, for all your saints at rest (*vv.1, 2k, 3*)
415	For the bread which you have broken
454	Forth in the peace of Christ we go
219	From heav'n you came, helpless babe
268	Hail, thou once-despised Jesus!
583	Jesu, my Lord, my God, my all
338	Jesus, stand among us
424	Jesus, stand among us at the meeting of our lives
652	Lead us, heavenly Father, lead us
305	O Breath of life, come sweeping through us
104	O for a thousand tongues to sing
279	O sons and daughters, let us sing! (*vv.1, 4–9*)
307	Our great Redeemer, as he breathed
505	Peace be to this congregation
675	Peace, perfect peace, in this dark world of sin?
288	Thine be the glory, risen, conquering Son

The Second Sunday of Easter   Year C
also called 'Low Sunday'

1st Reading		**Acts 5: 27–32**
	258	Christ the Lord is risen again!
	227	Man of sorrows! What a name
	248	We sing the praise of him who died

Alternative 1st Reading		**Job 42: 1–6**
	226	It is a thing most wonderful

Psalm		**Psalm 118: 14–29**
	683	All people that on earth do dwell
	326	Blessed city, heavenly Salem (*Christ is made the sure foundation*)
	327	Christ is our corner-stone
	714	Holy, holy, holy Lord, God of power and might
	715	Holy, holy, holy, Lord God, the Lord Almighty

334	I will enter his gates with thanksgiving in my heart
678	Ten thousand times ten thousand
78	This is the day that the Lord has made
493	Ye that know the Lord is gracious

Alternative Psalm **Psalm 150**

24	All creatures of our God and King
346	Angel voices, ever singing
453	Come to us, creative Spirit
321	Holy, holy, holy! Lord God almighty
360	Let all the world in every corner sing
705	New songs of celebration render
708	O praise ye the Lord! Praise him in the height
364	Praise him on the trumpet, the psaltery and harp
365	Praise to the Lord, the Almighty, the King of creation
368	Sing of the Lord's goodness
710	Sing to God new songs of worship

2nd Reading **Revelation 1: 4-8** *[1ABPr29B]*

454	Forth in the peace of Christ we go
646	Glorious things of thee are spoken
381	God has spoken—by his prophets
127	Hark what a sound, and too divine for hearing
321	Holy, holy, holy! Lord God almighty
130	Jesus came, the heavens adoring
132	[Lo! he comes with clouds descending]
373	To God be the glory! Great things he has done!

The Gospel **John 20: 19-31** *[E2AB]*

293	Breathe on me, Breath of God
255	Christ is risen, alleluia!
263	Crown him with many crowns
460	For all your saints in glory, for all your saints at rest *(vv.1, 2k, 3)*
415	For the bread which you have broken
454	Forth in the peace of Christ we go
219	From heav'n you came, helpless babe
268	Hail, thou once-despised Jesus
583	Jesu, my Lord, my God, my all
338	Jesus, stand among us
424	Jesus, stand among us at the meeting of our lives

652	Lead us, heavenly Father, lead us
305	O Breath of life, come sweeping through us
104	O for a thousand tongues to sing
279	O sons and daughters, let us sing! (vv.1, 4–9)
307	Our great Redeemer, as he breathed
505	Peace be to this congregation
675	Peace, perfect peace, in this dark world of sin?
288	Thine be the glory, risen, conquering Son

The Third Sunday of Easter   Year A

1st Reading   **Acts 2: 14a, 36–41**

259	Christ triumphant, ever reigning
478	Go forth and tell! O Church of God, awake!
277	Love's redeeming work is done
102	Name of all majesty
104	O for a thousand tongues to sing
306	O Spirit of the living God

Alternative 1st Reading   **Isaiah 43: 1–12**

642	Amazing grace (how sweet the sound!)
12	God is our strength and refuge
128	Hills of the north, rejoice
557	Rock of ages, cleft for me
595	Safe in the shadow of the Lord
22	You shall cross the barren desert

Psalm   **Psalm 116: 1–4, 12–19**

| 362 | O God beyond all praising |
| 363 | O Lord of heaven and earth and sea |

2nd Reading   **1 Peter 1: 17–23**

84	Alleluia! raise the anthem
525	Let there be love shared among us
432	Love is his word, love is his way

The Gospel   **Luke 24: 13–35**

629	Abide among us with thy grace
62	Abide with me, fast falls the eventide
253	As we walked home at close of day
260	Christ is alive! Let Christians sing

408	Come, risen Lord, and deign to be our guest
319	Father, of heaven, whose love profound
415	For the bread which you have broken
92	How sweet the name of Jesus sounds
272	Jesus lives: thy terrors now
338	Jesus, stand among us
424	Jesus, stand among us at the meeting of our lives
425	Jesus, thou joy of loving hearts
588	Light of the minds that know him
81	Lord, for the years your love has kept and guided
437	Now, my tongue, the mystery telling
106	O Jesus, King most wonderful
109	Sing alleluia to the Lord
72	Sun of my soul, thou Saviour dear

The Third Sunday of Easter   Year B

1st Reading   **Acts 3: 12–19** ✓

381	God has spoken—by his prophets
551	How can we sing with joy to God
99	Jesus, the name high over all
231	My song is love unknown ✓
104	O for a thousand tongues to sing
288	Thine be the glory, risen, conquering Son

Alternative 1st Reading   **Micah 4: 1–5**   [6–9]

118	Behold, the mountain of the Lord
501	Christ is the world's true light
263	Crown him with many crowns

Psalm   **Psalm 4** ✓

63	All praise to thee, my God, this night
652	Lead us, heavenly Father, lead us
620	O Lord, hear my prayer

2nd Reading   **1 John 3: 1–7** ✓

516	Beloved, let us love: love is of God
92	How sweet the name of Jesus sounds
226	It is a thing most wonderful
7	My God, how wonderful thou art
214	O Love, how deep, how broad, how high!

The Gospel   **Luke 24: 36b–48** ✓

256	Christ is risen as he said
263	Crown him with many crowns
264	Finished the strife of battle now
219	From heav'n you came, helpless babe
338	Jesus, stand among us
424	Jesus, stand among us at the meeting of our lives
104	O for a thousand tongues to sing
306	O Spirit of the living God
286	The strife is o'er, the battle done

The Third Sunday of Easter   Year C

1st Reading   **Acts 9: 1–6 (7–20)**

460	For all your saints in glory, for all your saints at rest (*vv. 1, 2a, 3*)
13	God moves in a mysterious way
581	I, the Lord of sea and sky

Alternative 1st Reading   **Jeremiah 32: 36–41**

80	Great is thy faithfulness, O God my Father

Psalm   **Psalm 30**   *[4LBPrl/Pr5C*/Pr8B/Pr9C]*

554	Lord Jesus, think on me
592	O Love that wilt not let me go
196	O worship the Lord in the beauty of holiness!
528	The Church's one foundation

2nd Reading   **Revelation 5: 11–14**

346	Angel voices, ever singing
332	Come, let us join our cheerful songs
351	From all that dwell below the skies
694	Glory, honour, endless praises
693	Glory in the highest to the God of heaven!
697	Great and wonderful your deeds
268	Hail, thou once-despised Jesus!
269	Hark ten thousand voices sounding
221	Hark! the voice of love and mercy
355	Holy, holy, holy is the Lord
97	Jesus shall reign where'er the sun
99	Jesus, the name high over all

276	Majesty, worship his majesty
104	O for a thousand tongues to sing
474	Such a host as none can number
678	Ten thousand times ten thousand

The Gospel **John 21: 1–19**

608	Be still and know that I am God
219	From heav'n you came, helpless babe
569	Hark, my soul, it is the Lord
226	It is a thing most wonderful
583	Jesu, my Lord, my God, my all
101	Jesus, the very thought of thee
229	My God, I love thee; not because
-366	Praise, my soul, the King of heaven
605	Will you come and follow me

The Fourth Sunday of Easter   Year A

1st Reading **Acts 2: 42–47**

397	Alleluia! Alleluia! Opening our hearts to him
522	In Christ there is no east or west
336	Jesus, where'er thy people meet
306	O Spirit of the living God

Alternative 1st Reading **Nehemiah 9: 6–15**

262	Come, ye faithful, raise the strain
353	Give to our God immortal praise
581	I, the Lord of sea and sky
6	Immortal, invisible, God only wise

Psalm 🐑 **Psalm 23**   [L4A/E4BC/PrIIB*/Pr23A*]

644	Faithful Shepherd, feed me
645	Father, hear the prayer we offer
466	Here from all nations, all tongues, and all peoples
467	How bright those glorious spirits shine!
655	Loving Shepherd of your sheep
433	My God, your table here is spread
235	[O sacred head, sore wounded]
365	Praise to the Lord, the Almighty, the King of creation
20	The King of love my shepherd is

21	The Lord's my shepherd, I'll not want
448	The trumpets sound, the angels sing

2nd Reading   **1 Peter 2: 19–25**

630	Blessed are the pure in heart
417	He gave his life in selfless love
436	Now let us from this table rise
593	O Jesus, I have promised
239	See, Christ was wounded for our sake
285	The head that once was crowned with thorns
9	There's a wideness in God's mercy
248	We sing the praise of him who died

The Gospel   **John 10: 1–10**

215	[Ah, holy Jesu, how hast thou offended]
683	All people that on earth do dwell
690	Come, worship God, who is worthy of honour
644	Faithful Shepherd, feed me
330	God is here! As we his people
614	Great Shepherd of your people, hear
649	Happy are they, they that love God
438	O thou, who at thy eucharist didst pray
244	There is a green hill far away

The Fourth Sunday of Easter   Year B

Ist Reading   ✎   **Acts 4: 5–12**

326	Blessed city, heavenly Salem
	(*Christ is made the sure foundation*)
327	Christ is our corner-stone
87	Christ is the world's Light, he and none other
211	Immortal love for ever full
99	Jesus, the name high over all
104	O for a thousand tongues to sing
340	Sing and be glad, for this is God's house!
117	To the name of our salvation
493	Ye that know the Lord is gracious

Alternative Ist Reading   **Ezekiel 34: 1–10**

589	Lord, speak to me that I may speak
438	O thou, who at thy eucharist didst pray
526	Risen Lord, whose name we cherish

| 20 | The King of love my shepherd is |
| 9 | There's a wideness in God's mercy |

Psalm   **Psalm 23**   *[L4A/E4AC/PrIIB*/Pr23A*]*

644	Faithful Shepherd, feed me
645	Father, hear the prayer we offer
466	Here from all nations, all tongues, and all peoples
467	How bright those glorious spirits shine!
655	Loving Shepherd of your sheep
433	My God, your table here is spread
235	[O sacred head, sore wounded]
365	Praise to the Lord, the Almighty, the King of creation
20	The King of love my shepherd is
21	The Lord's my shepherd, I'll not want
448	The trumpets sound, the angels sing

2nd Reading   **1 John 3: 16–24**

515	'A new commandment I give unto you'
516	Beloved, let us love: love is of God
517	Brother, sister, let me serve you
312	Gracious Spirit, Holy Ghost
523	Help us to help each other, Lord
421	I come with joy, a child of God
525	Let there be love shared among us
315	'This is my will, my one command'

The Gospel   **John 10: 11–18**

92	How sweet the name of Jesus sounds
655	Loving Shepherd of your sheep
509	Your kingdom come, O God!

The Fourth Sunday of Easter   Year C

1st Reading   **Acts 9: 36–43**

| 211 | Immortal love for ever full |
| 373 | To God be the glory! Great things he has done! |

Alternative 1st Reading   **Numbers 27: 12–23**

| 639 | O thou who camest from above |

Psalm		**Psalm 23**	[L4A/E4AB/PrIIB*/Pr23A*]
	644	Faithful Shepherd, feed me	
	645	Father, hear the prayer we offer	
	466	Here from all nations, all tongues, and all peoples	
	467	How bright those glorious spirits shine	
	655	Loving Shepherd of your sheep	
	433	My God, your table here is spread	
	235	[O sacred head, sore wounded]	
	365	Praise to the Lord, the Almighty, the King of creation	
	20	The King of love my shepherd is	
	21	The Lord's my shepherd, I'll not want	
	448	The trumpets sound, the angels sing	

2nd Reading   **Revelation 7: 9–17**   [ASA]

	250	All hail the power of Jesu's name
	398	Alleluia! sing to Jesus!
	346	Angel voices, ever singing
	562	Blessed assurance, Jesus is mine
	332	Come, let us join our cheerful songs
	463	Give us the wings of faith to rise
	694	Glory, honour, endless praises
	466	Here from all nations, all tongues, and all peoples
	321	Holy, holy, holy! Lord God almighty
	467	How bright those glorious spirits shine
	670	Jerusalem the golden
	275	Look, ye saints, the sight is glorious
	474	Such a host as none can number
	475	Who are these like stars appearing
	376	Ye holy angels bright
	492	Ye servants of God, your master proclaim

The Gospel   **John 10: 22–30**

	655	Loving Shepherd of your sheep
	660	Thine for ever! God of love

The Fifth Sunday of Easter Year A

1st Reading		**Acts 7: 55–60**
	460	For all your saints in glory, for all
		your saints at rest (*vv. 1, 2t, 3*)
	550	'Forgive our sins as we forgive'
	693	Glory in the highest to the God of heaven!
	696	God, we praise you! God we bless you!
	553	Jesu, lover of my soul
	8	The Lord is king! Lift up your voice
Alternative 1st Reading		**Deuteronomy 6: 20–25**
	262	Come, ye faithful, raise the strain
	383	Lord, be thy word my rule
Psalm		**Psalm 31: 1–5, 15–16**
	643	Be thou my vision, O Lord of my heart
	563	Commit your ways to God
	459	For all the saints, who from their labours rest
		(*vv. 1–3*)
	668	God is our fortress and our rock
	92	How sweet the name of Jesus sounds
	620	O Lord, hear my prayer
	557	Rock of ages, cleft for me
	595	Safe in the shadow of the Lord
2nd Reading		**1 Peter 2: 2–10**
	326	Blessed city, heavenly Salem
		(*Christ is made the sure foundation*)
	327	Christ is our corner-stone
	454	Forth in the peace of Christ we go
	380	God has spoken to his people, alleluia!
	125	Hail to the Lord's anointed
	569	Hark, my soul, it is the Lord
	92	How sweet the name of Jesus sounds
	486	People of God, arise
	340	Sing and be glad, for this is God's house!
	528	The Church's one foundation
	532	Who are we who stand and sing?
	493	Ye that know the Lord is gracious

The Gospel		**John 14: 1–14** $\qquad$ [5–1]
	87	Christ is the world's Light, he and none other
	610	Come, my Way, my Truth, my Life
	453	Come to us, creative Spirit
	566	Fight the good fight with all thy might!
	266	Hail the day that sees him rise
	270	I know that my Redeemer lives
	272	Jesus lives: thy terrors now
	100	Jesus loves me: this I know
	588	Light of the minds that know him
	619	Lord, teach us how to pray aright
	657	O God of Bethel, by whose hand
	625	Prayer is the soul's sincere desire
	626	'Set your troubled hearts at rest'
	109	Sing alleluia to the Lord
	20	The King of love my shepherd is
	21	The Lord's my shepherd, I'll not want
	660	Thine for ever! God of love
	115	Thou art the Way: to thee alone
	395	When Jesus taught by Galilee

The Fifth Sunday of Easter $\qquad$ Year B

1st Reading		**Acts 8: 26–40**
	390	Baptized into your name most holy
	273	Led like a lamb to the slaughter
	435	O God, unseen, yet ever near
	214	O Love, how deep, how broad, how high!
	306	O Spirit of the living God
	239	See, Christ was wounded for our sake

Alternative 1st Reading		**Deuteronomy 4: 32–40**
	51	Awake, my soul, and with the sun
	325	Be still, for the presence of the Lord, the Holy One, is here
	262	Come, ye faithful, raise the strain

Psalm		**Psalm 22: 25–31**
	✓581	I, the Lord of sea and sky
	8	The Lord is king! Lift up your voice
	492	Ye servants of God, your master proclaim

2nd Reading   **1 John 4: 7–21**

515   'A new commandment I give unto you'
216   Alleluia, my Father, for giving us your Son
218   And can it be that I should gain
516   Beloved, let us love: love is of God
 89   God is love—his the care
  3   God is love: let heaven adore him
312   Gracious Spirit, Holy Ghost
125   Hail to the Lord's anointed
422   In the quiet consecration
495   Jesu, Jesu, fill us with your love
525   Let there be love shared among us
634   Love divine, all loves excelling
432   Love is his word, love is his way
229   My God! I love thee; not because
102   Name of all majesty
214   O Love, how deep, how broad, how high!
367   Praise him, praise him, everybody praise him!
244   There is a green hill far away
315   'This is my will, my one command'
373   To God be the glory! Great things he has done!
530   Ubi caritas et amor
248   We sing the praise of him who died

The Gospel   **John 15: 1–8**

629   Abide among us with thy grace
 39   For the fruits of his creation
311   Fruitful trees, the Spirit's sowing
422   In the quiet consecration
524   May the grace of Christ our Saviour
451   We come as guests invited
394   We praise you, Lord, for Jesus Christ
          (*at a Baptism only*)

The Fifth Sunday of Easter   Year C

1st Reading		**Acts 11: 1–18**	
	250	All hail the power of Jesu's name	
	97	Jesus shall reign where'er the sun	

Alternative 1st Reading		**Leviticus 19: 1–2, 9–18**	*[3LAPr2A/Pr25A*]*
	515	A new commandment I give unto you	
	494	Beauty for brokenness	
	39	For the fruits of his creation	
	321	Holy, holy, holy! Lord God almighty	
	535	Judge eternal, throned in splendour	
	525	Let there be love shared among us	
	497	The Church of Christ, in every age	
	509	Your kingdom come, O God!	

Psalm		**Psalm 148**	*[ClABC]*
	682	All created things, bless the Lord	
	24	All creatures of our God and King	
	683	All people that on earth do dwell	
	711	All you heavens, bless the Lord (*Surrexit Christus*)	
	708	O praise ye the Lord! Praise him in the height	
	366	Praise, my soul, the King of heaven	
	709	Praise the Lord! You heavens, adore him	

2nd Reading		**Revelation 21: 1–6**	*[ASB]*
	512	From you all skill and science flow	
	646	Glorious things of thee are spoken	
	466	Here from all nations, all tongues, and all peoples	
	300	Holy Spirit, truth divine	
	670	Jerusalem the golden	
	553	Jesu, lover of my soul	
	425	Jesus, thou joy of loving hearts	
	⌃592	O Love, that wilt not let me go	
	473	Síormholadh is glóir duit, a Athair shíorai *(All glory and praise to you, Father, above)*	
	369	Songs of praise, the angels sang	
	138	Soon and very soon we are going to see the King	
	528	The Church's one foundation	
	681	There is a land of pure delight	
	144	Word of justice, alleluia	
	292	Ye choirs of new Jerusalem	

The Gospel   **John 13: 31–35**

515   'A new commandment I give unto you'
525   Let there be love shared among us
432   Love is his word, love is his way

The Sixth Sunday of Easter   Year A
Rogation Sunday

Ist Reading   **Acts 17: 22–31**

10   All my hope on God is founded
25   All things bright and beautiful
270   I know that my Redeemer lives
28   I sing the almighty power of God
581   I, the Lord of sea and sky
336   Jesus, where'er thy people meet
29   Lord of beauty, thine the splendour
363   O Lord of heaven and earth and sea
34   O worship the King all-glorious above
35   The spacious firmament on high
112   There is a Redeemer

Alternative Ist Reading   **Isaiah 41: 17–20**

29   Lord of beauty, thine the splendour
45   Praise, O praise our God and King
35   The spacious firmament on high

Psalm   **Psalm 66: 8–20**

657   O God of Bethel, by whose hand
640   Purify my heart

2nd Reading   **1 Peter 3: 13–22**

218   And can it be that I should gain
260   Christ is alive! Let Christians sing
257   Christ is the world's Redeemer
417   He gave his life in selfless love
553   Jesu, lover of my soul
431   Lord, enthroned in heavenly splendour
456   Lord, you give the great commission
102   Name of all majesty
392   Now is eternal life

214	O Love, how deep, how broad, how high!
439	Once, only once, and once for all
200	The sinless one to Jordan came
244	There is a green hill far away
372	Through all the changing scenes of life

The Gospel **John 14: 15–21**

398	Alleluia! sing to Jesus
516	Beloved, let us love: love is of God
294	Come down, O Love divine
300	Holy Spirit, truth divine
422	In the quiet consecration
307	Our great Redeemer, as he breathed
451	We come as guests invited

The Sixth Sunday of Easter

Year B

Rogation Sunday

1st Reading **Acts 10: 44–48**

298	Filled with the Spirit's power, with one accord
299	Holy Spirit, come, confirm us
92	How sweet the name of Jesus sounds
456	Lord, you give the great commission
306	O Spirit of the living God

Alternative 1st Reading **Isaiah 45: 11–13, 18–19**

| 581 | I, the Lord of sea and sky |

Psalm **Psalm 98** *[CPr3ABC/EVABC/Pr27C/Pr28C*]*

146	[A great and mighty wonder]
125	Hail to the Lord's anointed
166	[Joy to the world, the Lord is come!]
705	New songs of celebration render
710	Sing to God new songs of worship
369	Songs of praise the angels sang

2nd Reading **1 John 5: 1–6**

| 557 | Rock of ages, cleft for me |
| 528 | The Church's one foundation |

| **The Gospel** | | **John 15: 9–17** | *[5–14]* |

515	'A new commandment I give unto you'
516	Beloved, let us love: love is of God
523	Help us to help each other, Lord
421	I come with joy, a child of God
495	Jesu, Jesu, fill us with your love
525	Let there be love shared among us
75	Lord, dismiss us with your blessing
456	Lord, you give the great commission
231	My song is love unknown
315	'This is my will, my one command'
530	Ubi caritas et amor
451	We come as guests invited
627	What a friend we have in Jesus

The Sixth Sunday of Easter

Year C

Rogation Sunday

1st Reading		**Acts 16: 9–15**	
	350	For the beauty of the earth
	343	We love the place, O God

| **Alternative 1st Reading** | | **Joel 2: 21–27** | *[HTB]* |
| | 539 | Rejoice, O land, in God thy might |

| **Psalm** | | **Psalm 67** | *[Pr15A*/1–25]* |
| | 695 | God of mercy, God of grace |

2nd Reading		**Revelation 21: 10, 22 – 22: 5**	
	643	Be thou my vision, O Lord of my heart
	326	Blessed city, heavenly Salem
		(Christ is made the sure foundation)
	12	God is our strength and refuge
	670	Jerusalem the golden
	672	Light's abode, celestial Salem
	589	Lord, speak to me that I may speak
	677	Shall we gather at the river
	528	The Church's one foundation
	681	There is a land of pure delight
	376	Ye holy angels bright

The Gospel		**John 14: 23–29**
	294	Come down, O Love divine
	296	Come, Holy Ghost, our souls inspire
	549	Dear Lord and Father of mankind
	675	Peace, perfect peace, in this dark world of sin
	507	Put peace into each other's hands
	626	'Set your troubled hearts at rest'

Alternative Gospel		**John 5: 1–9**
	513	O Christ, the Healer, we have come
	104	O for a thousand tongues to sing

The Ascension Day Years A, B, C

1st Reading		**Acts 1: 1–11**
	250	All hail the power of Jesu's name
	398	Alleluia! sing to Jesus
	260	Christ is alive! Let Christians sing
	263	Crown him with many crowns (*vv. 1, 4–6*)
	695	God of mercy, God of grace
	266	Hail the day that sees him rise
	267	Hail the risen Lord, ascending
	268	Hail, thou once-despised Jesus!
	300	Holy Spirit, truth divine
	275	Look, ye saints, the sight is glorious
	431	Lord, enthroned in heavenly splendour
	104	O for a thousand tongues to sing
	307	Our great Redeemer, as he breathed
	285	The head that once was crowned with thorns

Alternative 1st Reading		**Daniel 7: 9–14**
	125	Hail to the Lord's anointed
	468	How shall I sing that majesty
	6	Immortal, invisible, God only wise
	130	Jesus came, the heavens adoring
	132	[Lo! he comes with clouds descending]
	276	Majesty, worship his majesty
	34	O worship the King all-glorious above
	678	Ten thousand times ten thousand
	73	The day thou gavest, Lord, is ended

Psalm	**Psalm 47**	
	275	Look, ye saints, the sight is glorious
	323	The God of Abraham praise

Alternative Psalm	**Psalm 93**	[Pr29B*]
	553	Jesu, lover of my soul
	276	Majesty, worship his majesty
	281	Rejoice, the Lord is King!
	8	The Lord is king! Lift up your voice
	492	Ye servants of God, your master proclaim

2nd Reading	**Ephesians 1: 15–23**	[Pr29A/ASC]
	250	All hail the power of Jesu's name
	643	Be thou my vision, O Lord of my heart
	326	Blessed city, heavenly Salem
		(*Christ is made the sure foundation*) (*omit v. 1*)
	296	Come, Holy Ghost, our souls inspire
	693	Glory in the highest to the God of heaven!
	324	God, whose almighty word
	266	Hail the day that sees him rise
	300	Holy Spirit, truth divine
	99	Jesus, the name high over all
	588	Light of the minds that know him
	281	Rejoice, the Lord is King!
	491	We have a gospel to proclaim

The Gospel	**Luke 24: 44–53**	
	398	Alleluia! sing to Jesus
	261	Christ, above all glory seated!
	266	Hail the day that sees him rise
	267	Hail the risen Lord, ascending
	634	Love divine, all loves excelling
	285	The head that once was crowned with thorns

The Seventh Sunday of Easter   Year A
The Sunday after the Ascension

1st Reading	**Acts 1: 6–14**	
	398	Alleluia! sing to Jesus
	259	Christ triumphant, ever reigning
	695	God of mercy, God of grace

266 Hail the day that sees him rise
267 Hail the risen Lord, ascending
268 Hail, thou once-despised Jesus!
300 Holy Spirit, truth divine
211 Immortal love for ever full
275 Look, ye saints, the sight is glorious
431 Lord, enthroned in heavenly splendour
104 O for a thousand tongues to sing
306 O Spirit of the living God
307 Our great Redeemer, as he breathed
109 Sing alleluia to the Lord
285 The head that once was crowned with thorns

Alternative 1st Reading   **Ezekiel 39: 21–39**

457 Pour out thy Spirit from on high

Psalm   **Psalm 68: 1–10, 32–35**

494 Beauty for brokenness
13 God moves in a mysterious way
368 Sing of the Lord's goodness
509 Your kingdom come, O God!

2nd Reading   **1 Peter 4: 12–14; 5: 6–11**

566 Fight the good fight with all thy might!
418 Here, O my Lord, I see thee face to face
635 Lord, be my guardian and my guide
618 Lord of all hopefulness, Lord of all joy
599 'Take up thy cross', the Saviour said
627 What a friend we have in Jesus

The Gospel   **John 17: 1–11**

518 Bind us together, Lord
86 Christ is the King! O friends, rejoice
456 Lord, you give the great commission
438 O thou, who at thy eucharist didst pray
526 Risen Lord, whose name we cherish
443 Sent forth by God's blessing, our true faith
     confessing
527 Son of God, eternal Saviour
285 The head that once was crowned with thorns

The Seventh Sunday of Easter
Year B
(The Sunday after the Ascension)

1st Reading		**Acts 1: 15–17, 21–26**
	461	For all thy saints, O Lord
	460	For all your saints in glory, for all your saints at rest (*vv. 1, 2f, 3*)
Alternative 1st Reading		**Exodus 28: 1–4, 9–10, 29–30**
	643	Be thou my vision, O Lord of my heart
Psalm		**Psalm 1** *[4LCPr1/Pr18C*/Pr20B/Pr25A*]*
	649	Happy are they, they that love God
	56	Lord, as I wake I turn to you
	383	Lord, be thy word my rule
2nd Reading		**1 John 5: 9–13**
	613	Eternal light, shine in my heart
The Gospel		**John 17: 6–19**
	518	Bind us together, Lord
	326	Blessed city, heavenly Salem (*Christ is made the sure foundation*)
	415	For the bread which you have broken
	438	O thou, who at thy eucharist didst pray
	526	Risen Lord, whose name we cherish
	527	Son of God, eternal Saviour
	285	The head that once was crowned with thorns
	531	Where love and loving-kindness dwell

The Seventh Sunday of Easter
Year C
(The Sunday after the Ascension)

1st Reading		**Acts 16: 16–34**
	320	Firmly I believe and truly
	92	How sweet the name of Jesus sounds
Alternative 1st Reading		**1 Samuel 12: 19–24**
	619	Lord, teach us how to pray aright
	625	Prayer is the soul's sincere desire

Psalm	**Psalm 97**	*[CPr2ABC/8–6]*

34	O worship the King all-glorious above
281	Rejoice, the Lord is King!
8	The Lord is king! Lift up your voice

2nd Reading   **Revelation 22: 12–14, 16–17, 20–21**

501	Christ is the world's true light
332	Come, let us join our cheerful songs
37	[Come, ye thankful people, come]
263	Crown him with many crowns
459	For all the saints, who from their labours rest
646	Glorious things of thee are spoken
381	God has spoken—by his prophets
127	Hark what a sound, and too divine for hearing
418	Here, O my Lord, I see thee face to face
300	Holy Spirit, truth divine
553	Jesu, lover of my soul
425	Jesus, thou joy of loving hearts
132	[Lo! he comes with clouds descending]
303	Lord of the Church, we pray for our renewing
634	Love divine, all loves excelling
137	Promised Lord and Christ is he
281	Rejoice, the Lord is King!
138	Soon and very soon we are going to see the King
144	Word of justice, alleluia
509	Your kingdom come, O God!

The Gospel   **John 17: 20–26**

518	Bind us together, Lord
326	Blessed city, heavenly Salem
	(*Christ is made the sure foundation*)
415	For the bread which you have broken
438	O thou, who at thy eucharist didst pray
526	Risen Lord, whose name we cherish
527	Son of God, eternal Saviour
285	The head that once was crowned with thorns
531	Where love and loving-kindness dwell

The Day of Pentecost
Year A

sometimes referred to as Whitsunday

1st Reading		**Acts 2: 1–21**	*[PBC]*
	296	Come, Holy Ghost, our souls inspire	
	318	Father, Lord of all creation	
	298	Filled with the Spirit's power, with one accord	
	301	Let every Christian pray	
	302	Lord God the Holy Ghost	
	303	Lord of the Church, we pray for our renewing	
	305	O Breath of life, come sweeping through us	
	306	O Spirit of the living God	
	639	O thou who camest from above	
	307	Our great Redeemer, as he breathed	
	308	Revive your Church, O Lord	
	341	Spirit divine, attend our prayers	
	386	Spirit of God, unseen as the wind	
	310	Spirit of the living God	
	313	The Spirit came, as promised	
	491	We have a gospel to proclaim	
	309	When God the Spirit came	
	204	When Jesus came to Jordan	
	395	When Jesus taught by Galilee	

Alternative 1st Reading		**Numbers 11: 24–30**	
	381	God has spoken—by his prophets	
	304	Loving Spirit, loving Spirit	
	386	Spirit of God, unseen as the wind	

Psalm		**Psalm 104: 24–34, 35b**	*[2LB/PBC]*
	346	Angel voices, ever singing	
	42	Good is the Lord, our heavenly King	
	356	I will sing, I will sing a song unto the Lord	
	357	I'll praise my maker while I've breath	
	6	Immortal, invisible, God only wise	
	305	O Breath of life, come sweeping through us	

2nd Reading		**1 Corinthians 12: 3b–13**	
	294	Come down, O Love divine	
	408	Come, risen Lord, and deign to be our guest	
	297	Come, thou Holy Spirit, come	
	318	Father, Lord of all creation	

312	Gracious Spirit, Holy Ghost
91	He is Lord, he is Lord
299	Holy Spirit, come, confirm us
421	I come with joy, a child of God
96	Jesus is Lord! Creation's voice proclaims it
102	Name of all majesty
306	O Spirit of the living God
438	O thou, who at thy eucharist didst pray
440	One bread, one body, one Lord of all
313	The Spirit came, as promised
491	We have a gospel to proclaim

The Gospel   **John 20: 19–23**

293	Breathe on me, Breath of God
263	Crown him with many crowns (*vv. 1, 3, 4, 5*)
338	Jesus, stand among us
424	Jesus, stand among us at the meeting of our lives
652	Lead us, heavenly Father, lead us
307	Our great Redeemer, as he breathed
505	Peace be to this congregation
675	Peace, perfect peace, in this dark world of sin?

Alternative Gospel   **John 7: 37–39**

646	Glorious things of thee are spoken
576	I heard the voice of Jesus say
553	Jesu, lover of my soul
303	Lord of the Church, we pray for our renewing

The Day of Pentecost   Year B
sometimes referred to as Whitsunday

1st Reading   **Acts 2: 1–21**   [PAC]

296	Come, Holy Ghost, our souls inspire
318	Father, Lord of all creation
298	Filled with the Spirit's power, with one accord
301	Let every Christian pray
302	Lord God the Holy Ghost
303	Lord of the Church, we pray for our renewing
305	O Breath of life, come sweeping through us
306	O Spirit of the living God

639	O thou who camest from above
307	Our great Redeemer, as he breathed
308	Revive your Church, O Lord
341	Spirit divine, attend our prayers
386	Spirit of God, unseen as the wind
310	Spirit of the living God
313	The Spirit came, as promised
491	We have a gospel to proclaim
309	When God the Spirit came
204	When Jesus came to Jordan
395	When Jesus taught by Galilee

Alternative Ist Reading   **Ezekiel 37: 1–14**   *[5LA/EVABC]*

293	Breathe on me, Breath of God
319	Father, of heaven, whose love profound
305	O Breath of life, come sweeping through us
306	O Spirit of the living God
308	Revive your Church, O Lord
310	Spirit of the living God

Psalm   **Psalm 104: 24–34, 35b**   *[2LB/PAC]*

346	Angel voices, ever singing
42	Good is the Lord, our heavenly King
356	I will sing, I will sing a song unto the Lord
357	I'll praise my maker while I've breath
6	Immortal, invisible, God only wise
305	O Breath of life, come sweeping through us

2nd Reading   **Romans 8: 22–27**

523	Help us to help each other, Lord
301	Let every Christian pray
654	Light of the lonely pilgrim's heart
49	Lord, bring the day to pass
619	Lord, teach us how to pray aright

The Gospel   **John 15: 26–27; 16: 4b–15**

294	Come down, O Love divine
295	Come, gracious Spirit, heavenly Dove
297	Come, thou Holy Spirit, come
324	God, whose almighty word
299	Holy Spirit, come, confirm us
300	Holy Spirit, truth divine

307	Our great Redeemer, as he breathed
310	Spirit of the living God
112	There is a Redeemer

The Day of Pentecost   Year C
sometimes referred to as Whitsunday

1st Reading		**Acts 2: 1–21**	*[PAB]*
	296	Come, Holy Ghost, our souls inspire
	318	Father, Lord of all creation
	298	Filled with the Spirit's power, with one accord
	301	Let every Christian pray
	302	Lord God the Holy Ghost
	303	Lord of the Church, we pray for our renewing
	305	O Breath of life, come sweeping through us
	306	O Spirit of the living God
	639	O thou who camest from above
	307	Our great Redeemer, as he breathed
	308	Revive your Church, O Lord
	341	Spirit divine, attend our prayers
	386	Spirit of God, unseen as the wind
	310	Spirit of the living God
	313	The Spirit came, as promised
	491	We have a gospel to proclaim
	309	When God the Spirit came
	204	When Jesus came to Jordan
	395	When Jesus taught by Galilee

| **Alternative 1st Reading** | | **Genesis 11: 1–9** |
| | 10 | All my hope on God is founded |

Psalm		**Psalm 104: 24–34, 35b**	*[2LB/PAB]*
	346	Angel voices, ever singing
	42	Good is the Lord, our heavenly King
	356	I will sing, I will sing a song unto the Lord
	357	I'll praise my maker while I've breath
	6	Immortal, invisible, God only wise
	305	O Breath of life, come sweeping through us

2nd Reading	**Romans 8: 14–17**
558	Abba Father, let me be
387	Thanks to God, whose Word was spoken
285	The head that once was crowned with thorns
The Gospel	**John 14: 8–17 (25–27)**
398	Alleluia! sing to Jesus
87	Christ is the world's Light, he and none other
294	Come down, O Love divine
295	Come, gracious Spirit, heavenly Dove
297	Come, thou Holy Spirit, come
324	God, whose almighty word
299	Holy Spirit, come, confirm us
300	Holy Spirit, truth divine
270	I know that my Redeemer lives
422	In the quiet consecration
310	Spirit of the living God

6 ORDINARY TIME

Trinity Sunday and the Sundays after Trinity

(PROPERS 4–24)

On the Sundays after Trinity a choice of readings from the Old Testament and the Psalms is provided in the Lectionary. The first option, marked (c) in the following pages, is a series of 'continuous' readings over the three-year period, giving in narrative form a salvation-history view of the Old Testament.

The second option, marked (p), is a series of 'paired' readings, following the pattern in the Roman Catholic and American Episcopal Church lectionaries, where the Old Testament reading has a somewhat thematic linking relationship with the New Testament readings that follow, usually the Gospel passage.

Either the first option (c) or the second option (p) should be adhered to for the whole period from the First Sunday after Trinity until the Sunday before Advent ('The Kingship of Christ'). This will determine from which options hymns should be chosen.

Trinity Sunday

Year A

1st Reading	**Genesis 1: 1 – 2: 4a**	*[EVABC]*
23	Álainn farraige spéirghlas	
	(*Beautiful the green-blue sea*)	
24	All creatures of our God and King	
25	All things bright and beautiful	
318	Father, Lord of all creation	
74	First of the week and finest day	
48	God in his love for us lent us this planet	
3	God is love: let heaven adore him	
26	God sends us refreshing rain	
4	God, who made the earth	
67	God, who made the earth and heaven	
27	God, who stretched the spangled heavens	
324	God, whose almighty word	
28	I sing the almighty power of God	
94	In the name of Jesus	
30	Let us, with a gladsome mind	
29	Lord of beauty, thine the splendour	
31	Lord of the boundless curves of space	
537	O God, our help in ages past	
32	O Lord my God! When I in awesome wonder	
33	O Lord of every shining constellation	
34	O worship the King all-glorious above	
35	The spacious firmament on high	
77	This day, at God's creating word	
36	We thank you, God our Father	

Alternative 1st Reading	**Isaiah 40: 12–17, 27–31**	
566	Fight the good fight with all thy might!	
306	O Spirit of the living God	
323	The God of Abraham praise	

Psalm	**Psalm 8**	*[TSC/Pr22B*/I–I]*
316	Bright the vision that delighted	
6	Immortal, invisible, God only wise	
362	O God beyond all praising	
32	O Lord my God! When I in awesome wonder	
33	O Lord of every shining constellation	

2nd Reading   **2 Corinthians 13: 11–13**

524   May the grace of Christ our Saviour
507   Put peace into each other's hands

The Gospel   **Matthew 28: 16–20**

398   Alleluia! sing to Jesus
86   Christ is the King! O friends, rejoice
454   Forth in the peace of Christ we go
478   Go forth and tell! O Church of God, awake!
455   Go forth for God; go forth to the world in peace
479   Go, tell it on the mountain
480   God forgave my sin in Jesus' name
322   I bind unto myself today (*vv. 1, 8, 9*)
104   O for a thousand tongues to sing
306   O Spirit of the living God
492   Ye servants of God, your master proclaim

Trinity Sunday   Year B

1st Reading   **Isaiah 6: 1–8**   [5LC]

316   Bright the vision that delighted
415   For the bread which you have broken
454   Forth in the peace of Christ we go
331   God reveals his presence
696   God, we praise you! God, we bless you!
355   Holy, holy, holy is the Lord
321   Holy, holy, holy! Lord God almighty
714   Holy, holy, holy Lord, God of power and might
715   Holy, holy, holy, Lord God, the Lord Almighty
581   I, the Lord of sea and sky
6   Immortal, invisible, God only wise
427   Let all mortal flesh keep silence
7   My God, how wonderful thou art
639   O thou who camest from above
370   Stand up, and bless the Lord
323   The God of Abraham praise

Psalm   **Psalm 29**   [EplABC]

349   Fill thou my life, O Lord my God
30   Let us, with a gladsome mind
431   Lord, enthroned in heavenly splendour

| 196 | O worship the Lord in the beauty of holiness! |
| 45 | Praise, O praise our God and King |

2nd Reading **Romans 8: 12–17**

558	Abba, Father, let me be
387	Thanks to God, whose Word was spoken
285	The head that once was crowned with thorns

The Gospel **John 3: 1–17** *[L2A]*

562	Blessed assurance, Jesus is mine
87	Christ is the world's Light, he and none other
319	Father, of heaven, whose love profound
352	Give thanks with a grateful heart
353	Give to our God immortal praise
226	It is a thing most wonderful
698	Jesus, Saviour of the world
484	Lift high the cross, the love of Christ proclaim
303	Lord of the Church, we pray for our renewing
227	Man of sorrows! What a name
102	Name of all majesty
305	O Breath of life, come sweeping through us
307	Our great Redeemer, as he breathed
108	Praise to the Holiest in the height
241	[Sing, my tongue, the glorious battle]
341	Spirit divine, attend our prayers
386	Spirit of God, unseen as the wind
373	To God be the glory! Great things he has done!

Trinity Sunday   Year C

1st Reading **Proverbs 8: 1–4, 22–31**

| 84 | Alleluia! raise the anthem |
| 537 | O God, our help in ages past |

Psalm **Psalm 8** *[TSA/Pr22B*/1–1]*

316	Bright the vision that delighted
6	Immortal, invisible, God only wise
362	O God beyond all praising
32	O Lord my God! When I in awesome wonder
33	O Lord of every shining constellation

2nd Reading		**Romans 5: 1–5**
	294	Come down, O Love divine
	652	Lead us, heavenly Father, lead us
	429	Lord Jesus Christ, you have come to us
	618	Lord of all hopefulness, Lord of all joy
	634	Love divine, all loves excelling
	636	May the mind of Christ my Saviour

The Gospel		**John 16: 12–15**
	324	God, whose almighty word
	300	Holy Spirit, truth divine
	112	There is a Redeemer

PROPER 4   Year A

The Sunday between May 29 and June 4 (if after Trinity Sunday)

(c) Ist Reading		**Genesis 6: 9–22; 7: 24; 8: 14–19**
	567	Forth, in thy name, O Lord, I go
	211	Immortal love for ever full
	637	O for a closer walk with God
	108	Praise to the Holiest in the height
	186	What Adam's disobedience cost

(c) Psalm		**Psalm 46**	*[EVABC/Pr29C*]*
	608	Be still and know that I am God	
	325	Be still, for the presence of the Lord, the Holy One, is here	
	646	Glorious things of thee are spoken	
	668	God is our fortress and our rock	
	12	God is our strength and refuge	
	92	How sweet the name of Jesus sounds	
	211	Immortal love for ever full	
	95	Jesu, priceless treasure	
	659	Onward, Christian soldiers	

(p) Ist Reading		**Deuteronomy 11: 18–21, 26–28**
	382	Help us, O Lord, to learn
	17	Lead me, Lord, lead me in thy righteousness *(Treoraigh mé, treoraigh mé, a Thiarna)*
	589	Lord, speak to me that I may speak
	601	Teach me, my God and King

142

(p) Psalm   **Psalm 31: 1–5, 19–24**

643	Be thou my vision, O Lord of my heart
563	Commit your ways to God
565	Father, I place into your hands
459	For all the saints, who from their labours rest (*vv. 1–3*)
668	God is our fortress and our rock
92	How sweet the name of Jesus sounds
15	If thou but suffer God to guide thee
620	O Lord, hear my prayer
557	Rock of ages, cleft for me
595	Safe in the shadow of the Lord

2nd Reading   **Romans 1: 16–17; 3: 22b–28 (29–31)**

84	Alleluia! raise the anthem
218	And can it be that I should gain
358	King of glory, King of peace
244	There is a green hill far away
373	To God be the glory! Great things he has done!

The Gospel   **Matthew 7: 21–29**

206	Come, let us to the Lord our God
92	How sweet the name of Jesus sounds
15	If thou but suffer God to guide thee
589	Lord, speak to me that I may speak
557	Rock of ages, cleft for me

PROPER 4   Year B

The Sunday between May 29 and June 4 (if after Trinity Sunday)

(c) 1st Reading   **1 Samuel 3: 1–10 (11–20)**   *[Ep2B]*

608	Be still and know that I am God
581	I, the Lord of sea and sky
589	Lord, speak to me that I may speak
624	Speak, Lord, in the stillness

(c) Psalm   **Psalm 139: 1–6, 13–18**   *[Ep2B/Prl8C]*

51	Awake, my soul, and with the sun
567	Forth, in thy name, O Lord, I go
226	It is a thing most wonderful
19	There is no moment of my life

(p) Ist Reading   **Deuteronomy 5: 12–15**

262   Come, ye faithful, raise the strain
55   Let this day be holy
383   Lord, be thy word my rule
76   Sweet is the work, my God and King

(p) Psalm   **Psalm 81: 1–10**

28   I sing the almighty power of God
360   Let all the world in every corner sing
362   O God beyond all praising
708   O praise ye the Lord! Praise him in the height
364   Praise him on the trumpet, the psaltery and harp
368   Sing of the Lord's goodness
369   Songs of praise the angels sang

2nd Reading   **2 Corinthians 4: 5–12**

52   Christ, whose glory fills the skies
613   Eternal light, shine in my heart
324   God, whose almighty word
569   Hark, my soul, it is the Lord
96   Jesus is Lord! Creation's voice proclaims it
195   Lord, the light of your love is shining
341   Spirit divine, attend our prayers

The Gospel   **Mark 2: 23 – 3: 6**

74   First of the week and finest day
513   O Christ, the Healer, we have come
104   O for a thousand tongues to sing
78   This is the day that the Lord has made

PROPER 4   Year C

The Sunday between May 29 and June 4 (if after Trinity Sunday)

(c) Ist Reading   **1 Kings 18: 20–21, (22–29) 30–39**

346   Angel voices, ever singing
614   Great Shepherd of your people, hear
321   Holy, holy, holy! Lord God almighty
323   The God of Abraham praise

(c) **Psalm**		**Psalm 96**	[C/ABC/Pr24A*]
	166	[Joy to the world, the Lord is come!]	
	705	New songs of celebration render	
	196	O worship the Lord in the beauty of holiness!	
	710	Sing to God new songs of worship	
	8	The Lord is king! Lift up your voice	
	373	To God be the glory! Great things he has done!	
	377	You shall go out with joy	

(p) **1st Reading**		**1 Kings 8: 22–23, 41–43**	
	51	Awake, my soul, and with the sun	
	321	Holy, holy, holy! Lord God almighty	

(p) **Psalm**		**Psalm 96: 1–9**	[Pr24A*]
	166	[Joy to the world, the Lord is come!]	
	705	New songs of celebration render	
	196	O worship the Lord in the beauty of holiness!	
	710	Sing to God new songs of worship	
	373	To God be the glory! Great things he has done!	

2nd Reading		**Galatians 1: 1–12**	
	486	People of God, arise	
	373	To God be the glory! Great things he has done!	
	491	We have a gospel to proclaim	

The Gospel		**Luke 7: 1–10**	
	65	At evening, when the sun had set	
	419	I am not worthy, holy Lord	
	603	When we walk with the Lord	
	144	Word of justice, alleluia	

PROPER 5   Year A

The Sunday between June 5 and 11 (if after Trinity Sunday)

(c) **1st Reading**		**Genesis 12: 1–9**	
	657	O God of Bethel, by whose hand	
	545	Sing of Eve and sing of Adam	
	323	The God of Abraham praise	
	372	Through all the changing scenes of life	

(c) Psalm		**Psalm 33: 1-12**
	539	Rejoice, O land, in God thy might
	369	Songs of praise the angels sang
	387	Thanks to God, Whose word was spoken

(p) Ist Reading		**Hosea 5: 15 – 6: 6**
	190	Brightest and best of the suns of the morning
	206	Come, let us to the Lord our God
	125	Hail to the Lord's anointed
	196	O worship the Lord in the beauty of holiness!

(p) Psalm		**Psalm 50: 7-15**
	361	Now thank we all our God

2nd Reading		**Romans 4: 13-25** [L2B]
	418	Here, O my Lord, I see thee face to face
	545	Sing of Eve and sing of Adam
	244	There is a green hill far away

The Gospel		**Matthew 9: 9-13, 18-26**
	549	Dear Lord and Father of mankind
	460	For all your saints in glory, for all your saints at rest (*vv. 1, 2p, 3*)
	417	He gave his life in selfless love
	211	Immortal love for ever full
	94	In the name of Jesus
	584	Jesus calls us! O'er the tumult
	130	Jesus came, the heavens adoring
	213	Jesus' hands were kind hands
	513	O Christ, the Healer, we have come
	113	There is singing in the desert, there is laughter in the skies
	605	Will you come and follow me

PROPER 5

The Sunday between June 5 and 11 (if after Trinity Sunday)

(c) 1st Reading   **1 Samuel 8: 4–11 (12–15), 16–20; (11: 14–15)**

131   Lift up your heads, you mighty gates

(c) Psalm   **Psalm 138**   *[5LC/Pr12C*/Pr16A*]*

250   All hail the power of Jesu's name
358   King of glory, King of peace
21   The Lord's my shepherd, I'll not want

(p) 1st Reading   **Genesis 3: 8–15**

250   All hail the power of Jesu's name
99   Jesus, the name high over all
484   Lift high the cross, the love of Christ proclaim
555   Lord of creation, forgive us, we pray
108   Praise to the Holiest in the height
545   Sing of Eve and sing of Adam
290   Walking in a garden at the close of day
186   What Adam's disobedience cost
292   [Ye choirs of new Jerusalem]

(p) Psalm   **Psalm 130**   *[L5A/Pr8B/Pr14B]*

564   Deus meus, adiuva me (*O my God, in help draw near*)
620   O Lord, hear my prayer
9   There's a wideness in God's mercy
627   What a friend we have in Jesus

2nd Reading   **2 Corinthians 4: 13 – 5: 1**

566   Fight the good fight with all thy might!
418   Here, O my Lord, I see thee face to face
277   [Love's redeeming work is done]

The Gospel   **Mark 3: 20–35**

522   In Christ there is no east or west
432   Love is his word, love is his way
197   Songs of thankfulness and praise
313   The Spirit came, as promised
662   Those who would valour see
      (*He who would valiant be*)

PROPER 5   ✗   Year C

The Sunday between June 5 and 11 (if after Trinity Sunday)

(c) Ist Reading   **1 Kings 17: 8–16 (17–24)** ✓   *[Pr27B*]*

517	Brother, sister, let me serve you
613	Eternal light, shine in my heart
647	Guide me, O thou great Jehovah
99	Jesus, the name high over all
104	O for a thousand tongues to sing
115	Thou art the Way: to thee alone

(c) Psalm   **Psalm 146**   *[Pr18B*/Pr21C*/Pr26B/Pr27B*]*

4	God, who made the earth
125	Hail to the Lord's anointed
92	How sweet the name of Jesus sounds
357	I'll praise my maker while I've breath
97	Jesus shall reign where'er the sun
99	Jesus, the name high over all
535	Judge eternal, throned in splendour
363	O Lord of heaven and earth and sea
708	O praise ye the Lord! Praise him in the height
712	Tell out, my soul, the greatness of the Lord
8	The Lord is king! Lift up your voice
376	Ye holy angels bright

(p) Ist Reading   **1 Kings 17: 17–24**

613	Eternal light, shine in my heart
99	Jesus, the name high over all
104	O for a thousand tongues to sing
115	Thou art the Way: to thee alone

(p) Psalm   **Psalm 30**   *[4LBPr1/E3C/Pr8B*/Pr9C]*

554	Lord Jesus, think on me
592	O Love that wilt not let me go
196	O worship the Lord in the beauty of holiness!
528	The Church's one foundation

2nd Reading   **Galatians 1: 11–24**

460	For all your saints in glory, for all your saints at rest (*vv. 1, 2a, 3*)
115	Thou art the Way: to thee alone
491	We have a gospel to proclaim

The Gospel   **Luke 7: 11–17**

   613 Eternal light, shine in my heart
    99 Jesus, the name high over all
  104 O for a thousand tongues to sing

PROPER 6   Year A

The Sunday between June 12 and 18 (if after Trinity Sunday)

(c) 1st Reading   **Genesis 18: 1–15; (21: 1–7)**

  545 Sing of Eve and sing of Adam
  323 The God of Abraham praise

(c) Psalm   **Psalm 116: 1–2, 12–19**   *[MTABC]*

   10 All my hope on God is founded
   51 Awake, my soul, and with the sun
  411 Draw near and take the body of the Lord
  362 O God beyond all praising
  363 O Lord of heaven and earth and sea

(p) 1st Reading   **Exodus 19: 2–8a**

  454 Forth in the peace of Christ we go
  323 The God of Abraham praise
  493 Ye that know the Lord is gracious

(p) Psalm   **Psalm 100**   *[Pr29A/HTC]*

  683 All people that on earth do dwell
  334 I will enter his gates with thanksgiving in my
        heart
  701 Jubilate, ev'rybody

2nd Reading   **Romans 5: 1–8**

  218 And can it be that I should gain
  294 Come down, O Love divine
  411 Draw near and take the body of the Lord
  268 Hail, thou once-despised Jesus
  671 Jesus, thy blood and righteousness
  652 Lead us, heavenly Father, lead us
  429 Lord Jesus Christ, you have come to us
  618 Lord of all hopefulness, Lord of all joy
  634 Love divine, all loves excelling

636	May the mind of Christ my Saviour
621	O Love divine, how sweet thou art!

The Gospel   **Matthew 9: 35 – 10: 8 (9–23)**

37	[Come, ye thankful people, come]
39	For the fruits of his creation
456	Lord, you give the great commission
441	Out to the world for Jesus
527	Son of God, eternal Saviour
197	Songs of thankfulness and praise
141	These are the days of Elijah
491	We have a gospel to proclaim
492	Ye servants of God, your master proclaim

PROPER 6   Year B

The Sunday between June 12 and 18 (if after Trinity Sunday)

(c) 1st Reading   **1 Samuel 15: 34 – 16: 13**

630	Blessed are the pure in heart
125	Hail to the Lord's anointed
306	O Spirit of the living God
498	What does the Lord require for praise and offering?

(c) Psalm   **Psalm 20**

643	Be thou my vision, O Lord of my heart
659	Onward, Christian soldiers
487	Soldiers of Christ, arise
488	Stand up, stand up for Jesus
243	The royal banners forward go

(p) 1st Reading   **Ezekiel 17: 22–24**

311	Fruitful trees, the Spirit's sowing

(p) Psalm   **Psalm 92: 1–4, 12–15**   *[2LPr3C]*

668	God is our fortress and our rock
361	Now thank we all our God
76	Sweet is the work, my God and King
36	We thank you, God our Father

2nd Reading		**2 Corinthians 5: 6–10 (11–13) 14–17**
	389	All who believe and are baptized
	416	Great God, your love has called us here
	226	It is a thing most wonderful
	672	Light's abode, celestial Salem
	634	Love divine, all loves excelling
	229	My God I love thee; not because
	528	The Church's one foundation

The Gospel		**Mark 4: 26–34**
	378	Almighty God, your word is cast
	37	[Come, ye thankful people, come]
	413	Father, we thank thee who hast planted
	39	For the fruits of his creation
	125	Hail to the Lord's anointed
	385	Rise and hear! The Lord is speaking

PROPER 6   Year C

The Sunday between June 12 and 18 (if after Trinity Sunday)

(c) Ist Reading		**1 Kings 21: 1–10 (11–14) 15–21a**
	548	Drop, drop, slow tears
	550	'Forgive our sins as we forgive'
	652	Lead us, heavenly Father, lead us

(c) Psalm		**Psalm 5: 1–8**
	80	Great is thy faithfulness, O God my Father
	321	Holy, holy, holy! Lord God almighty
	17	Lead me, Lord, lead me in thy righteousness
		(*Treoraigh mé, treoraigh mé, a Thiarna*)
	56	Lord, as I wake I turn to you

(p) Ist Reading		**2 Samuel 11: 26 – 12: 10, 13–15**
	548	Drop, drop, slow tears
	550	'Forgive our sins as we forgive'
	652	Lead us, heavenly Father, lead us
	385	Rise and hear! The Lord is speaking

(p) Psalm		**Psalm 32** *[LIA/L4C]*
	562	Blessed assurance, Jesus is mine
	92	How sweet the name of Jesus sounds

2nd Reading   **Galatians 2: 15–21**

218	And can it be that I should gain
268	Hail, thou once-despised Jesus
100	Jesus loves me: this I know
56	Lord, as I wake I turn to you
81	Lord, for the years your love has kept and guided
229	My God I love thee; not because
436	Now let us from this table rise
661	Through the night of doubt and sorrow

The Gospel   **Luke 7: 36 – 8: 3**

548	Drop, drop, slow tears
480	God forgave my sin in Jesus' name
92	How sweet the name of Jesus sounds
495	Jesu, Jesu, fill us with your love
553	Jesu, lover of my soul
590	My faith looks up to thee
557	Rock of ages, cleft for me
493	Ye that know the Lord is gracious

PROPER 7   Year A

The Sunday between June 19 and 25 (if after Trinity Sunday)

(c) 1st Reading   **Genesis 21: 8–21**

545	Sing of Eve and sing of Adam
323	The God of Abraham praise

(c) Psalm   **Psalm 86: 1–10, 16–17**

620	O Lord, hear my prayer
140	The Lord will come and not be slow
372	Through all the changing scenes of life
627	What a friend we have in Jesus

(p) 1st Reading   **Jeremiah 20: 7–13**

No suggested hymns

(p) Psalm   **Psalm 69: 7–10 (11–15) 16–18**

No suggested hymns

2nd Reading		**Romans 6: 1b–11**
	389	All who believe and are baptized
	84	Alleluia! raise the anthem
	403	Bread of the world, in mercy broken
	81	Lord, for the years your love has kept and guided
	392	Now is eternal life
	436	Now let us from this table rise
	703	Now lives the lamb of God
	638	O for a heart to praise my God
	286	The strife is o'er, the battle done
	661	Through the night of doubt and sorrow

The Gospel		**Matthew 10: 24–39**
	588	Light of the minds that know him
	108	Praise to the Holiest in the height
	599	'Take up thy cross', the Saviour said

PROPER 7

Year B

The Sunday between June 19 and 25 (if after Trinity Sunday)

(c) 1st Reading		**1 Samuel 17: 1a, 4–11, 19–23, 32–49**
	643	Be thou my vision, O Lord of my heart
	566	Fight the good fight with all thy might!
	668	God is our fortress and our rock
	593	O Jesus, I have promised
	487	Soldiers of Christ, arise
	488	Stand up, stand up for Jesus
	662	Those who would valour see
		(*He who would valiant be*)
	372	Through all the changing scenes of life

(c) Psalm		**Psalm 9: 9–20**
	668	God is our fortress and our rock
	12	God is our strength and refuge

or **(c)* 1st Reading**	**1 Samuel 17: 57 – 18: 5, 10–16**
	No suggested hymns

(c)* Psalm **Psalm 133** *[E2B/Pr15A/Unity]*

518	Bind us together, Lord
522	In Christ there is no east or west
525	Let there be love shared among us
438	O thou, who at thy eucharist didst pray
507	Put peace into each other's hands
661	Through the night of doubt and sorrow

(p) 1st Reading **Job 38: 1–11**

612	Eternal Father, strong to save
581	I, the Lord of sea and sky
369	Songs of praise the angels sang

(p) Psalm **Psalm 107: 1–3, 23–32**

683	All people that on earth do dwell
666	Be still, my soul: the Lord is on thy side
612	Eternal Father, strong to save
353	Give to our God immortal praise
128	Hills of the north, rejoice
584	Jesus calls us! O'er the tumult
652	Lead us, heavenly Father, lead us
30	Let us, with a gladsome mind
484	Lift high the cross, the love of Christ proclaim
384	Lord, thy word abideth
527	Son of God, eternal Saviour

2nd Reading **2 Corinthians 6: 1–13**

643	Be thou my vision, O Lord of my heart
566	Fight the good fight with all thy might!
417	He gave his life in selfless love
587	Just as I am, without one plea
652	Lead us, heavenly Father, lead us
487	Soldiers of Christ, arise
488	Stand up, stand up for Jesus

The Gospel **Mark 4: 35–41**

666	Be still, my soul: the Lord is on thy side
563	Commit your ways to God
612	Eternal Father, strong to save
2	Faithful one, so unchanging
648	God be with you till we meet again
300	Holy Spirit, truth divine

553	Jesu, lover of my soul
584	Jesus calls us! O'er the tumult
588	Light of the minds that know him
18	Lord, I come before your throne of grace
593	O Jesus, I have promised
527	Son of God, eternal Saviour
47	We plough the fields, and scatter
22	You shall cross the barren desert

If the continuous option of Old Testament and Psalm is being used, either the first set or the second set should be chosen in preference to choosing one item from each set.

PROPER 7   Year C

The Sunday between June 19 and 25 (if after Trinity Sunday)

(c) Ist Reading		**1 Kings 19: 1–4 (5–7) 8–15a**	
	325	Be still, for the presence of the Lord, the Holy One, is here	
	549	Dear Lord and Father of mankind	
	593	O Jesus, I have promised	
	624	Speak, Lord, in the stillness	
	387	Thanks to God, whose Word was spoken	

(c) Psalm		**Psalms 42 and 43**	*[EVABC]*
	607	As pants the hart for cooling streams	
	606	As the deer pants for the water	
	15	If thou but suffer God to guide thee	
	95	Jesu, priceless treasure	
	425	Jesus, thou joy of loving hearts	
	384	Lord, thy word abideth	
	434	My Jesus, pierced for love of me	

| **(p) Ist Reading** | **Isaiah 65: 1–9** |
| | *No suggested hymns* |

| **(p) Psalm** | | **Psalm 22: 19–28** |
| | 492 | Ye servants of God, your master proclaim |

155

2nd Reading		**Galatians 3: 23–29**	[6–24]
	250	All hail the power of Jesu's name	
	389	All who believe and are baptized	
	218	And can it be that I should gain	
	496	For the healing of the nations	
	522	In Christ there is no east or west	
	101	Jesus, the very thought of thee	
	358	King of glory, King of peace	

The Gospel		**Luke 8: 26–39**
	549	Dear Lord and Father of mankind
	554	Lord Jesus, think on me
	373	To God be the glory! Great things he has done!

PROPER 8   Year A

The Sunday between June 26 and July 2

(c) Ist Reading		**Genesis 22: 1–14**
	13	God moves in a mysterious way
	59	New every morning is the love
	601	Teach me, my God and King
	323	The God of Abraham praise

(c) Psalm		**Psalm 13**
	528	The Church's one foundation

(p) Ist Reading		**Jeremiah 28: 5–9**
	381	God has spoken—by his prophets

(p) Psalm		**Psalm 89: 1–4, 15–18**
	80	Great is thy faithfulness, O God my Father
	32	O Lord my God! When I in awesome wonder
	490	The Spirit lives to set us free
	374	When all thy mercies, O my God

2nd Reading		**Romans 6: 12–23**
	642	Amazing grace (how sweet the sound!)
	400	And now, O Father, mindful of the love
	87	Christ is the world's Light, he and none other

703	Now lives the Lamb of God
597	Take my life, and let it be
492	Ye servants of God, your master proclaim

The Gospel **Matthew 10: 40–42**

| 517 | Brother, sister, let me serve you |
| 495 | Jesu, Jesu, fill us with your love |

PROPER 8   Year B

The Sunday between June 26 and July 2

(c) Ist Reading **2 Samuel 1: 1, 17–27**

| 592 | O Love that wilt not let me go |

(c) Psalm **Psalm 130** *[L5A/Pr5B*/Prl4B]*

564	Deus meus, adiuva me (*O my God, in help draw near*)
620	O Lord, hear my prayer
9	There's a wideness in God's mercy
627	What a friend we have in Jesus

(p) Ist Reading **Wisdom 1: 13–15; 2: 23–24**

425	Jesus, thou joy of loving hearts
49	Lord, bring the day to pass
59	New every morning is the love

(p) Psalm **Psalm 30** *[4LBPrl/E3C/Pr5C*/Pr9C]*

554	Lord Jesus, think on me
592	O Love that wilt not let me go
196	O worship the Lord in the beauty of holiness!
528	The Church's one foundation

2nd Reading **2 Corinthians 8: 7–15**

352	Give thanks with a grateful heart
168	Lord, you were rich beyond all splendour
177	[Once in royal David's city (*vv. 1, 2, 6*)]
114	Thou didst leave thy throne and thy kingly crown

The Gospel		**Mark 5: 21–43**
	511	Father of mercy, God of consolation
	455	Go forth for God; go forth to the world in peace
	211	Immortal love for ever full
	513	O Christ, the Healer, we have come
	104	O for a thousand tongues to sing

PROPER 8   Year C

The Sunday between June 26 and July 2

(c) 1st Reading		**2 Kings 2: 1–2, 6–14**
	643	Be thou my vision, O Lord of my heart
	297	Come, thou Holy Spirit, come
	298	Filled with the Spirit's power, with one accord
	647	Guide me, O thou great Jehovah
	383	Lord, be thy word my rule
	386	Spirit of God, unseen as the wind
	310	Spirit of the living God

(c) Psalm		**Psalm 77: 1–2, 11–20**
	593	O Jesus, I have promised
	372	Through all the changing scenes of life
	529	Thy hand, O God, has guided

(p) 1st Reading		**1 Kings 19: 15–16, 19–21**
	125	Hail to the Lord's anointed

(p) Psalm		**Psalm 16**	*[EVABC/E2A/Pr28B/Pr28B*]*
	567	Forth, in thy name, O Lord, I go	
	300	Holy Spirit, truth divine	
	~ 553	Jesu, lover of my soul	
	652	Lead us, heavenly Father, lead us	
	392	Now is eternal life	
	289	[This joyful Eastertide]	

2nd Reading		**Galatians 5: 1, 13–25**
	297	Come, thou Holy Spirit, come
	320	Firmly I believe and truly
	39	For the fruits of his creation
	311	Fruitful trees, the Spirit's sowing

652	Lead us, heavenly Father, lead us
81	Lord, for the years your love has kept and guided
395	When Jesus taught by Galilee
144	Word of justice, alleluia

The Gospel   **Luke 9: 51–62**

608	Be still and know that I am God
219	From heav'n you came, helpless babe
421	I come with joy, a child of God
115	Thou art the Way: to thee alone
114	Thou didst leave thy throne and thy kingly crown

PROPER 9   Year A

The Sunday between July 3 and 9

(c) 1st Reading   **Genesis 24: 34–38, 42–49, 58–67**

| 383 | Lord, be thy word my rule |
| 323 | The God of Abraham praise |

(c) Psalm   **Psalm 45: 10–17**   *[9–8]*

| 528 | The Church's one foundation |
| 142 | Wake, O wake! With tidings thrilling |

(p) 1st Reading   **Zechariah 9: 9–12**

217	[All glory, laud, and honour]
347	Children of Jerusalem
125	Hail to the Lord's anointed
238	[Ride on, ride on in majesty]

(p) Psalm   **Psalm 145: 8–14**

24	All creatures of our God and King
42	Good is the Lord, our heavenly King
80	Great is thy faithfulness, O God my Father
125	Hail to the Lord's anointed
321	Holy, holy, holy! Lord God almighty
73	The day thou gavest, Lord, is ended
492	Ye servants of God, your master proclaim

2nd Reading		**Romans 7: 15–25a**
	51	Awake, my soul, and with the sun
	553	Jesu, lover of my soul

The Gospel		**Matthew 11: 16–19, 25–30**
	398	Alleluia! sing to Jesus
	567	Forth, in thy name, O Lord, I go
	127	Hark what a sound, and too divine for hearing
	418	Here, O my Lord, I see thee face to face
	92	How sweet the name of Jesus sounds
	576	I heard the voice of Jesus say
	97	Jesus shall reign where'er the sun
	587	Just as I am, without one plea
	103	O Christ the same, through all our story's pages
	363	O Lord of heaven and earth and sea
	451	We come as guests invited
	627	What a friend we have in Jesus
	22	You shall cross the barren desert

PROPER 9   Year B

The Sunday between July 3 and 9

(c) Ist Reading		**2 Samuel 5: 1–5, 9–10**
	12	God is our strength and refuge
	529	Thy hand, O God, has guided

(c) Psalm		**Psalm 48** [Ep4C]
	646	Glorious things of thee are spoken
	380	God has spoken to his people, alleluia!
	354	Great is the Lord and most worthy of praise
	593	O Jesus, I have promised

(p) Ist Reading		**Ezekiel 2: 1–5**
	381	God has spoken—by his prophets
	387	Thanks to God, whose Word was spoken

(p) Psalm		**Psalm 123** [Pr28A]
	696	God, we praise you! God, we bless you!
	208	[Hearken, O Lord, have mercy upon us]

2nd Reading ✓   **2 Corinthians 12: 2–10**

645   Father, hear the prayer we offer
352   Give thanks with a grateful heart
594   O Lord of creation, to you be all praise!
387   Thanks to God, whose Word was spoken

The Gospel ✓   **Mark 6: 1–13**

454   Forth in the peace of Christ we go
618   Lord of all hopefulness, Lord of all joy
197   Songs of thankfulness and praise

PROPER 9   Year C

The Sunday between July 3 and 9

(c) 1st Reading   **2 Kings 5: 1–14**   *[4LBPrl]*

553   Jesu, lover of my soul
587   Just as I am, without one plea
513   O Christ, the Healer, we have come
557   Rock of ages, cleft for me

(c) Psalm ✓   **Psalm 30**   *[4LBPrl/E3C/Pr5C*/Pr8B*]*

554   Lord Jesus, think on me
592   O Love that wilt not let me go
196   O worship the Lord in the beauty of holiness!
528   The Church's one foundation

(p) 1st Reading   **Isaiah 66: 10–14**

569   Hark, my soul, it is the Lord
16   Like a mighty river flowing

(p) Psalm   **Psalm 66: 1–9**

683   All people that on earth do dwell
701   Jubilate, ev'rybody
360   Let all the world in every corner sing
104   O for a thousand tongues to sing

2nd Reading   **Galatians 6: (1–6) 7–16**

561   Beneath the Cross of Jesus
523   Help us to help each other, Lord

225	In the cross of Christ I glory
634	Love divine, all loves excelling
528	The Church's one foundation
248	We sing the praise of him who died
247	When I survey the wondrous cross

The Gospel   **Luke 10: 1–11, 16–20**

37	[Come, ye thankful people, come]
39	For the fruits of his creation
454	Forth in the peace of Christ we go
478	Go forth and tell! O Church of God, awake!
455	Go forth for God; go forth to the world in peace
456	Lord, you give the great commission
305	O Breath of life, come sweeping through us
505	Peace be to this congregation
492	Ye servants of God, your master proclaim

PROPER 10   Year A

The Sunday between July 10 and 16

(c) 1st Reading   **Genesis 25: 19–34**

No suggested hymns

(c) Psalm   **Psalm 119: 105–112**   *[BSA]*

294	Come down, O Love divine
382	Help us, O Lord, to learn
384	Lord, thy word abideth
637	O for a closer walk with God
592	O Love that wilt not let me go
490	The Spirit lives to set us free
603	When we walk with the Lord

(p) 1st Reading   **Isaiah 55: 10–13**   *[2LCPr3]*

65	At evening, when the sun had set
454	Forth in the peace of Christ we go
384	Lord, thy word abideth
710	Sing to God new songs of worship
47	[We plough the fields, and scatter]
377	You shall go out with joy

| (p) **Psalm** | | **Psalm 65: (1–8) 9–13** | *[2LC/Pr25C/HTA]* |

	612	Eternal Father, strong to save
	645	Father, hear the prayer we offer
	42	Good is the Lord our heavenly King
	581	I, the Lord of sea and sky
	709	Praise the Lord! You heavens, adore him

2nd Reading **Romans 8: 1–11**

	218	And can it be that I should gain
	294	Come down, O Love divine
	319	Father, of heaven, whose love profound
	74	First of the week and finest day
	353	Give to our God immortal praise
	300	Holy Spirit, truth divine
	102	Name of all majesty
	104	O for a thousand tongues to sing
	373	To God be the glory! Great things he has done!

Gospel **Matthew 13: 1–9, 18–23**

	378	Almighty God, your word is cast
	413	Father, we thank thee who hast planted
	380	God has spoken to his people, alleluia!
	430	Lord, as the grain which once on upland acres
	75	Lord, dismiss us with your blessing
	385	Rise and hear! The Lord is speaking

PROPER 10

Year B

The Sunday between July 10 and 16

(c) 1st Reading **2 Samuel 6: 1–5, 12b–19**

| | 529 | Thy hand, O God, has guided |

(c) Psalm **Psalm 24** *[ASB]*

	48	God in his love for us lent us this planet
	266	[Hail the day that sees him rise]
	337	Lift up your heads, O ye gates
	131	Lift up your heads, you mighty gates
	134	Make way, make way, for Christ the King
	284	[The golden gates are lifted up]

(p) **1st Reading**		**Amos 7: 7–15**	
	381	God has spoken—by his prophets	

(p) **Psalm**		**Psalm 85: 8–13**	*[Pr14A*]*
	695	God of mercy, God of grace	
	539	Rejoice, O land, in God thy might	
	140	[The Lord will come and not be slow]	

2nd Reading		**Ephesians 1: 3–14**	*[C2ABC]*
	84	Alleluia! raise the anthem	
	189	[As with gladness men of old]	
	318	Father, Lord of all creation	
	352	Give thanks with a grateful heart	
	99	Jesus, the name high over all	
	652	Lead us, heavenly Father, lead us	
	524	May the grace of Christ our Saviour	
	363	O Lord of heaven and earth and sea	
	313	The Spirit came, as promised	
	9	There's a wideness in God's mercy	
	373	To God be the glory! Great things he has done!	
	451	We come as guests invited	

The Gospel		**Mark 6: 14–29**	
	460	For all your saints in glory, for all your saints at rest (*vv. 1, 2i, 3*)	

PROPER 10

Year C

The Sunday between July 10 and 16

(c) **1st Reading**		**Amos 7: 7–17**	
	381	God has spoken—by his prophets	

(c) **Psalm**		**Psalm 82**	*[Pr15C*]*
	125	Hail to the Lord's anointed	
	535	Judge eternal, throned in splendour	
	140	[The Lord will come and not be slow]	
	509	Your kingdom come, O God!	

(p) **1st Reading**		**Deuteronomy 30: 9–14**	
	211	Immortal love for ever full	

(p) **Psalm**		**Psalm 25: 1–10**	[AIC/LIB]
	17	Lead me, Lord, lead me in thy righteousness	
		(Treoraigh mé, treoraigh mé, a Thiarna)	
	652	Lead us, heavenly Father, lead us	
	712	Tell out, my soul, the greatness of the Lord	

2nd Reading **Colossians 1: 1–14**

- 84 Alleluia! raise the anthem
- 312 Gracious Spirit, Holy Ghost
- 523 Help us to help each other, Lord
- 619 Lord, teach us how to pray aright
- 639 O thou who camest from above
- 508 Peace to you
- 487 Soldiers of Christ, arise
- 624 Speak, Lord, in the stillness
- 9 There's a wideness in God's mercy
- 373 To God be the glory! Great things he has done!
- 344 When morning gilds the skies
- 493 Ye that know the Lord is gracious

The Gospel **Luke 10: 25–37**

- 517 Brother, sister, let me serve you
- 569 Hark, my soul, it is the Lord
- 523 Help us to help each other, Lord
- 499 When I needed a neighbour, were you there
- 500 Would you walk by on the other side

PROPER 11 — Year A

The Sunday between July 17 and 23

(c) 1st Reading **Genesis 28: 10–19a**

- 561 Beneath the Cross of Jesus
- 562 Blessed assurance, Jesus is mine
- 330 God is here! As we his people
- 331 God reveals his presence
- 67 God, who made the earth and heaven
- 656 Nearer, my God, to thee
- 657 O God of Bethel, by whose hand

(c) Psalm   **Psalm 139: 1–12, 23–24**

51	Awake, my soul, and with the sun
647	Guide me, O thou great Jehovah
579	I want to walk as a child of the light
226	It is a thing most wonderful
195	Lord, the light of your love is shining
71	Saviour, again to thy dear name we raise
19	There is no moment of my life

(p) 1st Reading   **Wisdom 12: 13, 16–19**

560	Alone with none but thee, my God
668	God is our fortress and our rock

(p) Alternative 1st Reading Isaiah 44: 6–8

2	[Faithful one, so unchanging]
381	God has spoken—by his prophets
668	God is our fortress and our rock
557	Rock of ages, cleft for me

(p) Psalm   **Psalm 86: 11–17**

349	Fill thou my life, O Lord my God
382	Help us, O Lord, to learn

2nd Reading   **Romans 8: 12–25**

558	Abba Father, let me be
523	Help us to help each other, Lord
301	Let every Christian pray
654	Light of the lonely pilgrim's heart
49	Lord, bring the day to pass
619	Lord, teach us how to pray aright
387	Thanks to God, whose Word was spoken
285	The head that once was crowned with thorns

The Gospel   **Matthew 13: 24–30, 36–43**

378	Almighty God, your word is cast
37	[Come, ye thankful people, come]
649	Happy are they, they that love God
95	Jesu, priceless treasure

PROPER 11

The Sunday between July 17 and 23

(c) 1st Reading   **2 Samuel 7: 1–14a**

342	Sweet is the solemn voice that calls
73	The day thou gavest, Lord, is ended
343	We love the place, O God

(c) Psalm   **Psalm 89: 20–37**

690	Come, worship God, who is worthy of honour
2	Faithful one, so unchanging
668	God is our fortress and our rock
557	Rock of ages, cleft for me

(p) 1st Reading   **Jeremiah 23: 1–6**   *[Pr29C/Pr29C*]*

250	All hail the power of Jesu's name
135	[O come, O come, Emmanuel]
442	Praise the Lord, rise up rejoicing
197	Songs of thankfulness and praise
323	The God of Abraham praise
20	The King of love my shepherd is

(p) Psalm   **Psalm 23**   *[L4A/E4ABC/Pr23A*]*

644	Faithful Shepherd, feed me
645	Father, hear the prayer we offer
466	Here from all nations, all tongues, and all peoples
467	How bright those glorious spirits shine!
655	Loving Shepherd of your sheep
433	My God, your table here is spread
235	O sacred head, sore wounded
365	Praise to the Lord, the Almighty, the King of creation
20	The King of love my shepherd is
21	The Lord's my shepherd, I'll not want
448	The trumpets sound, the angels sing

2nd Reading   **Ephesians 2: 11–22**

326	Blessed city, heavenly Salem *(Christ is made the sure foundation)*
327	Christ is our corner-stone

167

87	Christ is the world's Light, he and none other
501	Christ is the world's true light
421	I come with joy, a child of God
522	In Christ there is no east or west
306	O Spirit of the living God
675	Peace, perfect peace, in this dark world of sin?
507	Put peace into each other's hands
340	Sing and be glad, for this is God's house!
528	The Church's one foundation
313	The Spirit came, as promised
493	Ye that know the Lord is gracious

The Gospel　　　　　**Mark 6: 30–34, 53–56**

211	Immortal love for ever full
513	O Christ, the Healer, we have come
104	O for a thousand tongues to sing

PROPER II　　　　　　　　　　　Year C

The Sunday between July 17 and 23

(c) lst Reading　　　　　**Amos 8: 1–12**

No suggested hymns

(c) Psalm　　　　　**Psalm 52**

365	Praise to the Lord, the Almighty, the King of creation

(p) lst Reading　　　　　**Genesis 18: 1–10a**

545	Sing of Eve and sing of Adam
323	The God of Abraham praise

(p) Psalm　　　　　**Psalm 15**　　　　*[Ep4A/Pr17B*/5–14]*

631	God be in my head

2nd Reading　　　　　**Colossians 1: 15–28**

643	Be thou my vision, O Lord of my heart
220	Glory be to Jesus
268	Hail, thou once-despised Jesus
160	[Hark! the herald-angels sing]
421	I come with joy, a child of God

616	In my life, Lord, be glorified
94	In the name of Jesus
431	Lord, enthroned in heavenly splendour
303	Lord of the Church, we pray for our renewing
7	My God, how wonderful thou art
232	Nature with open volume stands
103	O Christ the same, through all our story's pages
306	O Spirit of the living God
675	Peace, perfect peace, in this dark world of sin?

The Gospel   **Luke 10: 38–42**

268	Hail, thou once-despised Jesus!
596	Seek ye first the kingdom of God
603	When we walk with the Lord

PROPER 12   Year A

The Sunday between July 17 and 24 ~~23~~

(c) 1st Reading   **Genesis 29: 15–28**

544	O perfect Love, all human thought transcending

(c) Psalm   **Psalm 105: 1–11, 45b**

321	Holy, holy, holy! Lord God almighty
597	Take my life, and let it be
323	The God of Abraham praise

(c) Alternative Psalm   **Psalm 128**

649	Happy are they, they that love God
539	Rejoice, O land, in God thy might
712	Tell out, my soul, the greatness of the Lord

(p) 1st Reading   **1 Kings 3: 5–12**

643	Be thou my vision, O Lord of my heart
533	God of grace and God of glory

(p) Psalm   **Psalm 119: 129–136**   [BSC]

382	Help us, O Lord, to learn
195	Lord, the light of your love is shining
384	Lord, thy word abideth
108	Praise to the Holiest in the height

2nd Reading **Romans 8: 26–39**

328	Come on and celebrate!
693	Glory in the highest to the God of heaven!
13	God moves in a mysterious way
266	[Hail the day that sees him rise]
226	It is a thing most wonderful
272	[Jesus lives: thy terrors now]
671	Jesus, thy blood and righteousness
358	King of glory, King of peace
619	Lord, teach us how to pray aright
392	Now is eternal life
638	O for a heart to praise my God
106	O Jesus, King most wonderful
363	O Lord of heaven and earth and sea
105	O the deep, deep love of Jesus
487	Soldiers of Christ, arise
288	Thine be the glory, risen, conquering Son
373	To God be the glory! Great things he has done!

The Gospel **Matthew 13: 31–33, 44–52**

665	Ag Críost an síol (*The seed is Christ's*)
643	Be thou my vision, O Lord of my heart
95	Jesu, priceless treasure
16	Like a mighty river flowing
384	Lord, thy word abideth

PROPER 12 Year B

The Sunday between July 17 and 23

(c) 1st Reading **2 Samuel 11: 1–15**

551	How can we sing with joy to God

(c) Psalm **Psalm 14** [Pr19C]

649	Happy are they, they that love God

(p) 1st Reading **2 Kings 4: 42–44**

44	Praise and thanksgiving, Father, we offer
497	The Church of Christ, in every age

(p) **Psalm**		**Psalm 145: 10–18**
	24	All creatures of our God and King
	42	Good is the Lord, our heavenly King
	80	Great is thy faithfulness, O God my Father
	125	Hail to the Lord's anointed
	321	Holy, holy, holy! Lord God almighty
	73	The day thou gavest, Lord, is ended
	492	Ye servants of God, your master proclaim

2nd Reading		**Ephesians 3: 14–21**
	294	Come down, O Love divine
	454	Forth in the peace of Christ we go
	616	In my life, Lord, be glorified
	589	Lord, speak to me that I may speak
	168	Lord, you were rich beyond all splendour
	621	O Love divine, how sweet thou art!
	105	O the deep, deep love of Jesus
	307	Our great Redeemer, as he breathed
	341	Spirit divine, attend our prayers
	313	The Spirit came, as promised
	373	To God be the glory! Great things he has done

The Gospel		**John 6: 1–21**
	665	Ag Críost an síol (*The seed is Christ's*)
	612	Eternal Father, strong to save
	39	For the fruits of his creation
	647	Guide me, O thou great Jehovah
	584	Jesus calls us! O'er the tumult
	587	Just as I am, without one plea
	652	Lead us, heavenly Father, lead us
	428	Let us break bread together, we are one
	657	O God of Bethel, by whose hand

PROPER 12

The Sunday between July ~~17~~ 24 and ~~23~~ 31

(c) **1st Reading**		**Hosea 1: 2–10**
	319	Father, of heaven, whose love profound
	569	Hark, my soul, it is the Lord

(c) Psalm   **Psalm 85**

695	God of mercy, God of grace
539	Rejoice, O land, in God thy might
140	[The Lord will come and not be slow]

(p) 1st Reading   **Genesis 18: 20–32**

619	Lord, teach us how to pray aright
8	The Lord is king! Lift up your voice

(p) Psalm   **Psalm 138**   [5LC/Pr5B/Pr16A*]

250	All hail the power of Jesu's name
358	King of glory, King of peace
21	The Lord's my shepherd, I'll not want

2nd Reading   **Colossians 2: 6–15 (16–19)**

389	All who believe and are baptized
261	Christ, above all glory seated!
523	Help us to help each other, Lord
102	Name of all majesty
248	We sing the praise of him who died

The Gospel   **Luke 11: 1–13**

550	'Forgive our sins as we forgive'
429	Lord Jesus Christ, you have come to us
619	Lord, teach us how to pray aright
657	O God of Bethel, by whose hand
623	Our heavenly Father, through your Son
625	Prayer is the soul's sincere desire
596	Seek ye first the kingdom of God
509	Your kingdom come, O God!

PROPER 13   Year A

The Sunday between July 31 and August 6

(c) 1st Reading   **Genesis 32: 22–31**   [Pr24C*]

418	Here, O my Lord, I see thee face to face
226	It is a thing most wonderful
592	O Love that wilt not let me go

(c) Psalm **Psalm 17: 1–7, 15**

635 Lord, be my guardian and my guide
620 O Lord, hear my prayer

(p) 1st Reading **Isaiah 55: 1–5**

646 Glorious things of thee are spoken
576 I heard the voice of Jesus say
557 Rock of ages, cleft for me
448 The trumpets sound, the angels sing

(p) Psalm **Psalm 145: 8–9, 14–21**

42 Good is the Lord, our heavenly King
365 Praise to the Lord, the Almighty, the King of
    creation

2nd Reading **Romans 9: 1–5**

303 Lord of the Church, we pray for our renewing
545 Sing of Eve and sing of Adam
323 The God of Abraham praise

The Gospel **Matthew 14: 13–21**

379 Break thou the bread of life
39 For the fruits of his creation
647 Guide me, O thou great Jehovah
428 Let us break bread together, we are one
435 O God, unseen, yet ever near

PROPER 13

Year B

The Sunday between July 31 and August 6

(c) 1st Reading **2 Samuel 11: 26 – 12: 13a**

548 Drop, drop, slow tears
550 'Forgive our sins as we forgive'
652 Lead us, heavenly Father, lead us
385 Rise and hear! The Lord is speaking

(c) Psalm **Psalm 51: 1–12** *[L5B]*

397 Alleluia! Alleluia! Opening our hearts to him
297 Come, thou Holy Spirit, come
614 Great Shepherd of your people, hear

	208	[Hearken, O Lord, have mercy upon us]
	553	Jesu, lover of my soul
	305	O Breath of life, come sweeping through us
	638	O for a heart to praise my God
	557	Rock of ages, cleft for me

(p) 1st Reading   **Exodus 16: 2–4, 9–15**

325	Be still, for the presence of the Lord, the Holy One, is here
549	Dear Lord and Father of mankind
647	Guide me, O thou great Jehovah
425	Jesus, thou joy of loving hearts
588	Light of the minds that know him
431	Lord, enthroned in heavenly splendour
589	Lord, speak to me that I may speak
445	Soul, array thyself with gladness

(p) Psalm   **Psalm 78: 23–29**

549	Dear Lord and Father of mankind
435	O God, unseen, yet ever near

2nd Reading   **Ephesians 4: 1–16**

518	Bind us together, Lord
86	Christ is the King! O friends, rejoice
501	Christ is the world's true light
294	Come down, O Love divine
408	Come, risen Lord, and deign to be our guest
318	Father, Lord of all creation
523	Help us to help each other, Lord
522	In Christ there is no east or west
438	O thou, who at thy eucharist didst pray
440	One bread, one body, one Lord of all
441	Out to the world for Jesus
507	Put peace into each other's hands
308	Revive your Church, O Lord
527	Son of God, eternal Saviour
369	Songs of praise the angels sang
528	The Church's one foundation
313	The Spirit came, as promised
661	Through the night of doubt and sorrow
529	Thy hand, O God, has guided

The Gospel		**John 6: 24–35**
	398	Alleluia! sing to Jesus
	403	Bread of the world, in mercy broken
	379	Break thou the bread of life
	408	Come, risen Lord, and deign to be our guest
	411	Draw near and take the body of the Lord
	647	Guide me, O thou great Jehovah
	418	Here, O my Lord, I see thee face to face
	420	'I am the bread of life'
	581	I, the Lord of sea and sky
	422	In the quiet consecration
	425	Jesus, thou joy of loving hearts
	588	Light of the minds that know him
	431	Lord, enthroned in heavenly splendour
	435	O God, unseen, yet ever near
	443	Sent forth by God's blessing, our true faith confessing
	445	Soul, array thyself with gladness
	624	Speak, Lord, in the stillness
	451	We come as guests invited

PROPER 13

Year C

The Sunday between July 31 and August 6

(c) 1st Reading		**Hosea 11: 1–11**
	518	Bind us together, Lord
	3	God is love: let heaven adore him
	569	Hark, my soul, it is the Lord
	211	Immortal love for ever full
	7	My God, how wonderful thou art
	231	My song is love unknown

(c) Psalm		**Psalm 107: 1–9, 43**
	683	All people that on earth do dwell
	353	Give to our God immortal praise
	30	Let us, with a gladsome mind
	484	Lift high the cross, the love of Christ proclaim
	361	Now thank we all our God ↓
	45	Praise, O praise our God and king
	372	Through all the changing scenes of life
	374	When all thy mercies, O my God

(p) **1st Reading**		**Ecclesiastes 1: 2, 12–14; 2: 18–23**
	563	Commit your ways to God

(p) **Psalm**		**Psalm 49: 1–12**
	10	All my hope on God is founded
	319	Father, of heaven, whose love profound
	533	God of grace and God of glory

2nd Reading		**Colossians 3: 1–11**
	260	Christ is alive! Let Christians sing
	501	Christ is the world's true light
	566	Fight the good fight with all thy might!
	268	Hail, thou once-despised Jesus!
	522	In Christ there is no east or west
	272	[Jesus lives: thy terrors now]
	427	Let all mortal flesh keep silence
	287	[The whole bright world rejoices now]

The Gospel		**Luke 12: 13–21**
	10	All my hope on God is founded
	643	Be thou my vision, O Lord of my heart
	533	God of grace and God of glory
	95	Jesu, priceless treasure
	196	O worship the Lord in the beauty of holiness!

PROPER 14   Year A

The Sunday between August 7 and 13

(c) **1st Reading**		**Genesis 37: 1–4, 12–28**
	647	Guide me, O thou great Jehovah

(c) **Psalm**		**Psalm 105: 1–6, 16–22, 45b**
	353	Give to our God immortal praise
	361	Now thank we all our God
	708	O praise ye the Lord! Praise him in the height
	365	Praise to the Lord, the Almighty, the King of creation

(p) Ist Reading **1 Kings 19: 9–18**

325 Be still, for the presence of the Lord,
    the Holy One, is here
549 Dear Lord and Father of mankind
593 O Jesus, I have promised
624 Speak, Lord, in the stillness
387 Thanks to God, whose Word was spoken

(p) Psalm **Psalm 85: 8–13** *[Pr10B*]*

695 God of mercy, God of grace
539 Rejoice, O land, in God thy might
140 [The Lord will come and not be slow]

2nd Reading **Romans 10: 5–15**

501 Christ is the world's true light
478 Go forth and tell! O Church of God, awake!
91 He is Lord, he is Lord
129 How lovely on the mountains are the feet of him
92 How sweet the name of Jesus sounds
94 In the name of Jesus
211 Immortal love for ever full
96 Jesus is Lord! Creation's voice proclaims it
425 Jesus, thou joy of loving hearts
303 Lord of the Church, we pray for our renewing
306 O Spirit of the living God
71 Saviour, again to thy dear name we raise
597 Take my life, and let it be
117 To the name of our salvation
491 We have a gospel to proclaim ⌐

The Gospel **Matthew 14: 22–33**

612 Eternal Father, strong to save
648 God be with you till we meet again
28 I sing the almighty power of God
553 Jesu, lover of my soul
584 Jesus calls us! O'er the tumult
587 Just as I am, without one plea
652 Lead us, heavenly Father, lead us
588 Light of the minds that know him
18 Lord, I come before your throne of grace
593 O Jesus, I have promised
34 O worship the King all-glorious above

366	Praise, my soul, the King of heaven
365	Praise to the Lord, the Almighty, the King of creation
527	Son of God, eternal Saviour
110	Tell me the stories of Jesus
47	[We plough the fields, and scatter]
680	Will your anchor hold in the storms of life
22	You shall cross the barren desert

PROPER 14   Year B

The Sunday between August 7 and 13

(c) 1st Reading   **2 Samuel 18: 5–9, 15, 31–33**

62	Abide with me, fast falls the eventide
590	My faith looks up to thee
592	O Love that wilt not let me go

(c) Psalm   **Psalm 130**   *[L5A/Pr5B*/Pr8B]*

564	Deus meus, adiuva me (*O my God, in help draw near*)
620	O Lord, hear my prayer
9	There's a wideness in God's mercy
627	What a friend we have in Jesus

(p) 1st Reading   **1 Kings 19: 4–8**

| 563 | Commit your ways to God |

(p) Psalm   **Psalm 34: 1–8**   *[Pr25B]*

86	Christ is the King! O friends, rejoice
99	Jesus, the name high over all
634	Love divine, all loves excelling
372	Through all the changing scenes of life
376	Ye holy angels bright

2nd Reading   **Ephesians 4: 25 – 5: 2**

24	All creatures of our God and King
550	'Forgive our sins as we forgive'
380	God has spoken to his people, alleluia!
520	God is love, and where true love is, God himself is there
523	Help us to help each other, Lord

503	Make me a channel of your peace
636	May the mind of Christ my Saviour
106	O Jesus, King most wonderful
526	Risen Lord, whose name we cherish
313	The Spirit came, as promised
244	There is a green hill far away
531	Where love and loving-kindness dwell

The Gospel   **John 6: 35, 41–51**

398	Alleluia! sing to Jesus
401	Be known to us in breaking bread
403	Bread of the world, in mercy broken
379	Break thou the bread of life
408	Come, risen Lord, and deign to be our guest
647	Guide me, O thou great Jehovah
420	'I am the bread of life'
581	I, the Lord of sea and sky
422	In the quiet consecration
425	Jesus, thou joy of loving hearts
588	Light of the minds that know him
431	Lord, enthroned in heavenly splendour
435	O God, unseen, yet ever near
472	Sing we of the blessed mother
445	Soul, array thyself with gladness
624	Speak, Lord, in the stillness
449	Thee we adore, O hidden Saviour, thee
451	We come as guests invited

PROPER 14   Year C

The Sunday between August 7 and 13

✕ **(c) lst Reading**   **Isaiah 1: 1, 10–20**

357	I'll praise my maker while I've breath
553	Jesu, lover of my soul
587	Just as I am, without one plea
446	Strengthen for service, Lord, the hands
498	What does the Lord require for praise and offering?

(c) Psalm **Psalm 50: 1–8, 22–23**

501	Christ is the world's true light
381	God has spoken—by his prophets
97	Jesus shall reign where'er the sun
131	Lift up your heads, you mighty gates
362	O God beyond all praising
140	[The Lord will come and not be slow]

(p) 1st Reading **Genesis 15: 1–6**

10	All my hope on God is founded
501	Christ is the world's true light
383	Lord, be thy word my rule
595	Safe in the shadow of the Lord
545	Sing of Eve and sing of Adam
323	The God of Abraham praise

(p) Psalm **Psalm 33: 12–22**

81	Lord, for the years your love has kept and guided
539	Rejoice, O land, in God thy might

2nd Reading **Hebrews 11: 1–3, 8–16**

326	Blessed city, heavenly Salem *(Christ is made the sure foundation)*
461	For all thy saints, O Lord
646	Glorious things of thee are spoken
469	In our day of thanksgiving one psalm let us offer
670	Jerusalem the golden
672	Light's abode, celestial Salem
658	One more step along the world I go
681	There is a land of pure delight
661	Through the night of doubt and sorrow

The Gospel **Luke 12: 32–40**

643	Be thou my vision, O Lord of my heart
86	Christ is the King! O friends, rejoice
363	O Lord of heaven and earth and sea
142	[Wake, O wake! With tidings thrilling]
145	You servants of the Lord

PROPER 15

PROPER 15

Year A

The Sunday between August 14 and 20

(c) 1st Reading		**Genesis 45: 1–15**	
	563	Commit your ways to God	
	649	Happy are they, they that love God	
	522	In Christ there is no east or west	
	525	Let there be love shared among us	
	527	Son of God, eternal Saviour	
	531	Where love and loving-kindness dwell	

(c) Psalm		**Psalm 133**	*[E2B/Pr7B/Unity]*
	518	Bind us together, Lord	
	522	In Christ there is no east or west	
	525	Let there be love shared among us	
	438	O thou, who at thy eucharist didst pray	
	507	Put peace into each other's hands	
	661	Through the night of doubt and sorrow	

(p) 1st Reading		**Isaiah 56: 1, 6–8**	
	342	Sweet is the solemn voice that calls	
	343	We love the place, O God	

(p) Psalm		**Psalm 67**	*[E6C/1–25]*
	695	God of mercy, God of grace	

2nd Reading		**Romans 11: 1–2a, 29–32**	
	218	And can it be that I should gain	
	9	There's a wideness in God's mercy	

The Gospel		**Matthew 15: (10–20) 21–28**	
	324	God, whose almighty word	
	716	Kyrie eleison	
	433	My God, your table here is spread	
	104	O for a thousand tongues to sing	
	514	We cannot measure how you heal	

PROPER 15

Year B

The Sunday between August 14 and 20

(c) Ist Reading		**1 Kings 2: 10–12; 3: 3–14**
	643	Be thou my vision, O Lord of my heart
	533	God of grace and God of glory

(c) Psalm		**Psalm 111** *[Ep4B/Pr23C*]*
	84	Alleluia! raise the anthem
	130	Jesus came, the heavens adoring
	529	Thy hand, O God, has guided
	373	To God be the glory! Great things he has done!

(p) Ist Reading		**Proverbs 9: 1–6**
	433	My God, your table here is spread

(p) Psalm		**Psalm 34: 9–14**
	507	Put peace into each other's hands
	372	Through all the changing scenes of life

2nd Reading		**Ephesians 5: 15–20**
	346	Angel voices, ever singing
	92	How sweet the name of Jesus sounds
	360	Let all the world in every corner sing
	369	Songs of praise the angels sang
	313	The Spirit came, as promised
	374	When all thy mercies, O my God
	458	When, in our music God is glorified
	344	When morning gilds the skies

The Gospel		**John 6: 51–58**
	398	Alleluia! sing to Jesus
	403	Bread of the world, in mercy broken
	411	Draw near and take the body of the Lord
	220	[Glory be to Jesus]
	647	Guide me, O thou great Jehovah
	420	'I am the bread of life'
	581	I, the Lord of sea and sky
	422	In the quiet consecration
	425	Jesus, thou joy of loving hearts
	435	O God, unseen, yet ever near

624   Speak, Lord, in the stillness
449   Thee we adore, O hidden Saviour, thee
451   We come as guests invited

PROPER 15   Year C

The Sunday between August 14 and 20

(c) 1st Reading	**Isaiah 5: 1–7**	*[Pr22A*]*
51	Awake, my soul, and with the sun	

(c) Psalm   **Psalm 80: 1–2, 8–19**

686   Bless the Lord, the God of our forebears
688   Come, bless the Lord, God of our forebears
695   God of mercy, God of grace
614   Great Shepherd of your people, hear
305   O Breath of life, come sweeping through us
657   O God of Bethel, by whose hand

(p) 1st Reading   **Jeremiah 23: 23–29**

381   God has spoken—by his prophets
388   Word of the living God

(p) Psalm	**Psalm 82**	*[Pr10C]*

125   Hail to the Lord's anointed
535   Judge eternal, throned in splendour
140   [The Lord will come and not be slow]
509   Your kingdom come, O God!

2nd Reading   **Hebrews 11: 29 – 12: 2**

566   Fight the good fight with all thy might!
352   Give thanks with a grateful heart
463   Give us the wings of faith to rise
696   God, we praise you! God, we bless you!
417   He gave his life in selfless love
636   May the mind of Christ my Saviour
285   The head that once was crowned with thorns
376   Ye holy angels bright

The Gospel   **Luke 12: 49–56**

550   'Forgive our sins as we forgive'
639   O thou who camest from above

PROPER 16   Year A

The Sunday between August 21 and 27

(c) 1st Reading	**Exodus 1: 8 – 2: 10**	
13	God moves in a mysterious way	
679	When Israel was in Egypt's land	

(c) Psalm	**Psalm 124**	*[Pr21B/12–28]*
642	Amazing grace (how sweet the sound!)	
553	Jesu, lover of my soul	
537	O God, our help in ages past	

(p) 1st Reading	**Isaiah 51: 1–6**	
481	God is working his purpose out as year succeeds to year	
102	Name of all majesty	
136	[On Jordan's bank the Baptist's cry]	

(p) Psalm	**Psalm 138**	*[5LC/Pr5B/Pr12C*]*
250	All hail the power of Jesu's name	
358	King of glory, King of peace	
21	The Lord's my shepherd, I'll not want	

2nd Reading	**Romans 12: 1–8**
408	Come, risen Lord, and deign to be our guest
567	Forth, in thy name, O Lord, I go
520	God is love, and where true love is, God himself is there
523	Help us to help each other, Lord
358	King of glory, King of peace
301	Let every Christian pray
438	O thou, who at thy eucharist didst pray
639	O thou who camest from above
597	Take my life, and let it be
313	The Spirit came, as promised
247	[When I survey the wondrous cross]
531	Where love and loving-kindness dwell

The Gospel	**Matthew 16: 13–20**	*[6–29]*
460	For all your saints in glory, for all your saints at rest (*vv. 1, 2j, 3*)	
659	Onward, Christian soldiers	
528	The Church's one foundation	

PROPER 16   Year B

The Sunday between August 21 and 27

(c) 1st Reading   **1 Kings 8: (1, 6, 10–11), 22–30, 41–43**

346   Angel voices, ever singing
614   Great Shepherd of your people, hear
321   Holy, holy, holy! Lord God almighty
323   The God of Abraham praise

(c) Psalm   **Psalm 84**   *[PresABC]*

400   And now, O Father, mindful of the love
333   How lovely are thy dwellings fair!
95   Jesu, priceless treasure
425   Jesus, thou joy of loving hearts
360   Let all the world in every corner sing
634   Love divine, all loves excelling
620   O Lord, hear my prayer
487   Soldiers of Christ, arise
342   Sweet is the solemn voice that calls
343   We love the place, O God

(p) 1st Reading   **Joshua 24: 1–2a, 14–18**

478   Go forth and tell! O Church of God, awake!
584   Jesus calls us! O'er the tumult
660   Thine for ever! God of love

(p) Psalm   **Psalm 34: 15–22**

657   O God of Bethel, by whose hand

2nd Reading   **Ephesians 6: 10–20**

643   Be thou my vision, O Lord of my heart
207   [Forty days and forty nights]
478   Go forth and tell! O Church of God, awake!
533   God of grace and God of glory
487   Soldiers of Christ, arise
488   Stand up, stand up for Jesus
313   The Spirit came, as promised

The Gospel   **John 6: 56–69**

398   Alleluia! sing to Jesus
403   Bread of the world, in mercy broken
420   'I am the bread of life'

581   I, the Lord of sea and sky
624   Speak, Lord, in the stillness
112   There is a Redeemer

PROPER 16   Year C

The Sunday between August 21 and 27

(c) 1st Reading   **Jeremiah 1: 4–10**   [1–25]

631   God be in my head
589   Lord, speak to me that I may speak
624   Speak, Lord, in the stillness
597   Take my life, and let it be

(c) Psalm   **Psalm 71: 1–6**

2   Faithful one, so unchanging
459   For all the saints, who from their labours rest
              (vv. 1–3)
668   God is our fortress and our rock
557   Rock of ages, cleft for me
595   Safe in the shadow of the Lord

(p) 1st Reading   **Isaiah 58: 9b–14**

206   Come, let us to the Lord our God
647   Guide me, O thou great Jehovah

X **(p) Psalm**   **Psalm 103: 1–8**

1   Bless the Lord, my soul
· 686   Bless the Lord, the God of our forebears
688   Come, bless the Lord, God of our forebears
349   Fill thou my life, O Lord my God
366   Praise, my soul, the King of heaven
365   Praise to the Lord, the Almighty, the King of
              creation
660   Thine for ever! God of love
47   [We plough the fields, and scatter]
374   When all thy mercies, O my God

2nd Reading   **Hebrews 12: 18–29**

646   Glorious things of thee are spoken
220   [Glory be to Jesus]
668   God is our fortress and our rock

619	Lord, teach us how to pray aright
638	O for a heart to praise my God
281	Rejoice, the Lord is King!

The Gospel   **Luke 13: 10–17**

124	[Hark the glad sound! the Saviour comes]
104	O for a thousand tongues to sing
514	We cannot measure how you heal

PROPER 17   Year A

The Sunday between August 21 and September 3

(c) 1st Reading   **Exodus 3: 1–15**

325	Be still, for the presence of the Lord, the Holy One, is here
262	Come, ye faithful, raise the strain
331	God reveals his presence
321	Holy, holy, holy! Lord God almighty
336	Jesus, where'er thy people meet
323	The God of Abraham praise

(c) Psalm   **Psalm 105: 1–6, 23–26, 45c**

| 321 | Holy, holy, holy! Lord God almighty |
| 679 | When Israel was in Egypt's land |

or   **Psalm 115**

| 668 | God is our fortress and our rock |

(p) 1st Reading   **Jeremiah 15: 15–21**

| 384 | Lord, thy word abideth |

(p) Psalm   **Psalm 26: 1–8**

| 343 | We love the place, O God |

2nd Reading   **Romans 12: 9–21**

219	From heav'n you came, helpless babe
455	Go forth for God; go forth to the world in peace
520	God is love, and where true love is, God himself is there
312	Gracious Spirit, Holy Ghost

523	Help us to help each other, Lord
300	Holy Spirit, truth divine
525	Let there be love shared among us
503	Make me a channel of your peace
507	Put peace into each other's hands
531	Where love and loving-kindness dwell

The Gospel   **Matthew 16: 21–28**

666	Be still, my soul: the Lord is on thy side
561	Beneath the Cross of Jesus
645	Father, hear the prayer we offer
588	Light of the minds that know him
59	New every morning is the love
108	Praise to the Holiest in the height
599	'Take up thy cross', the Saviour said
285	The head that once was crowned with thorns
605	Will you come and follow me

PROPER 17   Year B

The Sunday between August 21 and September 3

(c) 1st Reading   **Song of Solomon 2: 8–13**

262	[Come, ye faithful, raise the strain]

(c) Psalm   **Psalm 45: 1–2, 6–9**

88	Fairest Lord Jesus
125	Hail to the Lord's anointed
597	Take my life, and let it be
73	The day thou gavest, Lord, is ended

(p) 1st Reading   **Deuteronomy 4: 1–2, 6–9**

8	The Lord is king! Lift up your voice

(p) Psalm   **Psalm 15**   [Ep4A/PrIIC*/5–14]

631	God be in my head

2nd Reading   **James 1: 17–27**

62	Abide with me, fast falls the eventide
63	All praise to thee, my God, this night
494	Beauty for brokenness

566	Fight the good fight with all thy might!
350	For the beauty of the earth
512	From you all skill and science flow
80	Great is thy faithfulness, O God my Father
382	Help us, O Lord, to learn
6	Immortal, invisible, God only wise
362	O God beyond all praising
363	O Lord of heaven and earth and sea
601	Teach me, my God and King
47	[We plough the fields, and scatter]
374	When all thy mercies, O my God

The Gospel **Mark 7: 1–8, 14–15, 21–23**

630	Blessed are the pure in heart
131	Lift up your heads, you mighty gates
75	Lord, dismiss us with your blessing

PROPER 17   Year C

The Sunday between August 21 and September 3

✕(c) **1st Reading** **Jeremiah 2: 4–13**

645	Father, hear the prayer we offer
646	Glorious things of thee are spoken
553	Jesu, lover of my soul
303	Lord of the Church, we pray for our renewing
557	Rock of ages, cleft for me

✕ (c) **Psalm** **Psalm 81: 1, 10–16**

332	Come, let us join our cheerful songs
48	God in his love for us lent us this planet
360	Let all the world in every corner sing
44	Praise and thanksgiving, Father, we offer

(p) **1st Reading** **Sirach 10: 12–18**

630	Blessed are the pure in heart
294	Come down, O Love divine
638	O for a heart to praise my God

Alternative 1st Reading		**Proverbs 25: 6–7**
	630	Blessed are the pure in heart

(p) Psalm		**Psalm 112**
	591	O happy day that fixed my choice

✗ **2nd Reading**		**Hebrews 13: 1–8, 15–16**
	10	All my hope on God is founded
	516	Beloved, let us love: love is of God
	410	Dearest Jesus, at your word
	350	For the beauty of the earth
	525	Let there be love shared among us
	103	O Christ the same, through all our story's pages
	362	O God beyond all praising
	366	Praise, my soul, the King of heaven
	499	When I needed a neighbour, were you there

✗ **The Gospel**		**Luke 14: 1, 7–14**
	684	All praise to thee, for thou, O King divine
	630	Blessed are the pure in heart
	433	My God, your table here is spread
	712	Tell out, my soul, the greatness of the Lord
	451	We come as guests invited

PROPER 18   Year A

The Sunday between September 4 and 10

˙ **(c) 1st Reading**		**Exodus 12: 1–14**
	254	[At the Lamb's high feast we sing]
	258	[Christ the Lord is risen again!]
	328	Come on and celebrate!
	268	Hail, thou once-despised Jesus!
	431	Lord, enthroned in heavenly splendour
	703	Now lives the Lamb of God

(c) Psalm		**Psalm 149**	[ASC]
	346	Angel voices, ever singing	
	705	New songs of celebration render	
	368	Sing of the Lord's goodness	
	710	Sing to God new songs of worship	
	492	Ye servants of God, your master proclaim	

(p) Ist Reading   **Ezekiel 33: 7–11**

206	Come, let us to the Lord our God
479	Go, tell it on the mountain
589	Lord, speak to me that I may speak

(p) Psalm   **Psalm 119: 33–40**   *[3LAPr2]*

594	O Lord of creation, to you be all praise!

2nd Reading   **Romans 13: 8–14**

515	'A new commandment I give unto you'
549	Dear Lord and Father of mankind
74	First of the week and finest day
39	For the fruits of his creation
126	[Hark! a thrilling voice is sounding]
525	Let there be love shared among us
487	Soldiers of Christ, arise
488	Stand up, stand up for Jesus
145	You servants of the Lord

The Gospel   **Matthew 18: 15–20**

517	Brother, sister, let me serve you
550	'Forgive our sins as we forgive'
623	Our heavenly Father, through your Son
342	Sweet is the solemn voice that calls

PROPER 18   Year B

The Sunday between September 4 and 10

(c) Ist Reading   **Proverbs 22: 1–2, 8–9, 22–23**

494	Beauty for brokenness
523	Help us to help each other, Lord
432	Love is his word, love is his way

(c) Psalm   **Psalm 125**   *[6–29]*

3	God is love: let heaven adore him
34	O worship the King all-glorious above
595	Safe in the shadow of the Lord

(p) 1st Reading		**Isaiah 35: 4–7a**
	231	My song is love unknown (*vv. 1, 2, 4, 7*)
	104	O for a thousand tongues to sing
	113	There is singing in the desert, there is laughter in the skies

(p) Psalm		**Psalm 146** *[Pr5C/Pr21C*/Pr26B/Pr27B*]*
	4	God, who made the earth
	125	Hail to the Lord's anointed
	92	How sweet the name of Jesus sounds
	357	I'll praise my maker while I've breath
	97	Jesus shall reign where'er the sun
	99	Jesus, the name high over all
	535	Judge eternal, throned in splendour
	363	O Lord of heaven and earth and sea
	708	O praise ye the Lord! Praise him in the height
	712	Tell out, my soul, the greatness of the Lord
	8	The Lord is king! Lift up your voice
	376	Ye holy angels bright

2nd Reading		**James 2: 1–10 (11–13) 14–17**
	494	Beauty for brokenness
	317	Father all-loving, you rule us in majesty
	352	Give thanks with a grateful heart
	649	Happy are they, they that love God
	527	Son of God, eternal Saviour
	497	The Church of Christ, in every age

The Gospel		**Mark 7: 24–37**
	65	At evening, when the sun had set
	511	Father of mercy, God of consolation
	512	From you all skill and science flow
	614	Great Shepherd of your people, hear
	211	Immortal love for ever full
	513	O Christ, the Healer, we have come
	104	O for a thousand tongues to sing
	514	We cannot measure how you heal

PROPER 18   Year C

The Sunday between September 4 and 10

✗ (c) 1st Reading   **Jeremiah 18: 1–11**

No suggested hymns

✗ (c) Psalm   **Psalm 139: 1–6, 13–18**   *[Ep2B/Pr4B]*

51	Awake, my soul, and with the sun
567	Forth, in thy name, O Lord, I go
226	It is a thing most wonderful
19	There is no moment of my life

(p) 1st Reading   **Deuteronomy 30: 15–20**   *[4LAPrI]*

206	Come, let us to the Lord our God
56	Lord, as I wake I turn to you
591	O happy day that fixed my choice
597	Take my life, and let it be

(p) Psalm   **Psalm 1**   *[4LCPrI/E7B/Pr20B/Pr25A*]*

649	Happy are they, they that love God
56	Lord, as I wake I turn to you
383	Lord, be thy word my rule

✗ 2nd Reading   **Philemon 1–21**

517	Brother, sister, let me serve you
455	Go forth for God; go forth to the world in peace
523	Help us to help each other, Lord
597	Take my life, and let it be

✗ The Gospel   **Luke 14: 25–33**

588	Light of the minds that know him
59	New every morning is the love
108	Praise to the Holiest in the height
599	'Take up thy cross,' the Saviour said
605	Will you come and follow me

PROPER 19

Year A

The Sunday between September 11 and 17

(c) 1st Reading **Exodus 14: 19–31**

254 [At the Lamb's high feast we sing]
262 [Come, ye faithful, raise the strain]
647 Guide me, O thou great Jehovah
652 Lead us heavenly Father, lead us
657 O God of Bethel, by whose hand
537 O God, our help in ages past
661 Through the night of doubt and sorrow

(c) Psalm **Psalm 114** *[EVABC]*

325 Be still, for the presence of the Lord,
    the Holy One, is here
646 Glorious things of thee are spoken
557 Rock of ages, cleft for me

(p) 1st Reading **Genesis 50: 15–21**

550 'Forgive our sins as we forgive'

(p) Psalm **Psalm 103: (1–7) 8–13**

1 Bless the Lord, my soul
686 Bless the Lord, the God of our forebears
688 Come, bless the Lord, God of our forebears
349 Fill thou my life, O Lord my God
80 Great is thy faithfulness, O God my Father
33 O Lord of every shining constellation
366 Praise, my soul, the King of heaven
365 Praise to the Lord, the Almighty, the King of
    creation
660 Thine for ever! God of love
47 [We plough the fields, and scatter]
374 When all thy mercies, O my God

2nd Reading **Romans 14: 1–12**

147 [Angels, from the realms of glory]
94 In the name of Jesus
272 [Jesus lives: thy terrors now]
277 [Love's redeeming work is done]

The Gospel   **Matthew 18: 21–35**

550 'Forgive our sins as we forgive'
421 I come with joy, a child of God
503 Make me a channel of your peace
623 Our heavenly Father, through your Son

PROPER 19   Year B

The Sunday between September 11 and 17

(c) 1st Reading   **Proverbs 1: 20–33**

643 Be thou my vision, O Lord of my heart
11 Can we by searching find out God
324 God, whose almighty word

(c) Psalm   **Psalm 19**   *[Ep3C/L3B/EVABC/Pr22A]*

606 As the deer pants for the water
153 [Come, thou Redeemer of the earth]
351 From all that dwell below the skies
631 God be in my head
696 God, we praise you! God, we bless you!
616 In my life, Lord, be glorified
97 Jesus shall reign where'er the sun
384 Lord, thy word abideth
432 Love is his word, love is his way
638 O for a heart to praise my God
34 O worship the King all-glorious above
35 The spacious firmament on high

(c) Alternative Canticle for Psalm   **'Song of Wisdom' (Wisdom 7: 26 – 8: 1)**

643 Be thou my vision, O Lord of my heart
33 O Lord of every shining constellation

(p) 1st Reading   **Isaiah 50: 4–9a**   *[L6ABC/HW-WABC]*

230 My Lord, what love is this
235 O sacred head, sore wounded
239 See, Christ was wounded for our sake

(p) Psalm   **Psalm 116: 1–9**

494 Beauty for brokenness
374 When all thy mercies, O my God

2nd Reading   **James 3: 1–12**

589   Lord, speak to me that I may speak
33   O Lord of every shining constellation

The Gospel   **Mark 8: 27–38**

666   Be still, my soul: the Lord is on thy side
460   For all your saints in glory, for all
      your saints at rest (*vv. 1, 2j, 3*)
588   Light of the minds that know him
59   New every morning is the love
108   Praise to the Holiest in the height
599   'Take up thy cross,' the Saviour said
112   There is a Redeemer
605   Will you come and follow me

PROPER 19   Year C

The Sunday between September 11 and 17

(c) 1st Reading   ✗   **Jeremiah 4: 11–12, 22–28**

140   [The Lord will come and not be slow]
540   To thee our God we fly

(c) Psalm   **Psalm 14**   *[Pr12B]*

649   Happy are they, they that love God

(p) 1st Reading   **Exodus 32: 7–14**

584   Jesus calls us! O'er the tumult
358   King of glory, King of peace
372   Through all the changing scenes of life
374   When all thy mercies, O my God

(p) Psalm   **Psalm 51: 1–10**

397   Alleluia! Alleluia! Opening our hearts to him
297   Come, thou Holy Spirit, come
614   Great Shepherd of your people, hear
208   [Hearken, O Lord, have mercy upon us]
553   Jesu, lover of my soul
305   O Breath of life, come sweeping through us
638   O for a heart to praise my God
557   Rock of ages, cleft for me

X **2nd Reading**   **1 Timothy 1: 12–17**

6	Immortal, invisible, God only wise
553	Jesu, lover of my soul
429	Lord Jesus Christ, you have come to us
231	My song is love unknown
102	Name of all majesty
657	O God of Bethel, by whose hand
366	Praise, my soul, the King of heaven

X **The Gospel**   **Luke 15: 1–10**

683	All people that on earth do dwell
642	Amazing grace (how sweet the sound!)
328	Come on and celebrate!
644	Faithful Shepherd, feed me
319	Father, of heaven, whose love profound
587	Just as I am, without one plea
105	O the deep, deep love of Jesus
438	O thou, who at thy eucharist didst pray
20	The King of love my shepherd is
660	Thine for ever! God of love

PROPER 20   Year A

The Sunday between September 18 and 24

(c) 1st Reading   **Exodus 16: 2–15**

325	Be still, for the presence of the Lord, the Holy One, is here
549	Dear Lord and Father of mankind
647	Guide me, O thou great Jehovah
425	Jesus, thou joy of loving hearts
588	Light of the minds that know him
431	Lord, enthroned in heavenly splendour
589	Lord, speak to me that I may speak
445	Soul, array thyself with gladness

(c) Psalm   **Psalm 105: 1–6, 37–45**

398	Alleluia! sing to Jesus
411	Draw near and take the body of the Lord
647	Guide me, O thou great Jehovah
422	In the quiet consecration

588	Light of the minds that know him
708	O praise ye the Lord! Praise him in the height
365	Praise to the Lord, the Almighty, the King of creation
368	Sing of the Lord's goodness
624	Speak, Lord, in the stillness

(p) 1st Reading · **Jonah 3: 10 – 4: 11**

No suggested hymns

(p) Psalm · **Psalm 145: 1–8**

24	All creatures of our God and King
358	King of glory, King of peace
360	Let all the world in every corner sing
104	O for a thousand tongues to sing
368	Sing of the Lord's goodness
374	When all thy mercies, O my God

2nd Reading · **Philippians 1: 21–30**

566	Fight the good fight with all thy might!
461	For all thy saints, O Lord
272	[Jesus lives: thy terrors now]
425	Jesus, thou joy of loving hearts
588	Light of the minds that know him
81	Lord, for the years your love has kept and guided

The Gospel · **Matthew 20: 1–16**

645	Father, hear the prayer we offer
454	Forth in the peace of Christ we go
567	Forth, in thy name, O Lord, I go
219	From heav'n you came, helpless babe
636	May the mind of Christ my Saviour
446	Strengthen for service, Lord, the hands
597	Take my life, and let it be
8	The Lord is king! Lift up your voice
372	Through all the changing scenes of life
450	Upon thy table, Lord, we place
145	You servants of the Lord

PROPER 20 Year B

The Sunday between September 18 and 24

(c) 1st Reading   **Proverbs 31: 10–31**

350	For the beauty of the earth
543	Lord of the home, your only Son
524	May the grace of Christ our Saviour
544	O perfect Love, all human thought transcending

(c) Psalm   **Psalm 1**   *[4LCPr1/E7B/Pr18C*/Pr25A*]*

649	Happy are they, they that love God
56	Lord, as I wake I turn to you
383	Lord, be thy word my rule

(p) 1st Reading   **Wisdom 1: 16 – 2: 1, 12–22**

10	All my hope on God is founded
700	Holy God, we praise thy name

(p) Alternative 1st Reading   **Jeremiah 11: 18–20**

118	Behold, the mountain of the Lord
273	Led like a lamb to the slaughter
140	[The Lord will come and not be slow]

(p) Psalm   **Psalm 54**

218	And can it be that I should 'gain
638	O for a heart to praise my God
620	O Lord, hear my prayer

2nd Reading   **James 3: 13 – 4: 3, 7–8a**

10	All my hope on God is founded
297	Come, thou Holy Spirit, come
563	Commit your ways to God
311	Fruitful trees, the Spirit's sowing
533	God of grace and God of glory
551	How can we sing with joy to God
553	Jesu, lover of my soul
99	Jesus, the name high over all
619	Lord, teach us how to pray aright
593	O Jesus, I have promised
507	Put peace into each other's hands
8	The Lord is king! Lift up your voice

The Gospel   **Mark 9: 30-37**

219   From heav'n you came, helpless babe
651   Jesus, friend of little children
228   Meekness and majesty
231   My song is love unknown
439   Once, only once, and once for all
627   What a friend we have in Jesus
145   You servants of the Lord

PROPER 20   Year C

The Sunday between September 18 and 24

(c) 1st Reading   **Jeremiah 8: 18 - 9: 1**

62   Abide with me, fast falls the eventide

(c) Psalm   **Psalm 79: 1-9**

569   Hark, my soul, it is the Lord

(p) 1st Reading   **Amos 8: 4-7**

535   Judge eternal, throned in splendour
509   Your kingdom come, O God!

(p) Psalm   **Psalm 113**   [5–31]

501   Christ is the world's true light
360   Let all the world in every corner sing
718   O praise the Lord, ye servants of the Lord
719   Praise the Lord, all you servants of the Lord
712   Tell out, my soul, the greatness of the Lord
 73   The day thou gavest, Lord, is ended

2nd Reading   **1 Timothy 2: 1-7**   [HTB]

518   Bind us together, Lord
319   Father, of heaven, whose love profound
419   I am not worthy, holy Lord
 81   Lord, for the years your love has kept and guided
619   Lord, teach us how to pray aright
366   Praise, my soul, the King of heaven
540   To thee our God we fly

× **The Gospel**   **Luke 16: 1–13**

643 Be thou my vision, O Lord of my heart
567 Forth, in thy name, O Lord, I go
81 Lord, for the years your love has kept and guided
638 O for a heart to praise my God
527 Son of God, eternal Saviour
597 Take my life, and let it be
604 Teach me, my God and King

PROPER 21   Year A

The Sunday between September 25 and October 1

(c) 1st Reading   **Exodus 17: 1–7**   [L3A]

607 As pants the hart for cooling streams
606 As the deer pants for the water
645 Father, hear the prayer we offer
646 Glorious things of thee are spoken
647 Guide me, O thou great Jehovah
431 Lord, enthroned in heavenly splendour
557 Rock of ages, cleft for me

(c) Psalm   **Psalm 78: 1–4, 12–16**

254 [At the Lamb's high feast we sing]
262 [Come, ye faithful, raise the strain]
647 Guide me, O thou great Jehovah
557 Rock of ages, cleft for me

(p) 1st Reading   **Ezekiel 18: 1–4, 25–32**

638 O for a heart to praise my God

(p) Psalm   **Psalm 25: 1–9**

17 Lead me, Lord, lead me in thy righteousness
       (Treoraigh mé, treoraigh mé, a Thiarna)
652 Lead us, heavenly Father, lead us
712 Tell out, my soul, the greatness of the Lord

2nd Reading   **Philippians 2: 1–13**

250 All hail the power of Jesu's name
684 All praise to thee, for thou, O King divine
218 And can it be that I should gain

630   Blessed are the pure in heart
 91   He is Lord, he is Lord
523   Help us to help each other, Lord
211   Immortal love for ever full
 94   In the name of Jesus
275   Look, ye saints, the sight is glorious
168   Lord, you were rich beyond all splendour
636   May the mind of Christ my Saviour
228   Meekness and majesty
102   Name of all majesty
173   O Jesu so meek, O Jesu so kind
285   The head that once was crowned with thorns
112   There is a Redeemer
117   To the name of our salvation

The Gospel   **Matthew 21: 23–32**

 86   Christ is the King! O friends, rejoice
593   O Jesus, I have promised
136   [On Jordan's bank the Baptist's cry]

PROPER 21   Year B

The Sunday between September 25 and October 1

(c) 1st Reading   **Esther 7: 1–6, 9–10; 9: 20–22**

537   O God, our help in ages past
712   Tell out, my soul, the greatness of the Lord
372   Through all the changing scenes of life

(c) Psalm   **Psalm 124**   *[Pr16A]*

642   Amazing grace (how sweet the sound!)
553   Jesu, lover of my soul
537   O God, our help in ages past

(p) 1st Reading   **Numbers 11: 4–6, 10–16, 24–29**

381   God has spoken—by his prophets
304   Loving Spirit, loving Spirit
386   Spirit of God, unseen as the wind

(p) Psalm		**Psalm 19: 7–14**	[BSB]
	606	As the deer pants for the water	
	631	God be in my head	
	696	God, we praise you! God, we bless you!	
	616	In my life, Lord, be glorified	
	384	Lord, thy word abideth	
	432	Love is his word, love is his way	
	638	O for a heart to praise my God	

2nd Reading   **James 5: 13–20**

511   Father of mercy, God of consolation
614   Great Shepherd of your people, hear
635   Lord, be my guardian and my guide
619   Lord, teach us how to pray aright
369   Songs of praise the angels sang

The Gospel   **Mark 9: 38–50**

643   Be thou my vision, O Lord of my heart
455   Go forth for God; go forth to the world in peace
507   Put peace into each other's hands
527   Son of God, eternal Saviour
446   Strengthen for service, Lord, the hands

PROPER 21

Year C

The Sunday between September 25 and October 1

(c) 1st Reading   **Jeremiah 32: 1–3a, 6–15**

No suggested hymns

(c) Psalm   **Psalm 91: 1–6, 14–16**

63   All praise to thee, my God, this night
642   Amazing grace (how sweet the sound!)
66   Before the ending of the day
459   For all the saints, who from their labours rest
       (*vv. 1–3*)
668   God is our fortress and our rock
12   God is our strength and refuge
322   I bind unto myself today (*vv. 1, 6, 8, 9*)
357   I'll praise my maker while I've breath
553   Jesu, lover of my soul

366 Praise, my soul, the King of heaven
595 Safe in the shadow of the Lord
372 Through all the changing scenes of life

(p) Ist Reading

Amos 6: 1a, 4–7

630 Blessed are the pure in heart
498 What does the Lord require in praise and offering

✗ **(p) Psalm**

Psalm 146 *[Pr5C/Pr18B*/Pr26B/Pr27B*]*

4 God, who made the earth
125 Hail to the Lord's anointed
92 How sweet the name of Jesus sounds
357 I'll praise my maker while I've breath
97 Jesus shall reign where'er the sun
99 Jesus, the name high over all
535 Judge eternal, throned in splendour
363 O Lord of heaven and earth and sea
708 O praise ye the Lord! Praise him in the height
712 Tell out, my soul, the greatness of the Lord
8 The Lord is king! Lift up your voice
376 Ye holy angels bright

✗ **2nd Reading**

1 Timothy 6: 6–19

10 All my hope on God is founded
643 Be thou my vision, O Lord of my heart
566 Fight the good fight with all thy might!
353 Give to our God immortal praise
223 Hosanna, hosanna, hosanna in the highest
6 Immortal, invisible, God only wise
275 Look, ye saints, the sight is glorious
363 O Lord of heaven and earth and sea
281 Rejoice, the Lord is King!
485 Rise up and serve the Lord!
285 The head that once was crowned with thorns
8 The Lord is king! Lift up your voice

✗ **The Gospel**

Luke 16: 19–31

642 Amazing grace (how sweet the sound!)
630 Blessed are the pure in heart
517 Brother, sister, let me serve you
87 Christ is the world's Light, he and none other
318 Father, Lord of all creation

496	For the healing of the nations
495	Jesu, Jesu, fill us with your love
589	Lord, speak to me that I may speak
712	Tell out, my soul, the greatness of the Lord
497	The Church of Christ, in every age
498	What does the Lord require for praise and offering?
499	When I needed a neighbour, were you there

PROPER 22 Year A

The Sunday between October 2 and 8

(c) Ist Reading		**Exodus 20: 1–4, 7–9, 12–20**
	383	Lord, be thy word my rule
	135	[O come, O come, Emmanuel]
	638	O for a heart to praise my God
	76	Sweet is the work, my God and King

(c) Psalm		**Psalm 19** *[Ep3C/3LB/EVABC/Pr19B]*
	606	As the deer pants for the water
	153	[Come, thou Redeemer of the earth]
	351	From all that dwell below the skies
	631	God be in my head
	696	God, we praise you! God, we bless you!
	616	In my life, Lord, be glorified
	97	Jesus shall reign where'er the sun
	384	Lord, thy word abideth
	432	Love is his word, love is his way
	638	O for a heart to praise my God
	34	O worship the King all-glorious above
	35	The spacious firmament on high

(p) Ist Reading		**Isaiah 5: 1–7** *[Pr15C]*
	51	Awake, my soul, and with the sun

(p) Psalm		**Psalm 80: 7–15**
	695	God of mercy, God of grace

2nd Reading		**Philippians 3: 4b–14**	*[L5C]*

218	And can it be that I should gain
561	Beneath the Cross of Jesus
11	Can we by searching find out God
566	Fight the good fight with all thy might!
418	Here, O my Lord, I see thee face to face
99	Jesus, the name high over all
425	Jesus, thou joy of loving hearts
671	Jesus, thy blood and righteousness
588	Light of the minds that know him
81	Lord, for the years your love has kept and guided
248	We sing the praise of him who died
247	[When I survey the wondrous cross]
376	Ye holy angels bright

The Gospel **Matthew 21: 33–46**

215	[Ah, holy Jesu, how hast thou offended]
326	Blessed city, heavenly Salem
	(*Christ is made the sure foundation*)
327	Christ is our corner-stone
268	Hail, thou once-despised Jesus!
93	I danced in the morning when the world was begun
230	My Lord, what love is this
231	My song is love unknown
340	Sing and be glad, for this is God's house!
493	Ye that know the Lord is gracious

PROPER 22   Year B

The Sunday between October 2 and 8

(c) Ist Reading **Job 1: 1; 2: 1–10**

638	O for a heart to praise my God

(c) Psalm **Psalm 26**

343	We love the place, O God

(p) Ist Reading **Genesis 2: 18–24**

618	Lord of all hopefulness, Lord of all joy
634	Love divine, all loves excelling

(p) Psalm   **Psalm 8**   *[TSAC/1–1]*

316   Bright the vision that delighted
6   Immortal, invisible, God only wise
362   O God beyond all praising
32   O Lord my God! When I in awesome wonder
33   O Lord of every shining constellation

2nd Reading   **Hebrews 1: 1–4; 2: 5–12**

250   All hail the power of Jesu's name
259   Christ triumphant, ever reigning
263   Crown him with many crowns
381   God has spoken—by his prophets
696   God, we praise you! God, we bless you!
94   In the name of Jesus (*vv. 1–3, 8*)
276   Majesty, worship his majesty
228   Meekness and majesty (*omit v.2*)
7   My God, how wonderful thou art
175   [Of the Father's heart begotten]
387   Thanks to God, whose Word was spoken
285   The head that once was crowned with thorns
376   Ye holy angels bright

The Gospel   **Mark 10: 2–16**

630   Blessed are the pure in heart
318   Father, Lord of all creation
649   Happy are they, they that love God
651   Jesus, friend of little children
585   Jesus, good above all other
652   Lead us, heavenly Father, lead us
618   Lord of all hopefulness, Lord of all joy
543   Lord of the home, your only Son
634   Love divine, all loves excelling
524   May the grace of Christ our Saviour
361   Now thank we all our God
544   O perfect Love, all human thought transcending

PROPER 22

Year C

The Sunday between October 2 and 8

(c) Ist Reading		**Lamentations 1: 1–6**
	563	Commit your ways to God
	653	Lead, kindly Light, amid the encircling gloom
	135	[O come, O come, Emmanuel]
	372	Through all the changing scenes of life

(c) Psalm		**Psalm 137: 1–6**
	398	Alleluia! sing to Jesus
	135	[O come, O come, Emmanuel]

(p) Ist Reading		**Habakkuk 1: 1–4; 2: 1–4** [4ACPr26]
	643	Be thou my vision, O Lord of my heart
	509	Your kingdom come, O God!

(p) Psalm		**Psalm 37: 1–9**
	325	Be still, for the presence of the Lord, the Holy One, is here
	563	Commit your ways to God
	639	O thou who camest from above

2nd Reading		**2 Timothy 1: 1–14**
	102	Name of all majesty
	33	O Lord of every shining constellation
	639	O thou who camest from above
	175	[Of the Father's heart begotten]
	373	To God be the glory! Great things he has done!

The Gospel		**Luke 17: 5–10**
	563	Commit your ways to God
	549	Dear Lord and Father of mankind
	463	Give us the wings of faith to rise
	523	Help us to help each other, Lord
	446	Strengthen for service, Lord, the hands
	601	Teach me, my God and King
	372	Through all the changing scenes of life

PROPER 23

Year A

The Sunday between October 9 and 15

(c) 1st Reading		**Exodus 32: 1–14**
	584	Jesus calls us! O'er the tumult
	637	O for a closer walk with God
(c) Psalm		**Psalm 106: 1–6, 19–23**
	353	Give to our God immortal praise
	30	Let us, with a gladsome mind
	634	Love divine, all loves excelling
	45	Praise, O praise our God and King
	20	The King of love my shepherd is
(p) 1st Reading		**Isaiah 25: 1–9**
	512	From you all skill and science flow
	466	Here from all nations, all tongues, and all peoples
	467	How bright those glorious spirits shine!
	553	Jesu, lover of my soul
	135	[O come, O come, Emmanuel]
	280	[Our Lord Christ hath risen]
(p) Psalm		**Psalm 23** *[L4A/E4ABC/PrIIB*]*
	644	Faithful Shepherd, feed me
	645	Father, hear the prayer we offer
	466	Here from all nations, all tongues, and all peoples
	467	How bright those glorious spirits shine!
	655	Loving Shepherd of your sheep
	433	My God, your table here is spread
	235	O sacred head, sore wounded
	365	Praise to the Lord, the Almighty, the King of creation
	20	The King of love my shepherd is
	21	The Lord's my shepherd, I'll not want
	448	The trumpets sound, the angels sing
2nd Reading		**Philippians 4: 1–9**
	349	Fill thou my life, O Lord my God
	225	In the cross of Christ I glory
	16	Like a mighty river flowing
	636	May the mind of Christ my Saviour
	507	Put peace into each other's hands

	281	Rejoice, the Lord is King!
	71	Saviour, again to thy dear name we raise
	627	What a friend we have in Jesus

The Gospel   **Matthew 22: 1–14**

	406	Christians, lift your hearts and voices
	408	Come, risen Lord, and deign to be our guest
	418	Here, O my Lord, I see thee face to face
	421	I come with joy, a child of God
	587	Just as I am, without one plea
	433	My God, your table here is spread
	445	Soul, array thyself with gladness
	20	The King of love my shepherd is
	448	The trumpets sound, the angels sing
	529	Thy hand, O God, has guided
	451	We come as guests invited
	145	You servants of the Lord

PROPER 23   Year B

The Sunday between October 9 and 15

(c) 1st Reading   **Job 23: 1–9, 16–17**

| | 11 | Can we by searching find out God |

(c) Psalm   **Psalm 22: 1–15**

	671	Jesus, thy blood and righteousness
	361	Now thank we all our God ✓
	537	O God, our help in ages past

(p) 1st Reading   **Amos 5: 6–7, 10–15**

| | 509 | Your kingdom come, O God! |

(p) Psalm   **Psalm 90: 12–17**

| | 695 | God of mercy, God of grace |
| | 535 | Judge eternal, throned in splendour |

2nd Reading   **Hebrews 4: 12–16**

	218	And can it be that I should gain
	65	At evening, when the sun had set
	51	Awake, my soul, and with the sun

319	Father, of heaven, whose love profound
207	[Forty days and forty nights]
668	God is our fortress and our rock
652	Lead us, heavenly Father, lead us
431	Lord, enthroned in heavenly splendour
384	Lord, thy word abideth
657	O God of Bethel, by whose hand
439	Once, only once, and once for all
627	What a friend we have in Jesus
291	Where high the heavenly temple stands

The Gospel   **Mark 10: 17–31**

643	Be thou my vision, O Lord of my heart
11	Can we by searching find out God
295	Come, gracious Spirit, heavenly Dove
646	Glorious things of thee are spoken
553	Jesu, lover of my soul
584	Jesus calls us! O'er the tumult
637	O for a closer walk with God
363	O Lord of heaven and earth and sea
597	Take my life, and let it be
660	Thine for ever! God of love
662	Those who would valour see (*He who would valiant be*)
605	Will you come and follow me

PROPER 23   Year C

The Sunday between October 9 and 15

(c) 1st Reading   **Jeremiah 29: 1, 4–7**

No suggested hymns

(c) Psalm   **Psalm 66: 1–12**

683	All people that on earth do dwell
701	Jubilate, ev'rybody
360	Let all the world in every corner sing
104	O for a thousand tongues to sing
640	Purify my heart

(p) Ist Reading   **2 Kings 5: 1–3, 7–15c**

553	Jesu, lover of my soul
587	Just as I am, without one plea
513	O Christ, the Healer, we have come
557	Rock of ages, cleft for me

(p) Psalm   **Psalm 111**   [Ep4B/Pr15B]

84	Alleluia! raise the anthem
130	Jesus came, the heavens adoring
529	Thy hand, O God, has guided
373	To God be the glory! Great things he has done!

2nd Reading   **2 Timothy 2: 8–15**

488	Stand up, stand up for Jesus
599	'Take up thy cross,' the Saviour said
285	The head that once was crowned with thorns
661	Through the night of doubt and sorrow

The Gospel   **Luke 17: 11–19**   [HTA]

92	How sweet the name of Jesus sounds
211	Immortal love for ever full
361	Now thank we all our God
104	O for a thousand tongues to sing
366	Praise, my soul, the King of heaven
373	To God be the glory! Great things he has done!

PROPER 24   Year A

The Sunday between October 16 and 22

(c) Ist Reading   **Exodus 33: 12–23**

80	Great is thy faithfulness, O God my Father
557	Rock of ages, cleft for me

(c) Psalm   **Psalm 99**   [ILAC]

686	Bless the Lord, the God of our forebears
688	Come, bless the Lord, God of our forebears
431	Lord, enthroned in heavenly splendour
281	Rejoice, the Lord is King!
8	The Lord is king! Lift up your voice

(p) **Ist Reading**		**Isaiah 45: 1–7**	
	501	Christ is the world's true light	
	124	[Hark the glad sound! the Saviour comes]	
	321	Holy, holy, holy! Lord God almighty	
	6	Immortal, invisible, God only wise	
	97	Jesus shall reign where'er the sun	
	73	The day thou gavest, Lord, is ended	

(p) **Psalm**		**Psalm 96: 1–9 (10–13)**	*[CPrIABC/Pr4C*]*
	166	[Joy to the world, the Lord is come!]	
	705	New songs of celebration render	
	196	O worship the Lord in the beauty of holiness!	
	710	Sing to God new songs of worship	
	8	The Lord is king! Lift up your voice	
	373	To God be the glory! Great things he has done!	
	377	You shall go out with joy	

2nd Reading		**1 Thessalonians 1: 1–10**	
	86	Christ is the King! O friends, rejoice	
	320	Firmly I believe and truly	
	312	Gracious Spirit, Holy Ghost	
	523	Help us to help each other, Lord*	
	300	Holy Spirit, truth divine	
	584	Jesus calls us! O'er the tumult	
	637	O for a closer walk with God	
	639	O thou who camest from above	
	508	Peace to you	
	491	We have a gospel to proclaim	

The Gospel		**Matthew 22: 15–22**	
	10	All my hope on God is founded	
	259	Christ triumphant, ever reigning	
	263	Crown him with many crowns	
	353	Give to our God immortal praise	
	646	Glorious things of thee are spoken	
	94	In the name of Jesus	
	97	Jesus shall reign where'er the sun	
	535	Judge eternal, throned in splendour	
	102	Name of all majesty	
	363	O Lord of heaven and earth and sea	
	493	Ye that know the Lord is gracious	
	509	Your kingdom come, O God!	

PROPER 24

Year B

The Sunday between October 16 and 22

(c) 1st Reading		**Job 38: 1–7, (34–41)**
	581	I, the Lord of sea and sky
	29	Lord of beauty, thine the splendour
	174	[O little town of Bethlehem]
	34	O worship the King all-glorious above
	369	Songs of praise the angels sang
	35	The spacious firmament on high

(c) Psalm		**Psalm 104: 1–9, 24, 35c**
	250	All hail the power of Jesu's name
	6	Immortal, invisible, God only wise
	34	O worship the King all-glorious above
	35	The spacious firmament on high

(p) 1st Reading		**Isaiah 53: 4–12**
	404	Broken for me, broken for you
	259	Christ triumphant, ever reigning
	219	From heav'n you came, helpless babe
	268	Hail, thou once-despised Jesus!
	417	He gave his life in selfless love
	273	Led like a lamb to the slaughter
	231	My song is love unknown (*vv. 1–3, 7*)
	20	The King of love my shepherd is

(p) Psalm		**Psalm 91: 9–16**
	66	Before the ending of the day
	322	I bind unto myself today (*vv. 1, 6, 8, 9*)
	553	Jesu, lover of my soul
	366	Praise, my soul, the King of heaven
	372	Through all the changing scenes of life

2nd Reading		**Hebrews 5: 1–10**
	226	It is a thing most wonderful
	652	Lead us, heavenly Father, lead us
	228	Meekness and majesty
	177	[Once in royal David's city]
	291	Where high the heavenly temple stands

The Gospel		**Mark 10: 35–45**	*[7–25]*
	684	All praise to thee, for thou, O King divine	
	517	Brother, sister, let me serve you	
	294	Come down, O Love divine	
	319	Father, of heaven, whose love profound	
	219	From heav'n you came, helpless babe	
	417	He gave his life in selfless love	
	523	Help us to help each other, Lord	
	419	I am not worthy, holy Lord	
	495	Jesu, Jesu, fill us with your love	
	96	Jesus is Lord! Creation's voice proclaims it	
	589	Lord, speak to me that I may speak	
	231	My song is love unknown	
	135	[O come, O come, Emmanuel]	
	214	O Love how deep, how broad, how high!	
	366	Praise, my soul, the King of heaven	
	244	There is a green hill far away	
	247	[When I survey the wondrous cross]	

PROPER 24   Year C

The Sunday between October 16 and 22

(c) Ist Reading		**Jeremiah 31: 27–34**	
	125	Hail to the Lord's anointed	
	382	Help us, O Lord, to learn	
	638	O for a heart to praise my God	
(c) Psalm		**Psalm 119: 97–104**	*[BSA]*
	383	Lord, be thy word my rule	
(p) Ist Reading		**Genesis 32: 22–31**	*[Pr13A]*
	418	Here, O my Lord, I see thee face to face	
	226	It is a thing most wonderful	
	592	O Love that wilt not let me go	
(p) Psalm		**Psalm 121**	*[L2A/Rog]*
	349	Fill thou my life, O Lord my God	
	14	I lift my eyes to the quiet hills	
	16	Like a mighty river flowing	
	664	To Zion's hill I lift my eyes	

2nd Reading   ƒ   **2 Timothy 3: 14 – 4: 5**   *[BSB]*

324	God, whose almighty word
382	Help us, O Lord, to learn
383	Lord, be thy word my rule
81	Lord, for the years your love has kept and guided
384	Lord, thy word abideth
387	Thanks to God, whose Word was spoken

The Gospel   ⸙   **Luke 18: 1–8**

400	And now, O Father, mindful of the love
118	Behold, the mountain of the Lord
317	Father all-loving, you rule us in majesty
645	Father, hear the prayer we offer
353	Give to our God immortal praise
614	Great Shepherd of your people, hear
635	Lord, be my guardian and my guide
81	Lord, for the years your love has kept and guided
619	Lord, teach us how to pray aright
59	New every morning is the love
362	O God beyond all praising
657	O God of Bethel, by whose hand
625	Prayer is the soul's sincere desire
596	Seek ye first the kingdom of God

7 ORDINARY TIME
The Sundays before Advent

(PROPERS 25–29)

including All Saints

PROPER 25   Year A

The Fifth Sunday before Advent

The Sunday between October 23 and 29

(c) 1st Reading   **Deuteronomy 34: 1–12**

563	Commit your ways to God
567	Forth, in thy name, O Lord I go
653	Lead, kindly Light, amid the encircling gloom
657	O God of Bethel, by whose hand
323	The God of Abraham praise
681	There is a land of pure delight

(c) Psalm   **Psalm 90: 1–6, 13–17**

6	Immortal, invisible, God only wise
537	O God, our help in ages past

(p) 1st Reading   **Leviticus 19: 1–2, 15–18**   *[3LAPr2/E5C]*

515	'A new commandment I give unto you'
494	Beauty for brokenness
39	For the fruits of his creation
321	Holy, holy, holy! Lord God almighty
535	Judge eternal, throned in splendour
525	Let there be love shared among us
497	The Church of Christ, in every age
509	Your kingdom come, O God!

(p) Psalm   **Psalm 1**   *[4LCPr1/E7B/Pr18C*/Pr20B]*

649	Happy are they, they that love God
56	Lord, as I wake I turn to you
383	Lord, be thy word my rule

2nd Reading   **1 Thessalonians 2: 1–8**

645	Father, hear the prayer we offer
567	Forth, in thy name, O Lord, I go
653	Lead, kindly Light, amid the encircling gloom
593	O Jesus, I have promised
639	O thou who camest from above
662	Those who would valour see
	(*He who would valiant be*)

372	Through all the changing scenes of life
529	Thy hand, O God, has guided
491	We have a gospel to proclaim

The Gospel   **Matthew 22: 34–46**

515	'A new commandment I give unto you'
250	All hail the power of Jesu's name
517	Brother, sister, let me serve you
520	God is love, and where true love is, God himself is there
125	Hail to the Lord's anointed
523	Help us to help each other, Lord
495	Jesu, Jesu, fill us with your love
525	Let there be love shared among us
594	O Lord of creation, to you be all praise!
281	Rejoice, the Lord is King!
597	Take my life, and let it be

PROPER 25   Year B

The Fifth Sunday before Advent

The Sunday between October 23 and 29

(c) 1st Reading   **Job 42: 1–6, 10–17**

549	Dear Lord and Father of mankind
13	God moves in a mysterious way
226	It is a thing most wonderful

(c) Psalm   **Psalm 34: 1–8, (19–22)**   [Pr14B]

86	Christ is the King! O friends, rejoice
99	Jesus, the name high over all
634	Love divine, all loves excelling
372	Through all the changing scenes of life
376	Ye holy angels bright

(p) 1st Reading   **Jeremiah 31: 7–9**

128	Hills of the north, rejoice
593	O Jesus, I have promised
366	Praise, my soul, the King of heaven
20	The King of love my shepherd is

(p) Psalm   **Psalm 126**   *[A3B/L5C/7–25/HTB]*

567	Forth, in thy name, O Lord, I go
356	I will sing, I will sing a song unto the Lord
712	Tell out, my soul, the greatness of the Lord
373	To God be the glory! Great things he has done!

2nd Reading   **Hebrews 7: 23–28**

398	Alleluia! sing to Jesus
258	[Christ the Lord is risen again!]
454	Forth in the peace of Christ we go
266	[Hail the day that sees him rise (*vv. 1, 2, 5, 6*)]
268	Hail, thou once-despised Jesus!
431	Lord, enthroned in heavenly splendour
105	O the deep, deep love of Jesus
439	Once, only once, and once for all
527	Son of God, eternal Saviour

The Gospel   **Mark 10: 46–52**

642	Amazing grace (how sweet the sound!)
218	And can it be that I should gain
52	Christ, whose glory fills the skies
294	Come down, O Love divine
563	Commit your ways to God
613	Eternal light, shine in my heart
324	God, whose almighty word
357	I'll praise my maker while I've breath
553	Jesu, lover of my soul
587	Just as I am, without one plea
554	Lord Jesus, think on me
104	O for a thousand tongues to sing
374	When all thy mercies, O my God

PROPER 25   Year C

The Fifth Sunday before Advent

The Sunday between October 23 and 29

(c) 1st Reading   **Joel 2: 23–32**

10	All my hope on God is founded
293	Breathe on me, Breath of God
457	Pour out thy Spirit from on high

71	Saviour, again to thy dear name we raise
313	The Spirit came, as promised

(c) Psalm   **Psalm 65**   *[2LC/Pr10A*/HTA]*

612	Eternal Father, strong to save
645	Father, hear the prayer we offer
42	Good is the Lord our heavenly King
581	I, the Lord of sea and sky
709	Praise the Lord! You heavens, adore him

(p) Ist Reading   **Sirach 35: 12–17**

597	Take my life, and let it be

(p) Alternative Ist Reading **Jeremiah 14: 7–10, 19–22**

319	Father, of heaven, whose love profound
637	O for a closer walk with God
537	O God, our help in ages past

(p) Psalm   **Psalm 84: 1–7**

400	And now, O Father, mindful of the love
333	How lovely are thy dwellings fair!
95	Jesu, priceless treasure
425	Jesus, thou joy of loving hearts
360	Let all the world in every corner sing
634	Love divine, all loves excelling
620	O Lord, hear my prayer
487	Soldiers of Christ, arise
342	Sweet is the solemn voice that calls
343	We love the place, O God

2nd Reading   **2 Timothy 4: 6–8, 16–18**

218	And can it be that I should gain
566	Fight the good fight with all thy might!
459	For all the saints, who from their labours rest
478	Go forth and tell! O Church of God, awake!
668	God is our fortress and our rock
647	Guide me, O thou great Jehovah
277	[Love's redeeming work is done]
281	Rejoice, the Lord is King!
487	Soldiers of Christ, arise
662	Those who would valour see
	(*He who would valiant be*)

373	To God be the glory! Great things he has done!
376	Ye holy angels bright
493	Ye that know the Lord is gracious

The Gospel A   **Luke 18: 9–14**

684	All praise to thee, for thou, O King divine
642	Amazing grace (how sweet the sound!)
630	Blessed are the pure in heart
294	Come down, O Love divine
696	God, we praise you! God, we bless you!
553	Jesu, lover of my soul
587	Just as I am, without one plea
358	King of glory, King of peace
554	Lord Jesus, think on me
102	Name of all majesty
366	Praise, my soul, the King of heaven
712	Tell out, my soul, the greatness of the Lord
493	Ye that know the Lord is gracious

All Saints

Year A

November 1

These provisions may be used on the Sunday nearest to All Saints' Day instead of the appropriate Proper.

1st Reading   **Jeremiah 31: 31–34**   *[L5B]*

125	Hail to the Lord's anointed
382	Help us, O Lord, to learn
638	O for a heart to praise my God

Psalm   **Psalm 34: 1–10**

86	Christ is the King! O friends, rejoice
99	Jesus, the name high over all
634	Love divine, all loves excelling
372	Through all the changing scenes of life
376	Ye holy angels bright

2nd Reading   **Revelation 7: 9–17**   *[E4C]*

250	All hail the power of Jesu's name
398	Alleluia! sing to Jesus!
346	Angel voices, ever singing

332	Come, let us join our cheerful songs
463	Give us the wings of faith to rise
694	Glory, honour, endless praises
466	Here from all nations, all tongues, and all peoples
321	Holy, holy, holy! Lord God almighty
467	How bright those glorious spirits shine!
670	Jerusalem the golden
275	Look, ye saints, the sight is glorious
474	Such a host as none can number
475	Who are these like stars appearing
376	Ye holy angels bright
492	Ye servants of God, your master proclaim
476	Ye watchers and ye holy ones

Alternative 2nd Reading   **1 John 3: 1–3**

92	How sweet the name of Jesus sounds
226	It is a thing most wonderful
277	[Love's redeeming work is done]
7	My God, how wonderful thou art
177	[Once in royal David's city]

The Gospel   **Matthew 5: 1–12**   *[Ep4A]*

630	Blessed are the pure in heart
293	Breathe on me, Breath of God
503	Make me a channel of your peace
507	Put peace into each other's hands
308	Revive your Church, O Lord
712	Tell out, my soul, the greatness of the Lord
22	You shall cross the barren desert

ALSO SUITABLE

459	For all the saints, who from their labours rest
461	For all thy saints, O Lord
460	For all your saints in glory, for all your saints at rest
650	In Christ, our humble head
469	In our day of thanksgiving one psalm let us offer
471	Rejoice in God's saints, today and all days!

All Saints
November 1

Year B

These provisions may be used on the Sunday nearest to All Saints' Day instead of the appropriate Proper.

1st Reading		**Wisdom 3: 1–9**	
	459	For all the saints, who from their labours rest	
	461	For all thy saints, O Lord	
	463	Give us the wings of faith to rise	
	467	How bright those glorious spirits shine!	
	468	How shall I sing that majesty	
	474	Such a host as none can number	
	475	Who are these like stars appearing	
	476	Ye watchers and ye holy ones	

Alternative 1st Reading		**Isaiah 25: 6–9**	[EIB]
	251	[Alleluia! Alleluia! Hearts to heaven and voices raise]	
	254	[At the Lamb's high feast we sing]	
	264	[Finished the strife of battle now]	
	512	From you all skill and science flow	
	466	Here from all nations, all tongues, and all peoples	
	467	How bright those glorious spirits shine!	
	270	I know that my Redeemer lives	
	553	Jesu, lover of my soul	
	135	[O come, O come, Emmanuel]	
	280	[Our Lord Christ hath risen]	

Psalm		**Psalm 24**	[Pr10B]
	48	God in his love for us lent us this planet	
	266	[Hail the day that sees him rise]	
	337	Lift up your heads, O ye gates	
	131	Lift up your heads, you mighty gates	
	134	Make way, make way, for Christ the King	
	284	The golden gates are lifted up	

2nd Reading		**Revelation 21: 1–6a**	[E5C]
	326	Blessed city, heavenly Salem *(Christ is made the sure foundation)*	
	512	From you all skill and science flow	
	646	Glorious things of thee are spoken	

466	Here from all nations, all tongues, and all peoples
300	Holy Spirit, truth divine
670	Jerusalem the golden
553	Jesu, lover of my soul
425	Jesus, thou joy of loving hearts
592	O Love, that wilt not let me go
473	[Síormholadh is glóir duit, a Athair shíorai]
	[(All glory and praise to you, Father, above)]
369	Songs of praise, the angels sang
138	Soon and very soon we are going to see the King
528	The Church's one foundation
681	There is a land of pure delight
144	Word of justice, alleluia
292	[Ye choirs of new Jerusalem]

The Gospel   **John 11: 32–44**

569	Hark, my soul, it is the Lord
226	It is a thing most wonderful
671	Jesus, thy blood and righteousness
104	O for a thousand tongues to sing
308	Revive your Church, O Lord

ALSO SUITABLE
650	In Christ, our humble head
469	In our day of thanksgiving one psalm let us offer
471	Rejoice in God's saints, today and all days!

All Saints   Year C
November 1

*These provisions may be used on the Sunday nearest to All Saints' Day instead of
the appropriate Proper.*

1st Reading   **Daniel 7: 1–3, 15–18**

6	Immortal, invisible, God only wise
34	O worship the King all-glorious above
285	The head that once was crowned with thorns

Psalm   **Psalm 149**   *[Pr18A]*

346	Angel voices, ever singing
705	New songs of celebration render
368	Sing of the Lord's goodness

| 710 | Sing to God new songs of worship |
| 492 | Ye servants of God, your master proclaim |

2nd Reading   **Ephesians 1: 11–23**   *[An ABC / Pr 29 A]*

250	All hail the power of Jesu's name
643	Be thou my vision, O Lord of my heart
326	Blessed city, heavenly Salem
	(*Christ is made the sure foundation*) (*omit v. 1*)
296	Come, Holy Ghost, our souls inspire
263	Crown him with many crowns
693	Glory in the highest to the God of heaven!
324	God, whose almighty word
266	[Hail the day that sees him rise]
300	Holy Spirit, truth divine
99	Jesus, the name high over all
588	Light of the minds that know him
281	Rejoice, the Lord is King!
313	The Spirit came, as promised
451	We come as guests invited
491	We have a gospel to proclaim

The Gospel   **Luke 6: 20–31**

| 494 | Beauty for brokenness |
| 22 | You shall cross the barren desert |

ALSO SUITABLE

459	For all the saints, who from their labours rest
461	For all thy saints, O Lord
650	In Christ, our humble head
469	In our day of thanksgiving one psalm let us offer
471	Rejoice in God's saints, today and all days!
476	Ye watchers and ye holy ones

PROPER 26   Year A

The Fourth Sunday before Advent

The Sunday between October 30 and November 5

(c) 1st Reading   **Joshua 3: 7–17**

| 647 | Guide me, O thou great Jehovah |
| 323 | The God of Abraham praise |

(c) Psalm **Psalm 107: 1–7, 33–37**

683	All people that on earth do dwell
39	For the fruits of his creation
353	Give to our God immortal praise
128	Hills of the north, rejoice
30	Let us, with a gladsome mind
484	Lift high the cross, the love of Christ proclaim
45	Praise, O praise our God and king
372	Through all the changing scenes of life

(p) 1st Reading **Micah 3: 5–12**

535	Judge eternal, throned in splendour
306	O Spirit of the living God
509	Your kingdom come, O God!

(p) Psalm **Psalm 43**

10	All my hope on God is founded
384	Lord, thy word abideth

2nd Reading **1 Thessalonians 2: 9–13**

517	Brother, sister, let me serve you
523	Help us to help each other, Lord
634	Love divine, all loves excelling
361	Now thank we all our God
387	Thanks to God, whose Word was spoken
532	Who are we who stand and sing?

The Gospel **Matthew 23: 1–12**

630	Blessed are the pure in heart
517	Brother, sister, let me serve you
219	From heav'n you came, helpless babe
495	Jesu, Jesu, fill us with your love
627	What a friend we have in Jesus

PROPER 26   Year B

The Fourth Sunday before Advent

The Sunday between October 30 and November 5

(c) Ist Reading		**Ruth 1: 1–18**
	592	O Love that wilt not let me go
(c) Psalm		**Psalm 146** *[Pr5C/Pr18B*/Pr21C*/Pr27B*]*
	4	God, who made the earth
	125	Hail to the Lord's anointed
	92	How sweet the name of Jesus sounds
	357	I'll praise my maker while I've breath
	97	Jesus shall reign where'er the sun
	99	Jesus, the name high over all
	535	Judge eternal, throned in splendour
	363	O Lord of heaven and earth and sea
	708	O praise ye the Lord! Praise him in the height
	712	Tell out, my soul, the greatness of the Lord
	8	The Lord is king! Lift up your voice
	376	Ye holy angels bright
(p) Ist Reading		**Deuteronomy 6: 1–9**
	381	God has spoken—by his prophets
	649	Happy are they, they that love God
	543	Lord of the home, your only Son
	229	My God I love thee; not because
(p) Psalm		**Psalm 119: 1–8** *[4LAPr1/5–1]*
	630	Blessed are the pure in heart
	649	Happy are they, they that love God
	601	Teach me, my God and King
2nd Reading		**Hebrews 9: 11–14**
	411	Draw near and take the body of the Lord
	220	[Glory be to Jesus]
	417	He gave his life in selfless love
	418	Here, O my Lord, I see thee face to face
	671	Jesus, thy blood and righteousness
	439	Once, only once, and once for all
	528	The Church's one foundation
	9	There's a wideness in God's mercy

The Gospel   **Mark 12: 28–34**

515	'A new commandment I give unto you'
11	Can we by searching find out God
349	Fill thou my life, O Lord my God
520	God is love, and where true love is, God himself is there
649	Happy are they, they that love God
523	Help us to help each other, Lord
358	King of glory, King of peace
229	My God I love thee; not because

PROPER 26   Year C

The Fourth Sunday before Advent

The Sunday between October 30 and November 5

(c) 1st Reading   **Habakkuk 1: 1–4; 2: 1–4**   *[Pr22C*]*

643	Be thou my vision, O Lord of my heart
509	Your kingdom come, O God!

(c) Psalm   **Psalm 119: 137–144**

6	Immortal, invisible, God only wise
705	New songs of celebration render
144	Word of justice, alleluia

(p) 1st Reading ⸙ **Isaiah 1: 10–18**

357	I'll praise my maker while I've breath
553	Jesu, lover of my soul
446	Strengthen for service, Lord, the hands
498	What does the Lord require for praise and offering?

(p) Psalm ⸙ **Psalm 32: 1–7**

562	Blessed assurance, Jesus is mine
92	How sweet the name of Jesus sounds

2nd Reading   **2 Thessalonians 1: 1–4, 11–12**

92	How sweet the name of Jesus sounds
616	In my life, Lord, be glorified
639	O thou who camest from above
508	Peace to you
624	Speak, Lord, in the stillness

The Gospel   **Luke 19: 1–10**

629	Abide among us with thy grace
417	He gave his life in selfless love
421	I come with joy, a child of God
576	I heard the voice of Jesus say
132	[Lo! he comes with clouds descending]
637	O for a closer walk with God
214	O Love, how deep, how broad, how high!
9	There's a wideness in God's mercy
78	This is the day that the Lord has made

PROPER 27   Year A
The Third Sunday before Advent

The Sunday between November 6 and 12

(c) 1st Reading   **Joshua 24: 1–3a, 14–25**

584	Jesus calls us! O'er the tumult
660	Thine for ever! God of love

(c) Psalm   **Psalm 78: 1–7**

563	Commit your ways to God

(p) 1st Reading   **Wisdom 6: 12–16**

643	Be thou my vision, O Lord of my heart

(p) Alternative 1st Reading Amos 5: 18–24

125	Hail to the Lord's anointed
6	Immortal, invisible, God only wise
538	O Lord, the clouds are gathering

(p) Psalm   **Psalm 70**   *[HW-WABC]*

620	O Lord, hear my prayer
596	Seek ye first the kingdom of God

2nd Reading   **1 Thessalonians 4: 13–18**

666	Be still, my soul: the Lord is on thy side
126	Hark! a thrilling voice is sounding
132	Lo! he comes with clouds descending
634	Love divine, all loves excelling

227 Man of sorrows! What a name
281 Rejoice, the Lord is King!
197 Songs of thankfulness and praise
140 The Lord will come and not be slow
289 [This joyful Eastertide]

The Gospel   **Matthew 25: 1–13**

86 Christ is the King! O friends, rejoice
570 Give me oil in my lamp, keep me burning
       (Give me joy in my heart, keep me praising)
418 Here, O my Lord, I see thee face to face
427 Let all mortal flesh keep silence
131 Lift up your heads, you mighty gates
433 My God, your table here is spread
448 The trumpets sound, the angels sing
142 Wake, O wake! With tidings thrilling
143 Waken, O sleeper, wake and rise
145 You servants of the Lord

PROPER 27   Year B

The Third Sunday before Advent

The Sunday between November 6 and 12

(c) 1st Reading   **Ruth 3: 1–5; 4: 13–17**

43 [Holy is the seed-time, when the buried grain]
545 Sing of Eve and sing of Adam

(c) Psalm   **Psalm 127**

63 All praise to thee, my God, this night
481 God is working his purpose out as year succeeds
       to year
543 Lord of the home, your only Son
288 Thine be the glory, risen, conquering Son

(p) 1st Reading   **1 Kings 17: 8–16**   [Pr5C]

517 Brother, sister, let me serve you
647 Guide me, O thou great Jehovah

(p) Psalm	**Psalm 146**	*[Pr5C/Pr18B*/Pr21C*/Pr26B]*

4	God, who made the earth
125	Hail to the Lord's anointed
92	How sweet the name of Jesus sounds
357	I'll praise my maker while I've breath
97	Jesus shall reign where'er the sun
99	Jesus, the name high over all
535	Judge eternal, throned in splendour
363	O Lord of heaven and earth and sea
708	O praise ye the Lord! Praise him in the height
712	Tell out, my soul, the greatness of the Lord
8	The Lord is king! Lift up your voice
376	Ye holy angels bright

2nd Reading　　　**Hebrews 9: 24–28**

400	And now, O Father, mindful of the love
258	[Christ the Lord is risen again!]
266	[Hail the day that sees him rise]
431	Lord, enthroned in heavenly splendour
439	Once, only once, and once for all
140	The Lord will come and not be slow

The Gospel　　　**Mark 12: 38–44**

218	And can it be that I should gain
219	From heav'n you came, helpless babe
580	I want to walk with Jesus Christ
591	O happy day that fixed my choice
593	O Jesus, I have promised
639	O thou who camest from above
597	Take my life, and let it be
605	Will you come and follow me

PROPER 27　　　　　　　　　　　　　Year C

The Third Sunday before Advent

The Sunday between November 6 and 12

(c) 1st Reading　　　**Haggai 1: 15b – 2: 9**

501	Christ is the world's true light
527	Son of God, eternal Saviour
488	Stand up, stand up for Jesus

(c) Psalm **Psalm 145: 1–5, 17–21**

683 All people that on earth do dwell
321 Holy, holy, holy! Lord God almighty
357 I'll praise my maker while I've breath
358 King of glory, King of peace
360 Let all the world in every corner sing
365 Praise to the Lord, the Almighty, the King of
    creation

(c) Alternative Psalm **Psalm 98** *[CPr3ABC/EVABC/E6B/Pr28C*]*

146 [A great and mighty wonder]
125 Hail to the Lord's anointed
166 [Joy to the world, the Lord is come!]
705 New songs of celebration render
710 Sing to God new songs of worship
369 Songs of praise the angels sang

(p) 1st Reading **Job 19: 23–27a**

92 How sweet the name of Jesus sounds
270 I know that my Redeemer lives
226 It is a thing most wonderful
7 My God, how wonderful thou art

(p) Psalm **Psalm 17: 1–9**

635 Lord, be my guardian and my guide
620 O Lord, hear my prayer

2nd Reading **2 Thessalonians 2: 1–5, 13–17**

328 Come on and celebrate!
244 There is a green hill far away

The Gospel **Luke 20: 27–38**

325 Be still, for the presence of the Lord,
    the Holy One, is here
328 Come on and celebrate!
415 For the bread which you have broken
670 Jerusalem the golden
672 Light's abode, celestial Salem
277 [Love's redeeming work is done]
392 Now is eternal life
323 The God of Abraham praise

PROPER 28   Year A

The Second Sunday before Advent

The Sunday between November 13 and 19

(c) 1st Reading		**Judges 4: 1–7**	
		No suggested hymns	
(c) Psalm		**Psalm 123**	[Pr9B*]
	696	God, we praise you! God, we bless you!	
	208	[Hearken, O Lord, have mercy upon us]	
(p) 1st Reading		**Zephaniah 1: 7, 12–18**	
	51	Awake, my soul, and with the sun	
	635	Lord, be my guardian and my guide	
	140	The Lord will come and not be slow	
(p) Psalm		**Psalm 90: 1–8 (9–11) 12**	
	6	Immortal, invisible, God only wise	
	537	O God, our help in ages past	
2nd Reading		**1 Thessalonians 5: 1–11**	
	643	Be thou my vision, O Lord of my heart	
	219	From heav'n you came, helpless babe	
	126	Hark! a thrilling voice is sounding	
	523	Help us to help each other, Lord	
	487	Soldiers of Christ, arise	
	143	Waken, O sleeper, wake and rise	
The Gospel		**Matthew 25: 14–30**	
	346	Angel voices, ever singing	
	51	Awake, my soul, and with the sun	
	453	Come, to us, creative Spirit	
	567	Forth, in thy name, O Lord, I go	
	48	God in his love for us lent us this planet	
	363	O Lord of heaven and earth and sea	
	527	Son of God, eternal Saviour	
	597	Take my life, and let it be	
	598	Take this moment, sign and space	

PROPER 28

Year B

The Second Sunday before Advent

The Sunday between November 13 and 19

(c) 1st Reading		**1 Samuel 1: 4–20**
	391	[Father, now behold us (*at a Baptism only*)]
	16	Like a mighty river flowing
	625	Prayer is the soul's sincere desire

(c) Psalm		**Psalm 16**	*[EVABC/E2A/Pr8C*]*
	567	Forth, in thy name, O Lord, I go	
	300	Holy Spirit, truth divine	
	553	Jesu, lover of my soul	
	652	Lead us, heavenly Father, lead us	
	392	Now is eternal life	
	289	[This joyful Eastertide]	

(p) 1st Reading		**Daniel 12: 1–3**
	459	For all the saints, who from their labours rest
	461	For all thy saints, O Lord
	463	Give us the wings of faith to rise
	466	Here from all nations, all tongues, and all peoples
	467	How bright those glorious spirits shine!
	474	Such a host as none can number
	475	Who are these like stars appearing

(p) Psalm		**Psalm 16**	*[EVABC/E2A/Pr8C*]*
	567	Forth, in thy name, O Lord, I go	
	300	Holy Spirit, truth divine	
	553	Jesu, lover of my soul	
	652	Lead us, heavenly Father, lead us	
	392	Now is eternal life	
	289	[This joyful Eastertide]	

2nd Reading		**Hebrews 10: 11–14 (15–18) 19–25**
	218	And can it be that I should gain
	400	And now, O Father, mindful of the love
	411	Draw near and take the body of the Lord
	220	[Glory be to Jesus]
	693	Glory in the highest to the God of heaven!

696	God, we praise you! God, we bless you!
382	Help us, O Lord, to learn
431	Lord, enthroned in heavenly splendour
619	Lord, teach us how to pray aright
638	O for a heart to praise my God
439	Once, only once, and once for all
281	Rejoice, the Lord is King!
291	Where high the heavenly temple stands

The Gospel   **Mark 13: 1–8**

10	All my hope on God is founded
327	Christ is our corner-stone
646	Glorious things of thee are spoken
95	Jesu, priceless treasure
372	Through all the changing scenes of life
661	Through the night of doubt and sorrow

PROPER 28   Year C

The Second Sunday before Advent

The Sunday between November 13 and 19

(c) 1st Reading   **Isaiah 65: 17–25**   *[EIC]*

| 369 | Songs of praise the angels sang |
| 292 | [Ye choirs of new Jerusalem] |

(c) Psalm Canticle   **The Song of Isaiah (Isaiah 12: 1–6)**

370	Stand up, and bless the Lord
373	To God be the glory! Great things he has done!
492	Ye servants of God, your master proclaim

(p) 1st Reading   **Malachi 4: 1–2a**

52	Christ, whose glory fills the skies
37	[Come, ye thankful people, come]
324	God, whose almighty word
160	[Hark! the herald-angels sing]
128	Hills of the north, rejoice
535	Judge eternal, throned in splendour
199	The people that in darkness walked

(p) Psalm	**Psalm 98**	*[CPrABC/EVABC/E6B/Pr27C]*

146	[A great and mighty wonder]
125	Hail to the Lord's anointed
166	[Joy to the world, the Lord is come!]
705	New songs of celebration render
710	Sing to God new songs of worship
369	Songs of praise the angels sang

2nd Reading	**2 Thessalonians 3: 6–13**	*[Rog]*

523	Help us to help each other, Lord
436	Now let us from this table rise
446	Strengthen for service, Lord, the hands
498	What does the Lord require for praise and offering?

The Gospel   **Luke 21: 5–19**

10	All my hope on God is founded
327	Christ is our corner-stone
52	Christ, whose glory fills the skies
496	For the healing of the nations
15	If thou but suffer God to guide thee

PROPER 29   Year A

The Sunday before Advent
The Kingship of Christ

The Sunday between November 20 and 26

(c) 1st Reading   **Ezekiel 34: 11–16, 20–24**

670	Jerusalem the golden
20	The King of love my shepherd is

(c) Psalm	**Psalm 100**	*[PR6A*/HTC]*

683	All people that on earth do dwell
334	I will enter his gates with thanksgiving in my heart
701	Jubilate, ev'rybody

(p) 1st Reading   **Ezekiel 34: 11–16, 20–24**

442	Praise the Lord, rise up rejoicing
20	The King of love my shepherd is

(p) Psalm   **Psalm 95: 1–7a**

346	Angel voices, ever singing
327	Christ is our corner-stone
687	Come, let us praise the Lord
689	Come, sing praises to the Lord above
690	Come, worship God, who is worthy of honour
360	Let all the world in every corner sing
196	O worship the Lord in the beauty of holiness!
197	Songs of thankfulness and praise
529	Thy hand, O God, has guided

2nd Reading   **Ephesians 1: 15–23**   *[AnABC/ASC]*

250	All hail the power of Jesu's name
643	Be thou my vision, O Lord of my heart
326	Blessed city, heavenly Salem
	(*Christ is made the sure foundation*) (omit v. 1)
296	Come, Holy Ghost, our souls inspire
263	Crown him with many crowns
693	Glory in the highest to the God of heaven!
324	God, whose almighty word
266	[Hail the day that sees him rise]
300	[Holy Spirit, truth divine]
99	Jesus, the name high over all
588	Light of the minds that know him
281	Rejoice, the Lord is King!
491	We have a gospel to proclaim

The Gospel   **Matthew 25: 31–46**

517	Brother, sister, let me serve you
86	Christ is the King! O friends, rejoice
89	God is love—his the care
520	God is love, and where true love is, God himself is there
91	He is Lord, he is Lord
523	Help us to help each other, Lord
495	Jesu, Jesu, fill us with your love
427	Let all mortal flesh keep silence
281	Rejoice, the Lord is King!
527	Son of God, eternal Saviour
314	There's a spirit in the air
114	Thou didst leave thy throne and thy kingly crown
499	When I needed a neighbour, were you there
531	Where love and loving-kindness dwell

239

PROPER 29   Year B

The Sunday before Advent
The Kingship of Christ

The Sunday between November 20 and 26

(c) Ist Reading		**2 Samuel 23: 1–7**
	125	Hail to the Lord's anointed
(c) Psalm		**Psalm 132: 1–12 (13–18)**
	218	And can it be that I should gain
	275	Look, ye saints, the sight is glorious
	457	Pour out thy Spirit from on high

(p) Ist Reading		**Daniel 7: 9–10, 13–14**	[8–6]
	6	Immortal, invisible, God only wise	
	125	Hail to the Lord's anointed	
	468	How shall I sing that majesty	
	130	Jesus came, the heavens adoring	
	132	Lo! he comes with clouds descending	
	34	O worship the King all-glorious above	
	196	O worship the Lord in the beauty of holiness!	
	678	Ten thousand times ten thousand	
	73	The day thou gavest, Lord, is ended	
	323	The God of Abraham praise	

(p) Psalm		**Psalm 93**	[An ABC]
	553	Jesu, lover of my soul	
	276	Majesty, worship his majesty	
	281	Rejoice, the Lord is King!	
	8	The Lord is king! Lift up your voice	
	492	Ye servants of God, your master proclaim	

2nd Reading		**Revelation 1: 4b–8**	[E2C]
	454	Forth in the peace of Christ we go	
	646	Glorious things of thee are spoken	
	381	God has spoken—by his prophets	
	127	Hark what a sound, and too divine for hearing	
	321	Holy, holy, holy! Lord God almighty	
	130	Jesus came, the heavens adoring	
	132	Lo! he comes with clouds descending	
	373	To God be the glory! Great things he has done!	

The Gospel		**John 18: 33–37**
	684	All praise to thee, for thou, O King divine
	263	Crown him with many crowns
	268	Hail, thou once despised Jesus!
	97	Jesus shall reign where'er the sun
	431	Lord, enthroned in heavenly splendour
	227	Man of sorrows! What a name
	231	My song is love unknown
	281	Rejoice, the Lord is King!
	285	The head that once was crowned with thorns
	245	To mock your reign, O dearest Lord
	184	[Unto us is born a Son]
	292	[Ye choirs of new Jerusalem]

PROPER 29 — Year C

The Sunday before Advent
The Kingship of Christ

The Sunday between November 20 and 26

(c) **Ist Reading**		**Jeremiah 23: 1–6**	[PrIIB*/Pr29C*]
	250	All hail the power of Jesu's name	
	135	O come, O come, Emmanuel	
	442	\ Praise the Lord, rise up rejoicing	
	197	Songs of thankfulness and praise	
	323	The God of Abraham praise	
	20	The King of love my shepherd is	

(c) **Psalm Canticle**		**Benedictus (Luke 1: 68–79)**	[A2C]
	685	Blessed be the God of Israel	
	52	Christ, whose glory fills the skies	
	119	Come, thou long-expected Jesus	
	381	God has spoken—by his prophets	
	706	O bless the God of Israel	

(p) **Ist Reading**		**Jeremiah 23: 1–6**	[PrIIB*]
	250	All hail the power of Jesu's name	
	135	O come, O come, Emmanuel	
	442	Praise the Lord, rise up rejoicing	
	197	Songs of thankfulness and praise	

323   The God of Abraham praise
20   The King of love my shepherd is

(p) Psalm   **Psalm 46**   *[EVABC/Pr4A]*

608   Be still and know that I am God
325   Be still, for the presence of the Lord,
        the Holy One, is here
646   Glorious things of thee are spoken
668   God is our fortress and our rock
12   God is our strength and refuge
92   How sweet the name of Jesus sounds
211   Immortal love for ever full
95   Jesu, priceless treasure
659   Onward, Christian soldiers

2nd Reading   **Colossians 1: 11–20**

84   Alleluia! raise the anthem
643   Be thou my vision, O Lord of my heart
220   Glory be to Jesus
160   [Hark! the herald-angels sing]
94   In the name of Jesus
431   Lord, enthroned in heavenly splendour
303   Lord of the Church, we pray for our renewing
619   Lord, teach us how to pray aright
103   O Christ the same, through all our story's pages
172   [O come, all ye faithful (*Adeste, fideles*)]
363   O Lord of heaven and earth and sea
306   O Spirit of the living God
675   Peace, perfect peace, in this dark world of sin?
487   Soldiers of Christ, arise
323   The God of Abraham praise
9   There's a wideness in God's mercy
373   To God be the glory! Great things he has done!
344   When morning gilds the skies

The Gospel   **Luke 23: 33–43**

396   According to thy gracious word
215   [Ah, holy Jesu, how hast thou offended]
642   Amazing grace (how sweet the sound!)
400   And now, O Father, mindful of the love
459   For all the saints, who from their labours rest
        (*vv. 1, 2, 5–7*)
90   Hail Redeemer, King divine!

268 Hail, thou once-despised Jesus!
221 Hark! the voice of love and mercy
417 He gave his life in selfless love
210 Holy God, of righteous glory
574 I give you all the honour
617 Jesus, remember me, when you come into your
     kingdom
698 Jesus, Saviour of the world
275 Look, ye saints, the sight is glorious
429 Lord Jesus Christ, you have come to us
554 Lord Jesus, think on me
456 Lord, you give the great commission
277 [Love's redeeming work is done]
227 Man of sorrows! What a name
228 Meekness and majesty
231 My song is love unknown
102 Name of all majesty
673 O Christ, our hope, our hearts' desire
235 [O sacred head, sore wounded]
557 Rock of ages, cleft for me
239 See, Christ was wounded for our sake
241 [Sing, my tongue, the glorious battle]
444 Soul of my Saviour, sanctify my breast
285 The head that once was crowned with thorns
244 There is a green hill far away
373 To God be the glory! Great things he has done!
245 To mock your reign, O dearest Lord
491 We have a gospel to proclaim

Hymns for use with additional lectionaries on Saints' Days, Holy Days, and other special occasions

The foregoing sections have contained suggested hymns for use with the Revised Common Lectionary as recommended by the Interprovincial Consultation. This Consultation consists of representatives from the four Anglican Provinces in Great Britain and Ireland, viz. The Church of England, the Scottish Episcopal Church, the Church in Wales, and the Church of Ireland.

The following sections 8 and 9 suggest a selection of hymns for use on Saints' Days, Holy Days, and other special occasions based on the additional readings which have been drawn up by the Interprovincial Consultation. On the Saints' Days only hymns for use with the readings at the Holy Communion are suggested.

8 Saints' Days and Holy Days

The Naming and Circumcision of Jesus
January 1

1st Reading		**Numbers 6: 22–27**
	695	God of mercy, God of grace
	717	May the Lord bless you and keep you

Psalm		**Psalm 8**	[TSAC/Pr22B*]
	316	Bright the vision that delighted	
	6	Immortal, invisible, God only wise	
	362	O God beyond all praising	
	32	O Lord my God! When I in awesome wonder	
	33	O Lord of every shining constellation	

2nd Reading		**Galatians 4: 4–7**	[CIB/9–8]
	558	Abba Father, let me be	
	241	[Sing, my tongue, the glorious battle *(vv. 1, 2, 5)*]	
	185	Virgin-born, we bow before thee	

The Gospel		**Luke 2: 15–21**	[CIB]
	250	All hail the power of Jesu's name	
	147	Angels, from the realms of glory	
	149	Away in a manger, no crib for a bed	
	152	Come and join the celebration	
	158	God rest you merry, gentlemen	
	92	How sweet the name of Jesus sounds	
	162	In the bleak mid-winter	
	94	In the name of Jesus	
	583	Jesu, my Lord, my God, my all	
	98	Jesus! Name of wondrous love!	
	99	Jesus, the name high over all	
	101	Jesus, the very thought of thee	
	484	Lift high the cross, the love of Christ proclaim	
	195	Lord, the light of your love is shining	
	170	Love came down at Christmas	
	102	Name of all majesty	
	172	O come, all ye faithful (*Adeste, fideles*) (*vv. 1–3, 6, 7b*)	
	104	O for a thousand tongues to sing	
	179	See amid the winter's snow	
	180	Shepherds came, their praises bringing	
	182	Silent night, holy night	
	111	There is a name I love to hear	

| | 117 | To the name of our salvation |
| | 187 | When the crimson sun had set |

ALSO SUITABLE	81	Lord, for the years your love has kept and guided
on January 1	537	O God, our help in ages past
	83	The year is gone beyond recall

The Conversion of Saint Paul
January 25

1st Reading		**Jeremiah 1: 4–10**	*[Pr16C]*
	10	All my hope on God is founded
	631	God be in my head
	589	Lord, speak to me that I may speak
	597	Take my life, and let it be

| **Psalm** | | **Psalm 67** | *[E6C/Pr15A*]* |
| | 695 | God of mercy, God of grace |

2nd Reading		**Acts 9: 1–22**	
	218	And can it be that I should gain
	501	Christ is the world's true light
	460	For all your saints in glory, for all your saints at rest (*vv. 1, 2, 3*)
	581	I, the Lord of sea and sky
	94	In the name of Jesus
	588	Light of the minds that know him
	589	Lord, speak to me that I may speak
	195	Lord, the light of your love is shining
	594	O Lord of creation, to you be all praise!
	488	Stand up, stand up for Jesus
	597	Take my life, and let it be
	605	Will you come and follow me

Alternative 2nd Reading		**Acts 26: 9–21**	
	218	And can it be that I should gain
	501	Christ is the world's true light
	460	For all your saints in glory, for all your saints at rest (*vv. 1, 2a, 3*)
	94	In the name of Jesus
	588	Light of the minds that know him

589 Lord, speak to me that I may speak
195 Lord, the light of your love is shining
594 O Lord of creation, to you be all praise!
488 Stand up, stand up for Jesus
597 Take my life, and let it be
605 Will you come and follow me

The Gospel   **Matthew 19: 27–30**

147 [Angels, from the realms of glory]
97 Jesus shall reign where'er the sun
597 Take my life, and let it be
662 Those who would valour see
   (*He who would valiant be*)

Saint Brigid
February 1

1st Reading   **Hosea 6: 1–4**

206 Come, let us to the Lord our God
125 Hail to the Lord's anointed

Psalm   **Psalm 134**   *[Ember]*

718 O praise the Lord, ye servants of the Lord
719 Praise the Lord, all you servants of the Lord

2nd Reading   **1 John 1: 1–4**

349 Fill thou my life, O Lord my God
324 God, whose almighty word
81 Lord, for the years your love has kept and guided
624 Speak, Lord, in the stillness
343 We love the place, O God

The Gospel   **John 10: 7–16**

215 [Ah, holy Jesu, how hast thou offended]
87 Christ is the world's Light, he and none other
92 How sweet the name of Jesus sounds
421 I come with joy, a child of God
655 Loving Shepherd of your sheep
235 [O sacred head, sore wounded]
438 O thou, who at thy eucharist didst pray

526	Risen Lord, whose name we cherish
20	The King of love my shepherd is

ALSO SUITABLE	459	For all the saints, who from their labours rest
	461	For all thy saints, O Lord
	460	For all your saints in glory, for all your saints at rest (*vv. 1, 2b, 3*)
	471	Rejoice in God's saints, today and all days!

Saint Patrick
March 17

1st Reading	**Tobit 13: 1b–7**
	No suggested hymns

Alternative 1st Reading	**Deuteronomy 32: 1–9**
668	God is our fortress and our rock
539	Rejoice, O land, in God thy might
540	To thee our God we fly (*vv. 1–3, 7*)

Psalm	**Psalm 145: 1–13**
24	All creatures of our God and King
125	Hail to the Lord's anointed
321	Holy, holy, holy! Lord God almighty
358	King of glory, King of peace
360	Let all the world in every corner sing
104	O for a thousand tongues to sing
365	Praise to the Lord, the Almighty, the King of creation
368	Sing of the Lord's goodness
73	The day thou gavest, Lord, is ended
374	When all thy mercies, O my God
492	Ye servants of God, your master proclaim

2nd Reading	**2 Corinthians 4: 1–12**
52	Christ, whose glory fills the skies
613	Eternal light, shine in my heart
481	God is working his purpose out as year succeeds to year
324	God, whose almighty word
569	Hark, my soul, it is the Lord

96	Jesus is Lord! Creation's voice proclaims it
195	Lord, the light of your love is shining
228	Meekness and majesty
341	Spirit divine, attend our prayers

The Gospel **John 4: 31–38** *[Ember]*

305	O Breath of life, come sweeping through us
46	Tá an fómhar seo go haerach, céad buíochas le hÍosa (*The harvest is bright, all thanks be to Jesus*)
141	These are the days of Elijah

ALSO SUITABLE

611	Christ be beside me
459	For all the saints, who from their labours rest
461	For all thy saints, O Lord
460	For all your saints in glory, for all your saints at rest (*vv. 1, 2c, 3*)
464	God, whose city's sure foundation
322	I bind unto myself today
536	Lord, while for all the world we pray
471	Rejoice in God's saints, today and all days!
473	Síormholadh is glóir duit, a Athair shíorai (*All glory and praise to you, Father, above*)

The Annunciation of our Lord to the Blessed Virgin Mary
March 25

Ist Reading **Isaiah 7: 10–14**

151	Child in the manger
160	[Hark! the herald-angels sing]
168	Lord, you were rich beyond all splendour
135	[O come, O come, Emmanuel]
174	[O little town of Bethlehem]

Psalm **Psalm 40: 5–10**

597	Take my life, and let it be
712	Tell out, my soul, the greatness of the Lord
492	Ye servants of God, your master proclaim

2nd Reading		**Hebrews 10: 4–10**	
	400	And now, O Father, mindful of the love	
	431	Lord, enthroned in heavenly splendour	

The Gospel		**Luke 1: 26–28**	*[A4B]*
	119	[Come, thou long-expected Jesus]	
	462	For Mary, mother of our Lord	
	123	God the Father sends his angel	
	125	Hail to the Lord's anointed	
	92	How sweet the name of Jesus sounds	
	94	In the name of Jesus	
	97	Jesus shall reign where'er the sun	
	99	Jesus, the name high over all	
	133	Long ago, prophets knew	
	704	Mary sang a song, a song of love	
	175	[Of the Father's heart, begotten]	
	472	Sing we of the blessed mother	
	139	The angel Gabriel from heaven came (*omit v. 4*)	
	73	The day thou gavest, Lord, is ended	
	185	Virgin-born, we bow before thee	
	477	We praise you, Lord, today	

Saint Mark
April 25

1st Reading		**Proverbs 15: 28–33**	
	10	All my hope on God is founded	
	643	Be thou my vision, O Lord of my heart	

Alternative 1st Reading		**Isaiah 52: 7–10**	*[CPr3ABC/11–30]*
	479	Go, tell it on the mountain	
	125	Hail to the Lord's anointed	
	129	How lovely on the mountains are the feet of him	
	597	Take my life, and let it be	
	387	Thanks to God, whose Word was spoken	

Psalm		**Psalm 119: 9–16**	*[L5B]*
	383	Lord, be thy word my rule	
	384	Lord, thy word abideth	
	638	O for a heart to praise my God	

2nd Reading		**Ephesians 4: 7–16**
	523	Help us to help each other, Lord
	308	Revive your Church, O Lord
	369	Songs of praise the angels sang
The Gospel		**Mark 13: 5–13**
	95	Jesu, priceless treasure
	589	Lord, speak to me that I may speak
	491	We have a gospel to proclaim
ALSO SUITABLE	459	For all the saints, who from their labours rest
	461	For all thy saints, O Lord
	460	For all your saints in glory, for all your saints at rest (*vv. 1, 2d, 3*)
	471	Rejoice in God's saints, today and all days!

Saint Philip and Saint James
May 1

1st Reading		**Isaiah 30: 15–21**
	422	In the quiet consecration
	535	Judge eternal, throned in splendour
	115	Thou art the Way: to thee alone
Psalm		**Psalm 119: 1–8** *[4LAPr1/Pr26B*]*
	630	Blessed are the pure in heart
	649	Happy are they, they that love God
	601	Teach me, my God, and King
2nd Reading		**Ephesians 1: 3–10**
	84	Alleluia! raise the anthem
	189	[As with gladness men of old]
	352	Give thanks with a grateful heart
	99	Jesus, the name high over all
	652	Lead us, heavenly Father, lead us
	363	O Lord of heaven and earth and sea
	9	There's a wideness in God's mercy
	373	To God be the glory! Great things he has done!

The Gospel		**John 14: 1–14**	*[E5A]*
	87	Christ is the world's Light, he and none other	
	610	Come, my Way, my Truth, my Life	
	453	Come to us, creative Spirit	
	566	Fight the good fight with all thy might!	
	268	Hail, thou once-despised Jesus!	
	270	I know that my Redeemer lives	
	272	Jesus lives: thy terrors now	
	100	Jesus loves me: this I know	
	588	Light of the minds that know him	
	619	Lord, teach us how to pray aright	
	657	O God of Bethel, by whose hand	
	625	Prayer is the soul's sincere desire	
	626	'Set your troubled hearts at rest'	
	109	Sing alleluia to the Lord	
	20	The King of love my shepherd is	
	21	The Lord's my shepherd, I'll not want	
	660	Thine for ever! God of love	
	115	Thou art the Way: to thee alone	
	395	When Jesus taught by Galilee	

ALSO SUITABLE	459	For all the saints, who from their labours rest
	461	For all thy saints, O Lord
	460	For all your saints in glory, for all your saints at rest (*vv. 1, 2e, 3*)
	471	Rejoice in God's saints, today and all days!

Saint Matthias
May 14

1st Reading		**Isaiah 22: 15–25**	
	135	[O come, O come, Emmanuel]	
Psalm		**Psalm 15**	*[Ep4A/PrIIC*/PrI7B*]*
	631	God be in my head	
2nd Reading		**Acts 1: 15–26**	
	460	For all your saints in glory, for all your saints at rest (*vv. 1, 2f, 3*)	

256

The Gospel	**John 15: 9–17**	*[E6B]*

515	'A new commandment I give unto you'
516	Beloved, let us love: love is of God
523	Help us to help each other, Lord
421	I come with joy, a child of God
495	Jesu, Jesu, fill us with your love
525	Let there be love shared among us
75	Lord, dismiss us with your blessing
456	Lord, you give the great commission
231	My song is love unknown
315	'This is my will, my one command'
530	Ubi caritas et amor
451	We come as guests invited
627	What a friend we have in Jesus

ALSO SUITABLE	
459	For all the saints, who from their labours rest
461	For all thy saints, O Lord
471	Rejoice in God's saints, today and all days!

The Visitation of the Blessed Virgin Mary
May 31

1st Reading	**Zephaniah 3: 14–18**

86	Christ is the King! O friends, rejoice
646	Glorious things of thee are spoken
125	Hail to the Lord's anointed
281	Rejoice, the Lord is King!

Psalm	**Psalm 113**	*[Pr20C*]*

501	Christ is the world's true light
360	Let all the world in every corner sing
718	O praise the Lord, ye servants of the Lord
719	Praise the Lord, all you servants of the Lord
712	Tell out, my soul, the greatness of the Lord
73	The day thou gavest, Lord, is ended

2nd Reading	**Romans 12: 9–16**

515	'A new commandment I give unto you'
516	Beloved, let us love: love is of God
517	Brother, sister, let me serve you
219	From heav'n you came, helpless babe

523	Help us to help each other, Lord
525	Let there be love shared among us
503	Make me a channel of your peace

The Gospel **Luke 1: 39–49 (50–56)**

470	Let God's people join in worship
704	Mary sang a song, a song of love
472	Sing we of the blessed mother
712	Tell out, my soul, the greatness of the Lord
373	To God be the glory! Great things he has done!
185	Virgin-born, we bow before thee
476	Ye watchers and ye holy ones

Saint Columba
June 9

1st Reading **Micah 4: 1–5** *[E3B]*

118	Behold, the mountain of the Lord
501	Christ is the world's true light
263	Crown him with many crowns
496	For the healing of the nations
538	O Lord, the clouds are gathering
539	Rejoice, O land, in God thy might
509	Your kingdom come, O God!

Psalm **Psalm 34: 9–15**

| 507 | Put peace into each other's hands |
| 372 | Through all the changing scenes of life |

2nd Reading **Romans 15: 1–6** *[BSC]*

86	Christ is the King! O friends, rejoice
349	Fill thou my life, O Lord my God
381	God has spoken—by his prophets
380	God has spoken to his people, alleluia!
382	Help us, O Lord, to learn
523	Help us to help each other, Lord
386	Spirit of God, unseen as the wind
387	Thanks to God, whose Word was spoken
372	Through all the changing scenes of life

The Gospel		John 12: 20–26
	43	[Holy is the seed-time, when the buried grain]
	522	In Christ there is no east or west
	278	Now the green blade rises from the buried grain (*omit v. 3*)
ALSO SUITABLE	560	Alone with none but thee, my God
	257	Christ is the world's Redeemer
	459	For all the saints, who from their labours rest
	461	For all thy saints, O Lord
	460	For all your saints in glory, for all your saints at rest (*vv. 1, 2g, 3*)
	471	Rejoice in God's saints, today and all days!

Saint Barnabas
June 11

1st Reading		Job 29: 11–16
	569	Hark, my soul, it is the Lord
	104	O for thousand tongues to sing
Psalm		**Psalm 112: 1–9**
	591	O happy day that fixed my choice
2nd Reading		**Acts 11: 19–30**
	494	Beauty for brokenness
	294	Come down, O Love divine
	298	Filled with the Spirit's power, with one accord
	460	For all your saints in glory, for all your saints at rest (*vv. 1, 2h, 3*)
	456	Lord, you give the great commission
	527	Son of God, eternal Saviour
	314	There's a spirit in the air
The Gospel		**John 15: 12–17**
	515	'A new commandment I give unto you'
	516	Beloved, let us love: love is of God
	523	Help us to help each other, Lord
	421	I come with joy, a child of God
	495	Jesu, Jesu, fill us with your love

525	Let there be love shared among us
75	Lord, dismiss us with your blessing
456	Lord, you give the great commission
231	My song is love unknown
315	'This is my will, my one command'
530	Ubi caritas et amor
451	We come as guests invited
627	What a friend we have in Jesus

ALSO SUITABLE	459	For all the saints, who from their labours rest
	461	For all thy saints, O Lord
	471	Rejoice in God's saints, today and all days!

The Birth of Saint John the Baptist
June 24

1st Reading **Isaiah 40: 1–11** *[A2B]*

120	Comfort, comfort ye my people
122	[Drop down, ye heavens from above]
644	Faithful Shepherd, feed me
6	Immortal, invisible, God only wise
535	Judge eternal, throned in splendour
134	Make way, make way, for Christ the King
141	These are the days of Elijah

Psalm **Psalm 85: 7–13**

695	God of mercy, God of grace
539	Rejoice, O land, in God thy might
140	The Lord will come and not be slow

2nd Reading **Acts 13: 14b–26**

250	All hail the power of Jesu's name
689	Come, sing praises to the Lord above
460	For all your saints in glory, for all your saints at rest (*vv. 1, 2i, 3*)
125	Hail to the Lord's anointed
161	[I know a rose-tree springing]
135	[O come, O come, Emmanuel]
136	On Jordan's bank the Baptist's cry

Alternative 2nd Reading	**Galatians 3: 23–29**	*[Pr7C]*
250	All hail the power of Jesu's name	
389	All who believe and are baptized	
218	And can it be that I should gain	
496	For the healing of the nations	
522	In Christ there is no east or west	
101	Jesus, the very thought of thee	
358	King of glory, King of peace	

The Gospel	**Luke 1: 57–66, 80**	
685	Blessed be the God of Israel	
706	O bless the God of Israel	

ALSO SUITABLE	119	Come, thou long-expected Jesus
	459	For all the saints, who from their labours rest
	461	For all thy saints, O Lord
	126	Hark! a thrilling voice is sounding
	124	Hark the glad sound! the Saviour comes
	471	Rejoice in God's saints, today and all days!

Saint Peter
June 29

1st Reading	**Ezekiel 3: 4–11**	
589	Lord, speak to me that I may speak	

Alternative 1st Reading	**Ezekiel 3: 22–27**	
589	Lord, speak to me that I may speak	

Psalm	**Psalm 125**	*[Pr18B]*
3	God is love: let heaven adore him	
34	O worship the King all-glorious above	
595	Safe in the shadow of the Lord	

2nd Reading	**Acts 12: 1–11**	
218	And can it be that I should gain	
460	For all your saints in glory, for all your saints at rest (*vv. 1, 2j, 2m, 3*)	
124	[Hark the glad sound! the Saviour comes]	
97	Jesus shall reign where'er the sun	

99	Jesus, the name high over all
134	Make way, make way, for Christ the King
493	Ye that know the Lord is gracious

The Gospel **Matthew 16: 13–20** *[Pr16A]*

460	For all your saints in glory, for all your saints at rest (*vv. 1, 2j, 3*)
659	Onward, Christian soldiers
528	The Church's one foundation
493	Ye that know the Lord is gracious

ALSO SUITABLE

326	Blessed city, heavenly Salem (*Christ is made the sure foundation*)
327	Christ is our corner-stone
459	For all the saints, who from their labours rest
461	For all thy saints, O Lord
471	Rejoice in God's saints, today and all days!

Saint Thomas
July 3

1st Reading **Habakkuk 2: 1–4**

643	Be thou my vision, O Lord of my heart

Psalm **Psalm 31: 1–6**

459	For all the saints, who from their labours rest (*vv. 1–3*)
668	God is our fortress and our rock
620	O Lord, hear my prayer
557	Rock of ages, cleft for me
595	Safe in the shadow of the Lord

2nd Reading **Ephesians 2: 19–22** *[10–28/DFC]*

326	Blessed city, heavenly Salem (*Christ is made the sure foundation*)
327	Christ is our corner-stone
340	Sing and be glad, for this is God's house!
528	The Church's one foundation
313	The Spirit came, as promised
493	Ye that know the Lord is gracious

Alternative 2nd Reading   **Hebrews 10: 35 – 11: 1**

558	Abba Father, let me be
562	Blessed assurance, Jesus is mine
563	Commit your ways to God
566	Fight the good fight with all thy might!
463	Give us the wings of faith to rise
552	I hear thy welcome voice
590	My faith looks up to thee
623	Our heavenly Father, through your Son

The Gospel   **John 20: 24–29**

255	[Christ is risen, alleluia!]
263	Crown him with many crowns (*vv. 1–4*)
460	For all your saints in glory, for all your saints at rest (*vv. 1, 2k, 3*)
219	From heav'n you came, helpless babe
226	It is a thing most wonderful
583	Jesu, my Lord, my God, my all
338	Jesus, stand among us
424	Jesus, stand among us at the meeting of our lives
229	My God I love thee; not because
279	O sons and daughters, let us sing! (*omit vv. 2, 3*)
288	Thine be the glory, risen, conquering Son

ALSO SUITABLE

52	Christ, whose glory fills the skies
461	For all thy saints, O Lord
270	I know that my Redeemer lives
272	[Jesus lives: thy terrors now]
471	Rejoice in God's saints, today and all days!

Saint Mary Magdalene
July 22

1st Reading   **Hosea 6: 1–3**

206	Come, let us to the Lord our God
125	Hail to the Lord's anointed

Alternative 1st Reading   **Song of Solomon 3: 1–4**

592	O Love that wilt not let me go

Psalm	**Psalm 42: 1–7**
607	As pants the hart for cooling streams
606	As the deer pants for the water
15	If thou but suffer God to guide thee
95	Jesu, priceless treasure
425	Jesus, thou joy of loving hearts
434	My Jesus, pierced with love of me

2nd Reading	**2 Corinthians 5: 14–18**
416	Great God, your love has called us here
268	Hail, thou once-despised Jesus!
522	In Christ there is no east or west
226	It is a thing most wonderful
634	Love divine, all loves excelling
306	O Spirit of the living God
528	The Church's one foundation

The Gospel	**John 20: 1–2, 11–18**
74	First of the week and finest day
460	For all your saints in glory, for all your saints at rest (*vv. 1, 2l, 3*)
273	Led like a lamb to the slaughter
274	[Light's glittering morn bedecks the sky]
104	O for a thousand tongues to sing
288	Thine be the glory, risen, conquering Son
115	Thou art the Way: to thee alone
290	Walking in a garden at the close of day

ALSO SUITABLE	459 For all the saints, who from their labours rest
461	For all thy saints, O Lord
576	I heard the voice of Jesus say
272	[Jesus lives: thy terrors now]
58	Morning has broken
237	O my Saviour, lifted
279	O sons and daughters, let us sing! (*vv. 1–3, 9*)
471	Rejoice in God's saints, today and all days!
246	Were you there when they crucified my Lord?

Saint James
July 25

1st Reading   **Jeremiah 45: 1–5**
No suggested hymns

Psalm   **Psalm 126**   *[A3B/L5C/Pr25B*/HTB]*

567	Forth, in thy name, O Lord, I go
356	I will sing, I will sing a song unto the Lord
712	Tell out, my soul, the greatness of the Lord
373	To God be the glory! Great things he has done!

2nd Reading   **Acts 11: 27 – 12: 2**

494	Beauty for brokenness
460	For all your saints in glory, for all your saints at rest (*vv. 1, 2m, 3*)
527	Son of God, eternal Saviour
314	There's a spirit in the air

The Gospel   **Mark 10: 35–45**   *[Pr24B]*

684	All praise to thee, for thou, O King, divine
517	Brother, sister, let me serve you
294	Come down, O Love divine
319	Father, of heaven, whose love profound
219	From heav'n you came, helpless babe
417	He gave his life in selfless love
523	Help us to help each other, Lord
419	I am not worthy, holy Lord
495	Jesu, Jesu, fill us with your love
96	Jesus is Lord! Creation's voice proclaims it
589	Lord, speak to me that I may speak
231	My song is love unknown
135	[O come, O come, Emmanuel]
214	O Love, how deep, how broad, how high!
366	Praise, my soul, the King of heaven
244	There is a green hill far away

Alternative Gospel   **Matthew 20: 20–28**

319	Father, of heaven, whose love profound
219	From heav'n you came, helpless babe
417	He gave his life in selfless love

419	I am not worthy, holy Lord
135	[O come, O come, Emmanuel]
366	Praise, my soul, the King of heaven
244	There is a green hill far away

ALSO SUITABLE

459	For all the saints, who from their labours rest
461	For all thy saints, O Lord
471	Rejoice in God's saints, today and all days!

The Transfiguration of Our Lord
August 6

Ist Reading   **Daniel 7: 9–10, 13–14**   *[Pr29B*]*

6	Immortal, invisible, God only wise
125	Hail to the Lord's anointed
468	How shall I sing that majesty
130	Jesus came, the heavens adoring
132	[Lo! he comes with clouds descending]
34	O worship the King all-glorious above
196	O worship the Lord in the beauty of holiness!
678	Ten thousand times ten thousand
73	The day thou gavest, Lord, is ended
323	The God of Abraham praise

Alternative Ist Reading   **Exodus 34: 29–35**   *[ILC]*

325	Be still, for the presence of the Lord, the Holy One, is here

Psalm   **Psalm 97**   *[CPr2ABC/E7C]*

34	O worship the King all-glorious above
281	Rejoice, the Lord is King!
8	The Lord is king! Lift up your voice

2nd Reading   **2 Peter 1: 16–19**

501	Christ is the world's true light
52	Christ, whose glory fills the skies
613	Eternal light, shine in my heart
654	Light of the lonely pilgrim's heart

The Gospel		Luke 9: 28–36	*[ILC/L2C]*
	325	Be still, for the presence of the Lord, the Holy One, is here	
	643	Be thou my vision, O Lord of my heart	
	501	Christ is the world's true light	
	205	Christ, upon the mountain peak	
	52	Christ, whose glory fills the skies	
	331	God reveals his presence	
	209	Here in this holy time and place	
	101	Jesus, the very thought of thee	
	195	Lord, the light of your love is shining	
	102	Name of all majesty	
	60	O Jesus, Lord of heavenly grace	
	449	Thee we adore, O hidden Saviour, thee	
	112	There is a Redeemer	
	374	When all thy mercies, O my God	

Saint Bartholomew
August 24

1st Reading		Isaiah 43: 8–13
	122	[Drop down, ye heavens, from above]
	321	Holy, holy, holy! Lord God almighty
	557	Rock of ages, cleft for me
	323	The God of Abraham praise

Psalm		Psalm 145: 1–7
	24	All creatures of our God and King
	358	King of glory, King of peace
	360	Let all the world in every corner sing
	104	O for a thousand tongues to sing
	368	Sing of the Lord's goodness
	374	When all thy mercies, O my God

2nd Reading		Acts 5: 12–16
	511	Father of mercy, God of consolation
	697	Great and wonderful your deeds
	513	O Christ, the Healer, we have come

The Gospel		**Luke 22: 24–30**
	417	He gave his life in selfless love
	418	Here, O my Lord, I see thee face to face
	531	Where love and loving-kindness dwell
ALSO SUITABLE	459	For all the saints, who from their labours rest
	461	For all thy saints, O Lord
	460	For all your saints in glory, for all your saints at rest (*vv. 1, 2n, 3*)
	471	Rejoice in God's saints, today and all days!

The Birth of the Blessed Virgin Mary
September 8

1st Reading		**Isaiah 61: 10–11**
	218	And can it be that I should gain
	418	Here, O my Lord, I see thee face to face
	671	Jesus, thy blood and righteousness
	175	[Of the Father's heart begotten]

Alternative 1st Reading		**Genesis 3: 8–15, 20**
	250	All hail the power of Jesu's name
	99	Jesus, the name high over all
	484	Lift high the cross, the love of Christ proclaim
	555	Lord of creation, forgive us, we pray
	108	Praise to the Holiest in the height
	545	Sing of Eve and sing of Adam
	290	Walking in a garden at the close of day
	186	What Adam's disobedience cost
	292	[Ye choirs of new Jerusalem]

Psalm		**Psalm 45: 10–17**	*[Pr9A]*
	528	The Church's one foundation	
	142	[Wake, O wake! With tidings thrilling]	

2nd Reading		**Galatians 4: 4–7**	*[CIB/1–1]*
	558	Abba Father, let me be	
	241	[Sing, my tongue, the glorious battle]	
	185	Virgin-born, we bow before thee	

The Gospel **Luke 1: 46–55**

704 Mary sang a song, a song of love
712 Tell out, my soul, the greatness of the Lord
373 To God be the glory! Great things he has done!

ALSO SUITABLE 459 For all the saints, who from their labours rest
461 For all thy saints, O Lord
460 For all your saints in glory, for all your
      saints at rest (*vv. 1, 2o, 3]*
462 For Mary, mother of our Lord
471 Rejoice in God's saints, today and all days!
472 Sing we of the blessed mother
139 The angel Gabriel from heaven came (*omit v. 4*)
476 Ye watchers and ye holy ones

Saint Matthew
September 21

1st Reading **Proverbs 3: 13–18**

643 Be thou my vision, O Lord of my heart

Psalm **Psalm 119: 65–72**

432 Love is his word, love is his way
20 The King of love my shepherd is

2nd Reading **2 Corinthians 4: 1–6**

684 All praise to thee, for thou, O King divine!
613 Eternal light, shine in my heart
481 God is working his purpose out as year succeeds
      to year
324 God, whose almighty word
482 Jesus bids us shine with a pure clear light
484 Lift high the cross, the love of Christ proclaim
195 Lord, the light of your love is shining
228 Meekness and majesty
486 People of God, arise
341 Spirit divine, attend our prayers
490 The Spirit lives to set us free
491 We have a gospel to proclaim
493 Ye that know the Lord is gracious

The Gospel		**Matthew 9: 9–13**
	549	Dear Lord and Father of mankind
	460	For all your saints in glory, for all your saints at rest (*vv. 1, 2p, 3*)
	417	He gave his life in selfless love
	94	In the name of Jesus
	584	Jesus calls us! O'er the tumult
	130	Jesus came, the heavens adoring
	605	Will you come and follow me
ALSO SUITABLE	459	For all the saints, who from their labours rest
	461	For all thy saints, O Lord
	471	Rejoice in God's saints, today and all days!
	527	Son of God, eternal Saviour

Saint Michael and all Angels
also known as Michaelmas September 29

1st Reading		**Genesis 28: 10–17**
	561	Beneath the Cross of Jesus
	562	Blessed assurance, Jesus is mine
	330	God is here! As we his people
	331	God reveals his presence
	67	God, who made the earth and heaven
	656	Nearer, my God, to thee

Psalm		**Psalm 103: 19–22**
	682	All created things, bless the Lord
	250	All hail the power of Jesu's name
	453	Come to us, creative Spirit
	465	Hark, hark, my soul, angelic songs are swelling
	321	Holy, holy, holy! Lord God almighty
	708	O praise ye the Lord! Praise him in the height
	366	Praise, my soul, the King of heaven
	709	Praise the Lord! You heavens, adore him
	376	Ye holy angels bright

2nd Reading		**Revelation 12: 7–12**
	269	Hark ten thousand voices sounding
	487	Soldiers of Christ, arise
	112	There is a Redeemer
	492	Ye servants of God, your master proclaim

The Gospel		**John 1: 47–51**
	460	For all your saints in glory, for all your saints at rest (*vv. 1, 2n, 3*)
	97	Jesus shall reign where'er the sun
ALSO SUITABLE	346	Angel voices, ever singing
	316	Bright the vision that delighted
	332	Come, let us join our cheerful songs
	696	God, we praise you! God, we bless you!

Saint Luke
October 18

1st Reading		**Isaiah 35: 3–6**
	231	My song is love unknown (*vv. 1, 2, 4, 7*)
	104	O for a thousand tongues to sing
	113	There is singing in the desert, there is laughter in the skies
Alternative 1st Reading		**Sirach 38: 1–4**
	65	At evening, when the sun had set
	511	Father of mercy, God of consolation
	512	From you all skill and science flow
	513	O Christ, the Healer, we have come
	514	We cannot measure how you heal
Psalm		**Psalm 147: 1–7**
	104	O for a thousand tongues to sing
2nd Reading		**2 Timothy 4: 5–17**
	566	Fight the good fight with all thy might!
	459	For all the saints, who from their labours rest
	478	Go forth and tell! O Church of God, awake!
	277	[Love's redeeming work is done]
	281	Rejoice, the Lord is King!
	487	Soldiers of Christ, arise
	492	Ye servants of God, your master proclaim
Alternative 2nd Reading		**Acts 16: 6–12a**
	324	God, whose almighty word

The Gospel	**Luke 10: 1–9**
37	Come, ye thankful people, come
39	For the fruits of his creation
454	Forth in the peace of Christ we go
478	Go forth and tell! O Church of God, awake!
455	Go forth for God; go forth to the world in peace
456	Lord, you give the great commission
305	O Breath of life, come sweeping through us
505	Peace be to this congregation
492	Ye servants of God, your master proclaim

ALSO SUITABLE	461 For all thy saints, O Lord
550	'Forgive our sins as we forgive'
460	For all your saints in glory, for all your saints at rest (*vv. 1, 2q, 3*)
471	Rejoice in God's saints, today and all days!
712	Tell out, my soul, the greatness of the Lord

Saint Simon and Saint Jude
October 28

1st Reading	**Isaiah 28: 14–16**
326	Blessed city, heavenly Salem (*Christ is made the sure foundation*)
327	Christ is our corner-stone
340	Sing and be glad, for this is God's house!
528	The Church's one foundation
493	Ye that know the Lord is gracious

Psalm	**Psalm 119: 89–96**
80	Great is thy faithfulness, O God my Father
382	Help us, O Lord, to learn
573	I am thine, O Lord, I have heard thy voice
384	Lord, thy word abideth
638	O for a heart to praise my God

2nd Reading	**Ephesians 2: 19–22** *[7–3/DFC]*
326	Blessed city, heavenly Salem (*Christ is made the sure foundation*)
327	Christ is our corner-stone
413	Father, we thank thee who hast planted

522	In Christ there is no east or west
340	Sing and be glad, for this is God's house!
528	The Church's one foundation
313	The Spirit came, as promised
493	Ye that know the Lord is gracious

The Gospel   **John 15: 17–27**

515	'A new commandment I give unto you'
294	Come down, O Love divine
296	Come, Holy Ghost, our souls inspire
297	Come, thou Holy Spirit, come
299	Holy Spirit, come, confirm us
307	Our great Redeemer, as he breathed

ALSO SUITABLE

459	For all the saints, who from their labours rest
461	For all thy saints, O Lord
460	For all your saints in glory, for all your saints at rest (*vv. 1, 2r, 3*)
471	Rejoice in God's saints, today and all days!

Saint Andrew
November 30

1st Reading   **Isaiah 52: 7–10**   *[CPr3ABC/4–25]*

479	Go, tell it on the mountain
125	Hail to the Lord's anointed
129	How lovely on the mountains are the feet of him
597	Take my life, and let it be
387	Thanks to God, whose Word was spoken

Psalm   **Psalm 19: 1–6**

153	Come, thou Redeemer of the earth
351	From all that dwell below the skies
97	Jesus shall reign where'er the sun
34	O worship the King all-glorious above
35	The spacious firmament on high

2nd Reading   **Romans 10: 12–18**

478	Go forth and tell! O Church of God, awake!
522	In Christ there is no east or west
425	Jesus, thou joy of loving hearts

303	Lord of the Church, we pray for our renewing
71	Saviour, again to thy dear name we raise
597	Take my life, and let it be
117	To the name of our salvation

The Gospel — **Matthew 4: 18–22**

86	Christ is the King! O friends, rejoice
549	Dear Lord and Father of mankind
584	Jesus calls us! O'er the tumult
395	When Jesus taught by Galilee
605	Will you come and follow me

ALSO SUITABLE

459	For all the saints, who from their labours rest
461	For all thy saints, O Lord
460	For all your saints in glory, for all your saints at rest (vv. 1, 2s, 3)
324	God, whose almighty word
471	Rejoice in God's saints, today and all days!

Saint Stephen
December 26

1st Reading — **2 Chronicles 24: 20–22**

381	God has spoken—by his prophets

Alternative 1st Reading — **Jeremiah 26: 12–15**

381	God has spoken—by his prophets

Psalm — **Psalm 119: 161–168**

382	Help us, O Lord, to learn
358	King of glory, King of peace
16	Like a mighty river flowing
383	Lord, be thy word my rule
384	Lord, thy word abideth

2nd Reading — **Acts 7: 51–60**

460	For all your saints in glory, for all your saints at rest (vv. 1, 2t, 3)
550	'Forgive our sins as we forgive'
693	Glory in the highest to the God of heaven!

696	God, we praise you! God, we bless you!
553	Jesu, lover of my soul
8	The Lord is king! Lift up your voice

The Gospel   **Matthew 10: 17–22**

589	Lord, speak to me that I may speak
593	O Jesus, I have promised
597	Take my life, and let it be

ALSO SUITABLE

250	All hail the power of Jesu's name
459	For all the saints, who from their labours rest
461	For all thy saints, O Lord
471	Rejoice in God's saints, today and all days!

Saint John
December 27

1st Reading   **Exodus 33: 7–11a**

647	Guide me, O thou great Jehovah

Alternative 1st Reading   **Exodus 33: 18–23**

557	Rock of ages, cleft for me

Psalm   **Psalm 117**

351	From all that dwell below the skies
359	Laudate Dominum

2nd Reading   **1 John 1: 1–9**

613	Eternal light, shine in my heart
418	Here, O my Lord, I see thee face to face
553	Jesu, lover of my soul
587	Just as I am, without one plea
429	Lord Jesus Christ, you have come to us
81	Lord, for the years your love has kept and guided
104	O for a thousand tongues to sing
557	Rock of ages, cleft for me
490	The Spirit lives to set us free

The Gospel		**John 21: 19b–25**
	460	For all your saints in glory, for all your saints at rest (*vv. 1, 2u, 3*)
	226	It is a thing most wonderful
	605	Will you come and follow me
ALSO SUITABLE	146	A great and mighty wonder
	459	For all the saints, who from their labours rest
	461	For all thy saints, O Lord
	588	Light of the minds that know him
	172	O come, all ye faithful (*Adeste, fideles*) (*vv. 1, 2, 6, 7b*)
	471	Rejoice in God's saints, today and all days!

Holy Innocents
December 28

1st Reading		**Jeremiah 31: 15–17**
	460	For all your saints in glory, for all your saints at rest (*vv. 1, 2v, 3*)
	651	Jesus, friend of little children

Psalm		**Psalm 124**	*[Pr16A/Pr21B]*
	642	Amazing grace (how sweet the sound!)	
	553	Jesu, lover of my soul	
	537	O God, our help in ages past	

2nd Reading		**1 Corinthians 1: 26–29**
	632	I love to hear the story
	168	Lord, you were rich beyond all splendour
	600	The wise may bring their learning

The Gospel		**Matthew 2: 13–18**
	189	As with gladness men of old
	190	Brightest and best of the suns of the morning
	194	Earth has many a noble city
	172	O come all ye faithful (*Adeste, fideles*) (*omit vv. 3, 7a*)
	196	O worship the Lord in the beauty of holiness!
	198	The first Nowell the angel did say
	184	Unto us is born a Son
	201	We three kings of Orient are

9 Special Occasions

Dedication Festival

Year A

When the anniversary date of a consecration of a church is not known, a Dedication Festival is traditionally observed on the first Sunday in October. Other times of the year, however, may be chosen as pastorally convenient.

1st Reading		**Haggai 2: 6–9**	
	501	Christ is the world's true light	
	119	[Come, thou long-expected Jesus]	
	527	Son of God, eternal Saviour	
	678	Ten thousand times ten thousand	

Psalm		**Psalm 84: 1–4**	*[DFC]*
	333	How lovely are thy dwellings fair!	
	95	Jesu, priceless treasure	
	425	Jesus, thou joy of living hearts	
	360	Let all the world in every corner sing	
	634	Love divine, all loves excelling	

2nd Reading		**1 Peter 2: 4–10**	
	326	Blessed city, heavenly Salem	
		(Christ is made the sure foundation)	
	327	Christ is our corner-stone	
	454	Forth in the peace of Christ we go	
	380	God has spoken to his people, alleluia!	
	125	Hail to the Lord's anointed	
	569	Hark, my soul, it is the Lord	
	92	How sweet the name of Jesus sounds	
	486	People of God, arise	
	340	Sing and be glad, for this is God's house!	
	532	Who are we who stand and sing?	
	493	Ye that know the Lord is gracious	

The Gospel		**John 2: 13–22**	*[3LB]*
	453	Come to us, creative Spirit	
	336	Jesus, where'er thy people meet	
	343	We love the place, O God	

ALSO SUITABLE	*Any of the hymns recommended in the Church Hymnal for 'Consecration and Dedication of Buildings'*

Dedication Festival   Year B

When the anniversary date of a consecration of a church is not known, a Dedication Festival is traditionally observed on the first Sunday in October. Other times of the year, however, may be chosen as pastorally convenient.

1st Reading		**1 Kings 8: 22–30**
	346	Angel voices, ever singing
	614	Great Shepherd of your people, hear
	321	Holy, holy, holy! Lord God almighty
	323	The God of Abraham praise

Psalm		**Psalm 122**	*[AIA/DFC/Ember]*
	683	All people that on earth do dwell	
	670	Jerusalem the golden	
	506	Pray that Jerusalem may have	

2nd Reading		**Hebrews 12: 18–24**
	646	Glorious things of thee are spoken
	220	Glory be to Jesus
	638	O for a heart to praise my God

The Gospel		**John 10: 22–29**
	655	Loving shepherd of your sheep
	660	Thine for ever! God of love

ALSO SUITABLE   *Any of the hymns recommended in the Church Hymnal for 'Consecration and Dedication of Buildings'*

Dedication Festival   Year C

When the anniversary date of a consecration of a church is not known, a Dedication Festival is traditionally observed on the first Sunday in October. Other times of the year, however, may be chosen as pastorally convenient.

1st Reading		**Genesis 28: 11–18**
	561	Beneath the Cross of Jesus
	562	Blessed assurance, Jesus is mine
	330	God is here! As we his people
	331	God reveals his presence
	67	God, who made the earth and heaven
	656	Nearer, my God, to thee

Alternative 1st Reading		**1 Chronicles 29: 6–19**	
	346	Angel voices, ever singing	
	453	Come to us, creative Spirit	
	321	Holy, holy, holy! Lord God almighty	
	6	Immortal, invisible, God only wise	
	361	Now thank we all our God	
	363	O Lord of heaven and earth and sea	
	527	Son of God, eternal Saviour	
	323	The God of Abraham praise	

Psalm		**Psalm 122**	*[AIA/DFB/Ember]*
	683	All people that on earth do dwell	
	670	Jerusalem the golden	
	506	Pray that Jerusalem may have	

Alternative psalm		**Psalm 84: 1–4**	*[DFA]*
	333	How lovely are thy dwellings fair!	
	95	Jesu, priceless treasure	
	425	Jesus, thou joy of living hearts	
	360	Let all the world in every corner sing	
	634	Love divine, all loves excelling	

2nd Reading		**Ephesians 2: 19–22**	*[7–3/10–28]*
	326	Blessed city, heavenly Salem	
		(*Christ is made the sure foundation*)	
	327	Christ is our corner-stone	
	413	Father, we thank thee who hast planted	
	522	In Christ there is no east or west	
	340	Sing and be glad, for this is God's house!	
	528	The Church's one foundation	
	313	The Spirit came, as promised	
	493	Ye that know the Lord is gracious	

The Gospel		**Matthew 21: 12–16**	
	217	[All glory, laud, and honour]	
	347	Children of Jerusalem	
	570	Give me oil in my lamp, keep me burning	
		(*omit v. 1*) (*Give me joy in my heart, keep me praising*)	
	223	Hosanna, hosanna, hosanna in the highest	
	97	Jesus shall reign where'er the sun	
	231	My song is love unknown	

104	O for a thousand tongues to sing
343	We love the place, O God

ALSO SUITABLE *Any of the hymns recommended in the Church Hymnal for 'Consecration and Dedication of Buildings'*

Harvest Thanksgiving   Year A

1st Reading   **Deuteronomy 8: 7–18**

42	Good is the Lord, our heavenly King
647	Guide me, O thou great Jehovah
539	Rejoice, O land, in God thy might
557	Rock of ages, cleft for me

Psalm   **Psalm 65**   *[2LC/Pr10A*/Pr25C]*

612	Eternal Father, strong to save
645	Father, hear the prayer we offer
42	Good is the Lord, our heavenly King
581	I, the Lord of sea and sky
709	Praise the Lord! You heavens, adore him

2nd Reading   **2 Corinthians 9: 6–15**

10	All my hope on God is founded
38	Father, blessing every seed-time
40	Father of mercies, God of love
363	O Lord of heaven and earth and sea
47	We plough the fields, and scatter

The Gospel   **Luke 17: 11–19**   *[Pr23C]*

92	How sweet the name of Jesus sounds
211	Immortal love for ever full
361	Now thank we all our God
104	O for a thousand tongues to sing
366	Praise, my soul, the King of heaven
373	To God be the glory! Great things he has done!

ALSO SUITABLE *Any hymns in the Harvest section of the Church Hymnal*

Harvest Thanksgiving

Year B

1st Reading		**Joel 2: 21–27**	*[E6C]*
	539	Rejoice, O land, in God thy might	

Psalm		**Psalm 126**	*[A3B/L5C/Pr25B*/7–25]*
	567	Forth, in thy name, O Lord, I go	
	356	I will sing, I will sing a song unto the Lord	
	712	Tell out, my soul, the greatness of the Lord	
	373	To God be the glory! Great things he has done!	

2nd Reading		**1 Timothy 2: 1–7**	*[Pr20C]*
	518	Bind us together, Lord	
	319	Father, of heaven, whose love profound	
	419	I am not worthy, holy Lord	
	81	Lord, for the years your love has kept and guided	
	619	Lord, teach us how to pray aright	
	366	Praise, my soul, the King of heaven	
	540	To thee our God we fly	

The Gospel		**Matthew 6: 25–33**	
	28	I sing the almighty power of God	
	6	Immortal, invisible, God only wise	
	657	O God of Bethel, by whose hand	
	365	Praise to the Lord, the Almighty, the King of creation	
	596	Seek ye first the kingdom of God	

ALSO SUITABLE	*Any hymns in the Harvest section of the Church Hymnal*

Harvest Thanksgiving

Year C

1st Reading		**Deuteronomy 26: 1–11**	*[LIC]*
	39	For the fruits of his creation	

Psalm		**Psalm 100**	*[Pr6A*/Pr29A]*
	683	All people that on earth do dwell	
	701	Jubilate, ev'rybody	

2nd Reading   **Philippians 4: 4–9**

349	Fill thou my life, O Lord my God
225	In the cross of Christ I glory
16	Like a mighty river flowing
636	May the mind of Christ my Saviour
507	Put peace into each other's hands
281	Rejoice, the Lord is King!
71	Saviour, again to thy dear name we raise
627	What a friend we have in Jesus

The Gospel   **John 6: 25–35**

398	Alleluia! sing to Jesus
403	Bread of the world, in mercy broken
379	Break thou the bread of life
408	Come, risen Lord, and deign to be our guest
411	Draw near and take the body of the Lord
647	Guide me, O thou great Jehovah
418	Here, O my Lord, I see thee face to face
420	'I am the bread of life'
581	I, the Lord of sea and sky
422	In the quiet consecration
425	Jesus, thou joy of loving hearts
588	Light of the minds that know him
431	Lord, enthroned in heavenly splendour
435	O God, unseen, yet ever near
443	Sent forth by God's blessing, our true faith confessing
445	Soul, array thyself with gladness
624	Speak, Lord, in the stillness
451	We come as guests invited

ALSO SUITABLE   *Any hymns in the Harvest section of the Church Hymnal*

Bible Sunday   Year A

may be observed on the last Sunday of October or other convenient Sunday

1st Reading   **Nehemiah 8: 1–4 (5–6), 8–12**

381	God has spoken—by his prophets
380	God has spoken to his people, alleluia!
382	Help us, O Lord, to learn

383	Lord, be thy word my rule
384	Lord, thy word abideth
386	Spirit of God, unseen as the wind
387	Thanks to God, whose Word was spoken
388	Word of the living God

Psalm   **Psalm 119: 97–104**   *[Pr24C]*

383	Lord, be thy word my rule

Alternative Psalm   **Psalm 119: 105–112**   *[Pr10A]*

294	Come down, O Love divine
382	Help us, O Lord, to learn
384	Lord, thy word abideth
637	O for a closer walk with God
592	O Love that wilt not let me go
490	The Spirit lives to set us free
603	When we walk with the Lord

2nd Reading   **Colossians 3: 12–17**   *[CIC/L4MS]*

346	Angel voices, ever singing
294	Come down, O Love divine
550	'Forgive our sins as we forgive'
454	Forth in the peace of Christ we go
300	Holy Spirit, truth divine
360	Let all the world in every corner sing
525	Let there be love shared among us
503	Make me a channel of your peace
361	Now thank we all our God
369	Songs of praise the angels sang
601	Teach me, my God and King
374	When all thy mercies, O my God

The Gospel   **Matthew 24: 30–35**

86	Christ is the King! O friends, rejoice
126	[Hark! a thrilling voice is sounding]
162	[In the bleak mid-winter]
130	Jesus came, the heavens adoring
132	[Lo! he comes with clouds descending]
384	Lord, thy word abideth
281	Rejoice, the Lord is King!
369	Songs of praise the angels sang
73	The day thou gavest, Lord, is ended

Bible Sunday

Year B

may be observed on the last Sunday of October or other convenient Sunday

1st Reading		**Isaiah 55: 1–11**	*[EVABC]*
	646	Glorious things of thee are spoken	
	576	I heard the voice of Jesus say	
	557	Rock of ages, cleft for me	
	448	The trumpets sound, the angels sing	

Psalm		**Psalm 19: 7–14**	*[Pr21B*]*
	631	God be in my head	
	696	God, we praise you! God, we bless you!	
	616	In my life, Lord, be glorified	
	384	Lord, thy word abideth	
	432	Love is his word, love is his way	
	638	O for a heart to praise my God	

2nd Reading		**2 Timothy 3: 14 – 4: 5**	*[Pr24C]*
	324	God, whose almighty word	
	382	Help us, O Lord, to learn	
	81	Lord, for the years your love has kept and guided	
	384	Lord, thy word abideth	
	387	Thanks to God, whose Word was spoken	

The Gospel		**John 5: 36b–47**	
	321	Holy, holy, holy! Lord God almighty	
	6	Immortal, invisible, God only wise	

Bible Sunday

Year C

may be observed on the last Sunday of October or other convenient Sunday

1st Reading		**Isaiah 45: 22–25**	
	684	All praise to thee, for thou, O King divine!	
	147	[Angels, from the realms if glory]	
	255	[Christ is risen, alleluia!]	
	206	Come, let us to the Lord our God	
	91	He is Lord, he is Lord	
	356	I will sing, I will sing a song unto the Lord	
	94	In the name of Jesus	
	275	Look, ye saints, the sight is glorious	

Psalm **Psalm 119: 129–136** *[Pr12A*]*

382 Help us, O Lord, to learn
195 Lord, the light of your love is shining
384 Lord, thy word abideth
108 Praise to the Holiest in the height

2nd Reading **Romans 15: 1–6** *[6–9]*

86 Christ is the King! O friends, rejoice
349 Fill thou my life, O Lord my God
381 God has spoken—by his prophets
380 God has spoken to his people, alleluia!
523 Help us to help each other, Lord
382 Help us, O Lord, to learn
386 Spirit of God, unseen as the wind
387 Thanks to God, whose Word was spoken
372 Through all the changing scenes of life

The Gospel **Luke 4: 16–24**

218 And can it be that I should gain
494 Beauty for brokenness
501 Christ is the world's true light
119 [Come, thou long-expected Jesus]
380 God has spoken to his people, alleluia!
125 Hail to the Lord's anointed
569 Hark, my soul, it is the Lord
124 [Hark the glad sound! the Saviour comes]
357 I'll praise my maker while I've breath
97 Jesus shall reign where'er the sun
99 Jesus, the name high over all
134 Make way, make way, for Christ the King
706 O bless the God of Israel
104 O for a thousand tongues to sing
605 Will you come and follow me

Ember Days
being the Wednesday, Friday, and Saturday following
The First Sunday of Lent,
The Day of Pentecost,
Holy Cross Day (September 14),
St. Lucy's Day (December 13)

Any one reading from each of the following sections may be used

1st Reading		**Jeremiah 1: 4–9**	
	631	God be in my head	
	589	Lord, speak to me that I may speak	
	624	Speak, Lord, in the stillness	
	597	Take my life, and let it be	

or		**Numbers 11: 16–17, 24–29**	
	381	God has spoken—by his prophets	
	304	Loving Spirit, loving Spirit	
	386	Spirit of God, unseen as the wind	

or		**Numbers 27: 15–23**	
	456	Lord, you give the great commission	
	457	Pour out thy Spirit from on high	

Psalm		**Psalm 84: 8–12**	
	400	And now, O Father, mindful of the love	
	418	Here, O my Lord, I see thee face to face	
	620	O Lord, hear my prayer	
	343	We love the place, O God	

or		**Psalm 122**	*[AIA/DFBC]*
	683	All people that on earth do dwell	
	670	Jerusalem the golden	
	506	Pray that Jerusalem may have	

or		**Psalm 134**	*[2–1]*
	718	O praise the Lord, ye servants of the Lord	
	719	Praise the Lord, all you servants of the Lord	

2nd Reading		**Acts 20: 28–35**	
	373	To God be the glory! Great things he has done!	

or   **1 Corinthians 3: 5–11**

326	Blessed city, heavenly Salem
	(*Christ is made the sure foundation*)
327	Christ is our corner-stone
481	God is working his purpose out as year succeeds to year
42	[Good is the Lord, our heavenly King]
43	[Holy is the seed-time, when the buried grain]
303	Lord of the Church, we pray for our renewing
526	Risen Lord, whose name we cherish
340	Sing and be glad, for this is God's house!
528	The Church's one foundation
47	[We plough the fields, and scatter]
493	Ye that know the Lord is gracious

or   **1 Peter 4: 7–11**

51	Awake, my soul, and with the sun
516	Beloved, let us love: love is of God
517	Brother, sister, let me serve you
567	Forth, in thy name, O Lord, I go
523	Help us to help each other, Lord
495	Jesu, Jesu, fill us with your love
301	Let every Christian pray
525	Let there be love shared among us
487	Soldiers of Christ, arise
488	Stand up, stand up for Jesus
313	The Spirit came, as promised
373	To God be the glory! Great things he has done!

The Gospel   **Matthew 9: 35–38**   *[Ms]*

37	[Come, ye thankful people, come]
39	For the fruits of his creation
141	These are the days of Elijah
491	We have a gospel to proclaim

or   **Luke 12: 35–43**

86	Christ is the King! O friends, rejoice
570	Give me oil in my lamp, keep me burning
	(*Give me joy in my heart, keep me praising*)
142	Wake, O wake! With tidings thrilling
145	You servants of the Lord

or	**Luke 4: 16–21**

218	And can it be that I should gain
494	Beauty for brokenness
501	Christ is the world's true light
119	[Come, thou long-expected Jesus]
380	God has spoken to his people, alleluia!
125	Hail to the Lord's anointed
569	Hark, my soul, it is the Lord
124	[Hark the glad sound! the Saviour comes]
357	I'll praise my maker while I've breath
97	Jesus shall reign where'er the sun
99	Jesus, the name high over all
483	Jesus went to worship
134	[Make way, make way, for Christ the King]
706	O bless the God of Israel
104	O for a thousand tongues to sing
605	Will you come and follow me

or	**John 4: 31–38**	*[3–17]*

305	O Breath of life, come sweeping through us

Rogation Days

being the Monday, Tuesday, and Wednesday immediately preceding
The Ascension Day

Any one reading from each of the following sections may be used

1st Reading	**Deuteronomy 8: 1–10**

689	Come, sing praises to the Lord above
539	Rejoice, O land, in God thy might
596	Seek ye first the kingdom of God

or	**1 Kings 8: 35–40**

26	God sends us refreshing rain
620	O Lord, hear my prayer
625	Prayer is the soul's sincere desire
539	Rejoice, O land, in God thy might

or	**Job 28: 1–11**

6	Immortal, invisible, God only wise

49	Lord, bring the day to pass
29	Lord of beauty, thine the splendour
34	O worship the King all-glorious above

Psalm　　　　　　　**Psalm 104: 21–30**

567	Forth, in thy name, O Lord, I go
6	Immortal, invisible, God only wise
305	O Breath of life, come sweeping through us

or　　　　　　　**Psalm 107: 1–9**

683	All people that on earth do dwell
353	Give to our God immortal praise
30	Let us, with a gladsome mind
484	Lift high the cross, the love of Christ proclaim
361	Now thank we all our God
45	Praise, O praise our God and king
372	Through all the changing scenes of life
374	When all thy mercies, O my God

or　　　　　　　**Psalm 121**　　　　　　　*[L2A/Pr24C*]*

349	Fill thou my life, O Lord my God
14	I lift my eyes to the quiet hills
16	Like a mighty river flowing
664	To Zion's hill I lift my eyes

2nd Reading　　　　　　　**Philippians 4: 4–7**　　　　　　　*[A3C]*

349	Fill thou my life, O Lord my God
225	In the cross of Christ I glory
16	Like a mighty river flowing
636	May the mind of Christ my Saviour
507	Put peace into each other's hands
281	Rejoice, the Lord is King!
627	What a friend we have in Jesus

or　　　　　　　**2 Thessalonians 3: 6–13**　　　　　　　*[Pr28C]*

523	Help us to help each other, Lord
436	Now let us from this table rise
446	Strengthen for service, Lord, the hands
498	What does the Lord require for praise and offering?

or   **1 John 5: 12–15**

392   Now is eternal life
620   O Lord, hear my prayer

The Gospel   **Matthew 6: 1–15**

86   Christ is the King! O friends, rejoice
119   [Come, thou long-expected Jesus]
415   For the bread which you have broken
39   For the fruits of his creation
550   'Forgive our sins as we forgive'
668   God is our fortress and our rock
635   Lord, be my guardian and my guide
619   Lord, teach us how to pray aright
503   Make me a channel of your peace
657   O God of Bethel, by whose hand
438   O thou, who at thy eucharist didst pray
623   Our heavenly Father, through your Son
625   Prayer is the soul's sincere desire
539   Rejoice, O land, in God thy might
527   Son of God, eternal Saviour
47   We plough the fields, and scatter
509   Your kingdom come, O God!

or   **Mark 11: 22–24**

312   Gracious Spirit, Holy Ghost
596   Seek ye first the kingdom of God

or   **Luke 11: 5–13**

101   Jesus, the very thought of thee
425   Jesus, thou joy of loving hearts
336   Jesus, where'er thy people meet
596   Seek ye first the kingdom of God
47   We plough the fields, and scatter

The Guidance of the Holy Spirit

1st Reading   **Isaiah 61: 1–3**

218   And can it be that I should gain
494   Beauty for brokenness
481   God is working his purpose out as year succeeds
         to year

324	God, whose almighty word
125	Hail to the Lord's anointed
124	Hark the glad sound! the Saviour comes
357	I'll praise my maker while I've breath
97	Jesus shall reign where'er the sun
99	Jesus, the name high over all
134	Make way, make way, for Christ the King
706	O bless the God of Israel
104	O for a thousand tongues to sing

Psalm   **Psalm 86: 9–12, 16–17**

349	Fill thou my life, O Lord my God
125	Hail to the Lord's anointed
382	Help us, O Lord, to learn

2nd Reading   **1 Corinthians 12: 4–13**

294	Come down, O Love divine
408	Come, risen Lord, and deign to be our guest
297	Come, thou Holy Spirit, come
318	Father, Lord of all creation
312	Gracious Spirit, Holy Ghost
299	Holy Spirit, come, confirm us
421	I come with joy, a child of God
102	Name of all majesty
306	O Spirit of the living God
438	O thou, who at thy eucharist didst pray
440	One bread, one body, one Lord of all
441	Out to the world for Jesus
313	The Spirit came, as promised
491	We have a gospel to proclaim

The Gospel   **John 14: 15–26**

398	Alleluia! sing to Jesus
516	Beloved, let us love: love is of God
294	Come down, O Love divine
297	Come, thou Holy Spirit, come
300	Holy Spirit, truth divine
422	In the quiet consecration
307	Our great Redeemer, as he breathed
310	Spirit of the living God
451	We come as guests invited

Mission

1st Reading		**Isaiah 49: 1–6**
	685	Blessed be the God of Israel
	691	Faithful vigil ended
	481	God is working his purpose out as year succeeds to year
	192	How brightly beams the morning star!
	706	O bless the God of Israel
	595	Safe in the shadow of the Lord
Psalm		**Psalm 96: 1–4, 10**
	705	New songs of celebration render
	281	Rejoice, the Lord is King!
	710	Sing to God new songs of worship
	370	Stand up, and bless the Lord
	8	The Lord is king! Lift up your voice
2nd Reading		**Ephesians 2: 13–18**
	87	Christ is the world's Light, he and none other
	501	Christ is the world's true light
	421	I come with joy, a child of God
	522	In Christ there is no east or west
	306	O Spirit of the living God
	675	Peace, perfect peace, in this dark world of sin?
	507	Put peace into each other's hands
	373	To God be the glory! Great things he has done!
The Gospel		**Matthew 9: 35–38** *[Ember]*
	37	Come, ye thankful people, come
	39	For the fruits of his creation
	141	These are the days of Elijah
	491	We have a gospel to proclaim

Peace

1st Reading		**Micah 4: 3–5**
	501	Christ is the world's true light
	263	Crown him with many crowns (*vv. 1, 4–6*)
	509	Your kingdom come, O God!

Psalm		**Psalm 29: 1–4, 9–10**
	349	Fill thou my life, O Lord my God
	431	Lord, enthroned in heavenly splendour
	196	O worship the Lord in the beauty of holiness!

2nd Reading		**1 Timothy 2: 1–5**
	518	Bind us together, Lord
	81	Lord, for the years your love has kept and guided
	540	To thee our God we fly

The Gospel		**Matthew 5: 43–48**
	516	Beloved, let us love: love is of God
	517	Brother, sister, let me serve you
	523	Help us to help each other, Lord
	503	Make me a channel of your peace
	513	O Christ, the Healer, we have come
	504	O let us spread the pollen of peace throughout our land
	499	When I needed a neighbour, were you there
	531	Where love and loving-kindness dwell
	500	Would you walk by on the other side

ALSO SUITABLE	502	God! As with silent hearts we bring to mind
for Remembrance	535	Judge eternal, throned in splendour
Sunday observance	538	O Lord, the clouds are gathering
	527	Son of God, eternal Saviour

Unity

1st Reading		**Ezekiel 37: 15–22**
	518	Bind us together, Lord

Psalm		**Psalm 133**	*[E2B/Pr7B/Prl5A]*
	518	Bind us together, Lord	
	522	In Christ there is no east or west	
	525	Let there be love shared among us	
	438	O thou, who at thy eucharist didst pray	
	507	Put peace into each other's hands	
	661	Through the night of doubt and sorrow	

2nd Reading   **Ephesians 4: 1–6**

518   Bind us together, Lord
501   Christ is the world's true light
294   Come down, O Love divine
408   Come, risen Lord, and deign to be our guest
507   Put peace into each other's hands
527   Son of God, eternal Saviour
528   The Church's one foundation
313   The Spirit came, as promised
661   Through the night of doubt and sorrow
529   Thy hand, O God, has guided

The Gospel   **John 17: 11–23**

326   Blessed city, heavenly Salem (*omit v. 1*)
           (*Christ is made the sure foundation*)
86   Christ is the King! O friends, rejoice
422   In the quiet consecration
303   Lord of the Church, we pray for our renewing
438   O thou, who at thy eucharist didst pray
526   Risen Lord, whose name we cherish
527   Son of God, eternal Saviour

Control Hymns

The following hymns are those which are related to more than one reading on a specific Sunday or occasion. They might well be hymns to which priority should be given when making a suitable selection for public worship. They are, therefore, referred to as 'Control Hymns'.

The numbers and letters following each hymn refer to the readings on which the hymn is based. The codes are interpreted as follows:

I	1st Reading
P	Psalm
2	2nd Reading
G	Gospel

The number 2 following any of the above codes indicates that the hymn is based on the second choice for a particular reading. A I and 2 following the code means that the hymn is based on both the first and second choices for the reading.

The letters 'c' and 'p' on the Sundays after Trinity refer to the 'continuous' readings and the 'paired' readings respectively.

The First Sunday of Advent

Year B	132	Lo! he comes with clouds descending	I,G

The Second Sunday of Advent

Year A	250	All hail the power of Jesu's name	I,2
	481	God is working his purpose out	I,P
Year B	134	Make way, make way, for Christ the King	I,G
Year C	134	Make way, make way, for Christ the King	I:2,G

The Third Sunday of Advent

Year A	535	Judge eternal, throned in splendour	P,2
Year B	124	Hark the glad sound! the Saviour comes	I,G
	134	Make way, make way, for Christ the King	I,G
Year C	281	Rejoice, the Lord is King!	I,2

The Fourth Sunday of Advent

Year A	160	Hark! the herald-angels sing	I,G
	168	Lord, you were rich beyond all splendour	I,G
	135	O come, O come, Emmanuel	I,G
	174	O little town of Bethlehem	I,G

| Year B | 704 | Mary sang a song, a song of love | P,G |
| | 175 | Of the Father's heart begotten | 2,G |

Christmas Day

Years A, B, C
Proper 1 | 151 | Child in the manger | 1,G

Proper 3	146	A great and mighty wonder	P,G
	84	Alleluia! raise the anthem	2,G
	125	Hail to the Lord's anointed	1,P
	387	Thanks to God, whose Word was spoken	1,2

The Second Sunday of Christmas

| Years A, B, C | 84 | Alleluia! raise the anthem | 2,G |

The Epiphany of our Lord

| Years A, B, C | 190 | Brightest and best of the suns of the morning | 1,G |
| | 196 | O worship the Lord in the beauty of holiness! | 1,G |

The First Sunday of Epiphany   The Baptism of Christ

| Year A | 197 | Songs of thankfulness and praise | 2,G |

| Year B | 341 | Spirit divine, attend our prayers | 1,G |

The Second Sunday of Epiphany

Year A	268	Hail, thou once-despised Jesus!	2,G
	431	Lord, enthroned in heavenly splendour	2,G
	112	There is a Redeemer	2,G
	492	Ye servants of God, your master proclaim	P,G

| Year C | 528 | The Church's one foundation | 1,G |

The Third Sunday of Epiphany

Year A	52	Christ, whose glory fills the skies	1,G
	362	O God beyond all praising	1,P
	199	The people that in darkness walked	1,G

| Year B | 381 | God has spoken—by his prophets | 1,P |

Year C	380	God has spoken to his people, alleluia!	1,G
	97	Jesus shall reign where'er the sun	P,G
	384	Lord, thy word abideth	1,P

The Fourth Sunday of Epiphany

| Year B | | 529 | Thy hand, O God, has guided | P, 2 |
| Year C | | 634 | Love divine, all loves excelling | 2, G |

The Presentation of Christ in the Temple   February 2 Candlemas Day

| Years A, B, C | | 634 | Love divine, all loves excelling | I, G |
| | | 134 | Make way, make way, for Christ the King | I, P |

The Fifth Sunday before Lent   (Proper 0)

| Year B | | 306 | O Spirit of the living God | I, 2 |
| Year C | | 454 | Forth in the peace of Christ we go | I, G |

The Fourth Sunday before Lent

| Year B | | 553 | Jesu, lover of my soul | I, G |

The Third Sunday before Lent

| Year C | | 563 | Commit your ways to God | I, P |

The Second Sunday before Lent

Year A	Option B	569	Hark, my soul, it is the Lord	I, P
		6	Immortal invisible, God only wise	I, G
Year B	Option A	84	Alleluia! raise the anthem	I, G
		160	[Hark! the herald-angels sing]	2, G
Year C	Option A	612	Eternal Father, strong to save	P, G
	Option B	668	God is our fortress and our rock	P, G
		526	Risen Lord, whose name we cherish	2, G

The Sunday before Lent   Transfiguration Sunday

Year A		325	Be still, for the presence of the Lord	I, G
		501	Christ is the world's true light	2, G
		52	Christ, whose glory fills the skies	2, G
Year B		643	Be thou my vision, O Lord of my heart	I, G
		501	Christ is the world's true light	P, G
Year C		325	Be still, for the presence of the Lord	I, G
		195	Lord, the light of your love is shining	2, G

The First Sunday of Lent

Year A		108	Praise to the Holiest in the height	I, 2
Year B		652	Lead us, heavenly Father, lead us	P, G
		200	The sinless one to Jordan came	2, G

299

| Year C | 66 | Before the ending of the day (*vv. 1, 2, 3d*) | P,G |
| | 595 | Safe in the shadow of the Lord | P,G |

The Second Sunday of Lent

Year A	349	Fill thou my life, O Lord my God	1,P
Year B	545	Sing of Eve and sing of Adam	1,2
Year C	501	Christ is the world's true light	1,P
	566	Fight the good fight with all thy might!	P,2

The Third Sunday of Lent

Year A	646	Glorious things of thee are spoken	1,G
	557	Rock of ages, cleft for me	1,G
Year C	646	Glorious things of thee are spoken	1,2
	557	Rock of ages, cleft for me	1,2

The Fourth Sunday of Lent   Mothering Sunday

Year B	352	Give thanks with a grateful heart	2,G
	353	Give to our God immortal praise	P,G
	484	Lift high the cross, the love of Christ proclaim	P,G
Year C	268	Hail, thou once-despised Jesus!	2,G

The Fifth Sunday of Lent

Year A	293	Breathe on me, Breath of God	1,G
	319	Father, of heaven, whose love profound	1,2
	308	Revive your Church, O Lord	1,G
Year B	638	O for a heart to praise my God	1,P

The Sixth Sunday of Lent   Palm Sunday

Year A	714	Holy, holy, holy Lord God of power and might	G,P (*Palms*)
	715	Holy, holy, holy, Lord God, the Lord Almighty	G,P (*Palms*)
	230	My Lord, what love is this	1,G (*Passion*)
Year B	714	Holy, holy, holy Lord, God of power and might	G,P (*Palms*)
	715	Holy, holy, holy, Lord God, the Lord Almighty	G,P (*Palms*)
	285	The head that once was crowned with thorns	2,G (*Passion*)

Year C	714	Holy, holy, holy Lord, God of power and might	G,P (Palms)
	715	Holy, holy, holy, Lord God, the Lord Almighty	G,P (Palms)

The Tuesday of Holy Week

Years A, B, C	643	Be thou my vision, O Lord of my heart	P, 2
	484	Lift high the cross, the love of Christ proclaim	2,G
	595	Safe in the shadow of the Lord	I,P
	241	Sing, my tongue, the glorious battle	2,G

The Wednesday of Holy Week

Years A, B, C	230	My Lord, what love is this	I,G

Maundy Thursday

Years A, B, C	411	Draw near and take the body of the Lord	P, 2
	432	Love is his word, love is his way	2,G
	438	O thou, who at thy eucharist didst pray	2,G

Good Friday

Years A, B, C	215	Ah, holy Jesu, how hast thou offended	I,G
	220	Glory be to Jesus	2,G
	417	He gave his life in selfless love	I,G
	226	It is a thing most wonderful	2:2,G
	227	Man of sorrows! What a name	I,G
	231	My song is love unknown	I,G
	233	O dearest Lord, thy sacred head	P,G
	237	O my Saviour, lifted	2,G
	235	O sacred head, sore wounded	I,G
	239	See, Christ was wounded for our sake	I,G
	240	Sweet the moments, rich in blessing	P,G
	247	When I survey the wondrous cross	P,G

Easter Day   The First Sunday of Easter

Year A	264	Finished the strife of battle now	I,P2
	271	Jesus Christ is risen today	I,G2
	286	The strife is o'er, the battle done	I,P2
	491	We have a gospel to proclaim	I,G2
Year B	258	Christ the Lord is risen again!	P2,GI2
	264	Finished the strife of battle now	I2,P2
	271	Jesus Christ is risen today	I,G2
	286	The strife is o'er, the battle done	I,P2, 2
	491	We have a gospel to proclaim	I,G2

Year C	258	Christ the Lord is risen again!	P2,G12
	264	Finished the strife of battle now	1,P2,G2
	271	Jesus Christ is risen today	1,G2
	102	Name of all majesty	1,2
	108	Praise to the Holiest in the height	P2,2
	286	The strife is o'er, the battle done	1,P2

The Second Sunday of Easter

Year A	567	Forth, in thy name, O Lord, I go	1,P
	652	Lead us, heavenly Father, lead us	P,G
	289	This joyful Eastertide	1,P

| Year B | 557 | Rock of ages, cleft for me | 1:2,2 |
| | 505 | Peace be to this congregation | 1:2,G |

| Year C | 454 | Forth in the peace of Christ we go | 2,G |
| | 321 | Holy, holy, holy! Lord God almighty | P2,2 |

The Third Sunday of Easter

| Year B | 104 | O for a thousand tongues to sing | 1,G |

The Fourth Sunday of Easter

| Year B | 655 | Loving Shepherd of your sheep | P,G |

Year C	466	Here from all nations, all tongues	P,2
	467	How bright those glorious spirits shine!	P,2
	655	Loving Shepherd of your sheep	P,G

The Fifth Sunday of Easter

| Year A | 92 | How sweet the name of Jesus sounds | P,2 |

| Year B | 422 | In the quiet consecration | 2,G |
| | 214 | O Love, how deep, how broad, how high! | 1,2 |

| Year C | 515 | A new commandment I give unto you | 1:2,G |
| | 525 | Let there be love shared among us | 1:2,G |

The Sixth Sunday of Easter   Rogation Sunday

| Year A | 29 | Lord of beauty, thine the splendour | 1,2 |
| | 35 | The spacious firmament on high | 1,2 |

| Year B | 456 | Lord, you give the great commission | 1,G |

The Ascension Day

Years A, B, C	250	All hail the power of Jesu's name	1,2
	398	Alleluia! sing to Jesus	1,G
	266	Hail the day that sees him rise	1,G

267	Hail the risen Lord, ascending	*1,G*
276	Majesty, worship his majesty	*1:2,P2*
281	Rejoice, the Lord is King!	*P2,2*
285	The head that once was crowned with thorns	*1,G*

The Seventh Sunday of Easter

| Year A | 285 | The head that once was crowned with thorns | *1,G* |

| Year C | 281 | Rejoice, the Lord is King! | *P,2* |

Pentecost   Whitsunday

Year A	318	Father, Lord of all creation	*1,2*
	303	Lord of the Church, we pray for our renewing	*1,G2*
	305	O Breath of life, come sweeping through us	*1,P*
	306	O Spirit of the living God	*1,2*
	313	The Spirit came, as promised	*1,2*
	491	We have a gospel to proclaim	*1,2*

Year B	305	O Breath of life, come sweeping through us	*1,P*
	307	Our great Redeemer, as he breathed	*1,G*
	310	Spirit of the living God	*1,G*

| Year C | 305 | O Breath of life, come sweeping through us | *1,P* |
| | 310 | Spirit of the living God | *1,G* |

Trinity Sunday

Year A	32	O Lord my God! When I in awesome wonder	*1,P*
	33	O Lord of every shining constellation	*1,P*
	306	O Spirit of the living God	*1:2,G*

Proper 4

Year A	92	How sweet the name of Jesus sounds	*Pcp,G*
	15	If thou but suffer God to guide thee	*Pp,G*
	211	Immortal love for ever full	*Ic,c*
	557	Rock of ages, cleft for me	*Pp,G*

| Year C | 373 | To God be the glory! Great things he has done! | *Pcp,2* |

Proper 5

Year A	545	Sing of Eve and sing of Adam	*Ic,2*
Year C	613	Eternal light, shine in my heart	*Ic,G/Ip,G*
	104	O for a thousand tongues to sing	*Ic,G/Ip,G*
	99	Jesus, the name high over all	*Ic,Pc,G*
	115	Thou art the Way: to thee alone	*Icp,2*

Proper 6

Year A	411	Draw near and take the body of the Lord	*Pc,2*
Year B	125	Hail to the Lord's anointed	*Ic,G*
Year C	56	Lord, as I wake I turn to you	*Pc,2*
	92	How sweet the name of Jesus sounds	*Pp,G*

Proper 7

Year B	666	Be still, my soul: the Lord is on thy side	*Pp,G*
	643	Be thou my vision, O Lord of my heart	*Icl,2*
	612	Eternal Father, strong to save	*Ip,G*
	566	Fight the good fight with all thy might!	*Icl,2*
	668	God is our fortress and our rock	*Icl,Pcl*
	593	O Jesus, I have promised	*Icl,G*
	487	Soldiers of Christ, arise	*Icl,2*
	527	Son of God, eternal Saviour	*Pp,G*
	488	Stand up, stand up for Jesus	*Icl,2*
Year C	549	Dear Lord and Father of mankind	*Ic,G*

Proper 8

Year C	297	Come, thou Holy Spirit, come	*Ic,2*
	652	Lead us, heavenly Father, lead us	*Pp,2*

Proper 9

Year B	387	Thanks to God, whose Word was spoken	*Ip,2*
Year C	528	The Church's one foundation	*Pc,2*

Proper 10

Year A	294	Come down, O Love divine	*Pc,2*
Year C	523	Help us to help each other, Lord	*2,G*

Proper 11

Year B	20	The King of love my shepherd is	*Ip,Pp*
Year C	268	Hail, thou once-despised Jesus!	*2,G*

Proper 12

Year A	643	Be thou my vision, O Lord of my heart	*Ip,G*
	384	Lord, thy word abideth	*Pp,G*
Year C	619	Lord, teach us how to pray aright	*Ip,G*

Proper 13

Year B	408	Come, risen Lord, and deign to be our guest	*2,G*
	647	Guide me, O thou great Jehovah	*Ip,G*
	588	Light of the minds that know him	*Ip,G*
	431	Lord, enthroned in heavenly splendour	*Ip,G*
	435	O God, unseen, yet ever near	*Pp,G*
	445	Soul, array thyself with gladness	*Ip,G*
Year C	10	All my hope on God is founded	*Pp,G*
	533	God of grace and God of glory	*Pp,G*

Proper 14

| Year A | 593 | O Jesus, I have promised | *Ip,G* |
| | 365 | Praise to the Lord, the Almighty | *Pc,G* |

Proper 15

| Year A | 522 | In Christ there is no east or west | *Ic,Pc* |
| | 525 | Let there be love shared among us | *Ic,Pc* |

Proper 16

| Year B | 478 | Go forth and tell! O Church of God, awake! | *Ip,2* |

Proper 17

| Year A | 321 | Holy, holy, holy! Lord God almighty | *Ic,Pc* |
| Year C | 630 | Blessed are the pure in heart | *Ip,G* |

Proper 18

Year B	494	Beauty for brokenness	*Ic,2*
	104	O for a thousand tongues to sing	*Ip,G*
Year C	56	Lord, as I wake I turn to you	*Ip,Pp*
	597	Take my life, and let it be	*Ip,2*

Proper 19

Year A	550	'Forgive our sins as we forgive'	*Ip,G*
Year B	643	Be thou my vision, O Lord of my heart	*Ic,Pc2*
	33	O Lord of every shining constellation	*Pc2,2*

	366	Praise, my soul, the King of heaven	Pp,G
	35	The spacious firmament on high	Ic,Pc
Year C	382	Help us, O Lord, to learn	Ic,2
	383	Lord, be thy word my rule	Pc,2
	81	Lord, for the years your love has kept	2,G

Proper 25 The Fifth Sunday before Advent

Year A	515	'A new commandment I give unto you'	Ip,G
	567	Forth, in thy name, O Lord, I go	Ic,2
	653	Lead, kindly light, amid the encircling gloom	Ic,2
	525	Let there be love shared among us	Ip,G
Year C	487	Soldiers of Christ, arise	Pp,2
	493	Ye that know the Lord is gracious	2,G

All Saints November I or the nearest Sunday

Year A	376	Ye holy angels bright	P,2
Year B	512	From you all skill and science flow	I:2,2
	466	Here from all nations, all tongues	I:2,2
	553	Jesu, lover of my soul	I:2,2

Proper 26 The Fourth Sunday before Advent

Year A	517	Brother, sister, let me serve you	2,G
Year B	649	Happy are they, they that love God	Ip,Pp,G
	229	My God I love thee; not because	Ip,G
Year C	92	How sweet the name of Jesus sounds	Pp,2

Proper 27 The Third Sunday before Advent

| Year C | 328 | Come on and celebrate! | 2,G |

Proper 28 The Second Sunday before Advent

| Year C | 52 | Christ, whose glory fills the skies | Ip-G |

Proper 29 The Sunday before Advent – The Kingship of Christ

Year A	281	Rejoice, the Lord is King!	2,G
Year B	132	Lo! he comes with clouds descending	Ip,2
	281	Rejoice, the Lord is King!	Pp,G
Year C	323	The God of Abraham praise	Ic,2
	373	To God be the glory!	2,G

The Conversion of Saint Paul January 25

597	Take my life, and let it be	1,2,G

The Visitation of the Blessed Virgin Mary May 31

712	Tell out, my soul, the greatness of the Lord	P,G

Saint Columba June 9

372	Through all the changing scenes of life	P,2

Saint Barnabas June 11

456	Lord, you give the great commission	2,G

Saint Peter June 29

493	Ye that know the Lord is gracious	2,G

The Transfiguration of our Lord August 6

325	Be still, for the presence of the Lord	1:2,G
501	Christ is the world's true light	2,G
52	Christ, whose glory fills the skies	2,G
34	O worship the King all-glorious above	1,P

Saint Luke October 18

478	Go forth and tell! O Church of God, awake!	2,G
492	Ye servants of God, your master proclaim	2,G

Saint Simon and Saint Jude October 28

326	Blessed city, heavenly Salem	1,2
	(*Christ is made the sure foundation*)	
327	Christ is our corner-stone	1,2
340	Sing and be glad, for this is God's house!	1,2
528	The Church's one foundation	1,2
493	Ye that know the Lord is gracious	1,2

Saint Andrew November 30

597	Take my life, and let it be	1,2

Saint John December 27

557	Rock of ages, cleft for me	1:2,2

Harvest Thanksgiving

Year A	42	Good is the Lord, our heavenly King	*I,P*

Bible Sunday

Year A	294	Come down, O Love divine	*P2,2*
	382	Help us, O Lord, to learn	*I,P2*
	383	Lord, be thy word my rule	*I,P*
	384	Lord, thy word abideth	*I,P2,G*
	369	Songs of praise the angels sang	*2,G*

Year B	384	Lord, thy word abideth	*P,2*

Year C	380	God has spoken to his people, alleluia!	*2,G*
	382	Help us, O Lord, to learn	*P,2*

The Guidance of the Holy Spirit

	294	Come down, O Love divine	*2,G*
	297	Come, thou Holy Spirit, come	*2,G*
	125	Hail to the Lord's anointed	*I,P*

Unity

	518	Bind us together, Lord	*I,P,2*
	507	Put peace into each other's hands	*P,2*
	527	Son of God, eternal Saviour	*2,G*
	661	Through the night of doubt and sorrow	*P,2*

Index of Suggested Hymns
suitable for use with the Revised Common Lectionary and additional lectionaries in the foregoing pages

Table of Scriptural References
from the Revised Common Lectionary and additional lectionaries
showing the codes of occasions and the page numbers on which the biblical references are to be found

A code showing an asterisk on the 'Proper' Sundays after Trinity indicates a 'paired' reading

Old Testament

Apocrypha

New Testament